HYPER
LEVERAGE

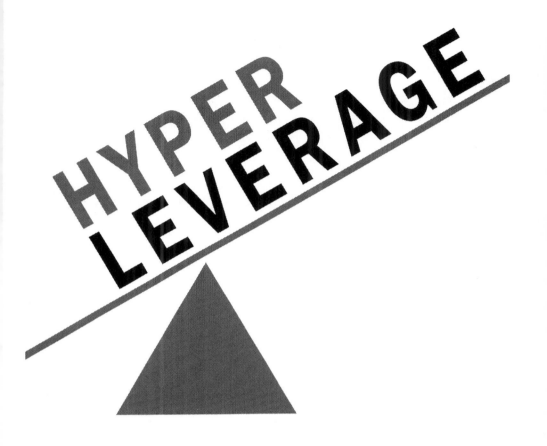

HYPER LEVERAGE

Do More with What You Have for Exceptional Results

JOEL GOOBICH

Published in Austin, TX, U.S.A. by Big Picture Advisors llc

Paperback ISBN: 978-1-950282-86-9
eBook ISBN: 978-1-950282-87-6
Hardcover ISBN: 978-1-64704-034-5

Printed in the United States of America

Distributed by Bublish, Inc.

Names: Goobich, Joel, author.
Title: Hyperleverage : do more with what you have for exceptional results / Joel Goobich.
Other Titles: Hyper leverage
Description: Austin, TX, U.S.A. : Big Picture Advisors, [2019] |
[Mount Pleasant, South Carolina] : Bublish, Inc., [2019]
Identifiers: ISBN 9781950282869 | ISBN 9781950282876 (ebook)
Subjects: LCSH: Business enterprises--Finance. | Financial
leverage. | Strategic planning. | Success in business.
Classification: LCC HG4026 .G66 2019 (print) | LCC
HG4026 (ebook) | DDC 658.15--dc23

CONTENTS

DEDICATION

I dedicate this book to my wife, Bonnie, whose unwavering
support, encouragement, and love I have leveraged time
and again to achieve my life and career ambitions.

'm not a tall man. I'll never be a pro basketball player or be chosen first for the next pickup game at the gym. I'm at peace with my height now, but back in middle school when I was playing basketball, I viewed it as a major liability. My perspective changed during the last game of my seventh-grade year. We were playing our archrivals from across town, a team with players three and four years older than us. As they entered the gym, they looked like giants to me—tall, huge, and muscular. We were toast!

By the fourth quarter, we were losing badly. Since it was a lost cause, our coach decided he could safely insert me—all 4'6" of me— into the game. He had nothing to lose. Finally, it was my moment to shine. Darting all over the court, I managed to steal the ball and began dribbling toward our basket. People started cheering. I was headed toward an easy layup when the other team's tallest player stepped directly in my path. He stood solidly staring me down from the foul line, only a few yards away. He had to be at least a foot and a half taller than me—a virtual Mount Everest.

I had only seconds to assess the situation. Though I was faster, I knew I couldn't get around my opponent. Suddenly, a crazy idea came to me. I crouched down as low as I could and drove straight for my opponent's crotch. Yep, I was going to run right between his legs. The boy was so shocked watching my maneuver—and the crowd started laughing so hard when they realized what I was aiming to do—I was able to make a quick pivot at the last second and take my shot. It went in, but unfortunately didn't change the outcome. We still lost by a wide margin, but I had my moment. In that moment, my biggest liability, my height, had become my leverage by allowing me the agility, speed and size to overcome the challenge that lay directly in my path.

To this day, I use this memory from my short-lived basketball career as a reminder that, if you're willing to think outside the box and be proactive, there's almost always a way around any obstacle. To gain an advantage in life or business, we must actively train ourselves to jump the next hurdle. What can we leverage? Most of the time, we have more options at our disposal than we think we do. Leverage enables people to amplify influence in a system or environment. When you understand the leverage you have at your fingertips, you can invest the right amount of effort through the proper channels to yield the greatest return for your business.

Today, as a business strategist and executive management consultant, I experience the power of leverage every day. Leverage is like air— vital to our existence and, even though we can't see it, we know it's there. We've learned to leverage and do all sorts of important things with air. We've built windmills to capture its energy, pressurized it in chambers to treat patients' wounds, and channeled it to help those struggling for breath. Despite its invisibility, we've learned to recognize air's power, figured out how to harness it, and reaped impactful benefits as a result. That's exactly how leverage works in business. It can turn the resources around us into revenue and profit generators.

Companies, teams, and professionals learn how to leverage their assets. Whether those assets are time, money, knowledge, expertise, relationships, people, talents, influence, or power, companies can use leverage to achieve exceptional results.

As you will learn through the many examples in this book, the story of business is the story of leverage. Without leverage, there would be inefficient or non-existent accumulation, replenishment, and utilization of assets. There would be less return on investments. The application of leverage is essential to the growth, maintenance, and longevity of any business entity. The importance of maximizing and actively searching for leverage, the central theme of this book, is often overlooked within companies.

Too often, organizations fail to recognize, explore, or appreciate the potential opportunities they have at their disposal. They become conservative, bogged down in bureaucracy, and accepting of mediocrity. Complacency sets in and leverage, if it happens at all, is mostly by happenstance and not by design.

> **Leverage:** The ability to influence a business system or environment in a way that multiplies your efforts or magnifies your potential.

The thing about leverage is that, without action, it is ephemeral. Its potential goes untapped and is wasted. Over time, companies that fail to master leverage are destined to lose their edge, to struggle, and to work harder than they need to for a minimal return. Over time, they will stagnate. In today's highly competitive marketplace, that's a death knell. Leverage is a business necessity, and to be at the top of your game, you need something more: you need HyperLeverage, the intentional exploitation of leverage opportunities, to yield exceptional results.

This book will show you how to identify and benefit from HyperLeverage and create a culture and approach that will give you and your business ongoing competitive advantage in today's marketplace. The strategies presented in this book will help you identify the resources you can leverage to grow your business and fatten your bottom line. Let's dive right in and find out more about HyperLeverage.

Why HyperLeverage?

Like air, leverage is invisible but crucial. We sense the existence of air, but most of the time we can't see or touch it. We depend on it, but we often take it for granted. In business, leverage is similar to air. It's all around us, but we often don't notice it. We rely on it, but we often fail to harness its power.

Leverage is the ability to influence a system or environment in a way that multiplies your efforts. To get the most out of the leverage opportunities in your company, you must invest the right amount of effort through the proper channels to yield a greater return than you might have experienced without leverage. In other words, leverage turns the potential found in existing resources and assets into innovation, growth, and revenue.

Let's define HyperLeverage and how it differs from simple leverage (see below).

HyperLeverage (noun) – The proactive, intentional, and systematic search for and acquisition,refinement, and exploitation of leverageable assets and resources.

HyperLeverage (verb) – To consciously exploit every existing leverage opportunity, asset or resource for maximum benefit and impactful results.

To be actively looking to acquire, refine, and deploy meaningful assets—either inside or outside your organization—you need to be hyper-focused on leverage as a business strategy. You must develop what I call a HyperLeverage Mindset at your company. This mindset means always being cognizant of and taking advantage of all leverage opportunities. It must be hardwired into the DNA of your business.

If HyperLeverage is a central business strategy for your leadership team, it means you do business differently. You have made a commitment to support and nurture the active and meaningful acquisition, refinement, or deployment of key assets. Finding leverage by chance is great, but HyperLeverage means your team's search for leverage is intentional. The pursuit of HyperLeverage shifts the way you and your team think, plan, and execute in your business. It requires a systematic reshaping of what I call the 4 Ps: People, Planning, Performance, and Progress, which are common to almost every professional work environment. We'll explore how leverage and HyperLeverage work within the 4 Ps later in the book.

People make HyperLeverage happen. If you want to experience HyperLeverage, you need your team to have a HyperLeverage Mindset. First, they need to learn to leverage their capabilities, skills, and experience. Second, they need to be empowered with the skills and freedom to seek and assess opportunities to leverage company assets. As Michael Mankins explains in *Time, Talent and Energy*, the truly scarce resources now confronting companies are the time, talent, and energy of the people in an organization—resources which are often squandered. Access to financial capital is cheap and abundant today, and therefore no longer as strong an advantage as it was in the past. What's needed today are organizational solutions that can unleash a company's full productive power and enable it to outpace competitors.

Planning is how HyperLeverage becomes part of the culture. Few organizations can thrive, and few professionals can succeed in their jobs, without taking a proactive approach to planning. Throughout the book, I address the concept of thinking backwards from the end goal. This allows you to view the entire canvas, the proverbial "big picture," to come into focus. It allows companies to craft more effective and creative strategies and roadmaps. It must be supported by the active and ongoing collection, organization and effective management of the select information to make smart decisions that are crucial in the development of action plans, and identification of important milestones.

Johnson and Scholes explain in *Exploring Corporate Strategy*, that "Strategy is the direction and scope of an organization over the long-term: which achieves advantage (sic leverage) for the organization through its configuration of resources within a challenging environment, to meet the needs of markets and to fulfill stakeholder expectations." What they are saying is that developing a strategy provides the leverage to peek into the future from a present point in time.

Performance is the third wheel that leads to successful HyperLeverage. Having the right people in place, devising the correct strategy, developing the appropriate plans, and collecting and refining the necessary assets are critical elements of success. Leverage requires action to achieve HyperLeverage. Albert Einstein, the most famous and perhaps the greatest scientific mind of the 20th century, concisely summarized, "Nothing happens until something moves." Performance is the connective glue in a leverage ecosystem.

We live in a world of dynamic change where old paradigms are being disrupted by innovation and technology. The ability to embrace these changes and to exploit them effectively has become the doorway to progress through which successful startups and smart businesses are beginning to implement. These windows of opportunity do not stay open long before closing on those organizations that can't or won't introduce and leverage progressive changes.

Businesses and professionals are often stymied by over-planning and over-thinking. Paralysis by analysis then sets in. In today's increasingly high-velocity global economy, advantages are bestowed upon those who take bold and decisive action. As an example, Fred Smith, the founder of Federal Express, was certainly not the first person who recognized how incompetent and bloated the U.S. Postal Service had become. Others probably had ideas of starting a private delivery service that could compete with the USPS and deliver better service to the customer and, at the same time, turn a healthy profit. What differentiates Smith from this pack was HyperLeverage—his ability to hit the gas pedal with the right objectives, the right teams, and the right assets.

The emphasis of this book is on laying the foundation for understanding leverage in a different context and understanding the system of achieving HyperLeverage that would apply to most companies and professionals. For most leaders, the 4 Ps of HyperLeverage, People, Planning, Performance and Progress are the core of their business activities.

Developing A Systematic Approach To Leverage

Most companies don't have a HyperLeverage system in place. They haven't yet assessed the 4 Ps to see how they can use and enhance what they already have to reap the many benefits of HyperLeverage. Many companies, even successful ones, learn about the power of HyperLeverage by accident, or the hard way. Take the story of Disney and its relationship with Pixar in the mid-1990s.

In 1995, Pixar was a little-known animation studio that had gone out on a limb to create its first feature-length movie. Though they were talented creators, the Pixar team had no expertise when it came to film distribution. When Disney picked up Pixar's first movie, *Toy Story*, Disney was king of movie tie-ins and merchandising. Disney executives fully understood the financial upside to licensing, but their animation department had become stale and didn't realize what a jewel they'd found in *Toy Story*. They also underestimated the appeal of the *Toy Story* characters. Disney put most of its eggs and merchandising emphasis on the upcoming *Hunchback of Notre Dame* animated movie, which had been produced in-house. While Disney offered licensing deals for *Toy Story* to the big toy manufacturers, Mattel and Hasbro, these companies passed on the offer—most likely because they did not sense that Disney was fully vested in *Toy Story*'s success. As a result, Disney was caught unprepared for the movie's huge appeal to not only children but to adults. The company missed the boat due to internal conflicts and a lack of adequate planning. It failed to capitalize fully on the original *Toy Story*'s huge success.

Disney ended up cutting a licensing deal with Thinkway Toys, a small Toronto-based manufacturer of talking coin banks in early 1995—a scant eleven months before the release of the film. In supply chain terms, that would be considered a "just in time" inventory item. It was barely enough time to create the prototype, set up production lines, create enough inventory, and get the product to distribution and eventually on store shelves. With that short a time frame, it was impossible for Disney to leverage the merchandising potential generated by the huge success of *Toy Story*.

Albert Chan, Thinkway's owner and toy designer, was ecstatic. This was his big break. He did all he could to HyperLeverage this unexpected opportunity. According to John Lassiter, the CEO of Pixar at the time, Chan put his own money into making 250,000 Woody and Buzz Lightyear dolls. Within the first week of the movie's release, there were orders for another 1.6 million. To date, Thinkway has produced more than 25 million Buzz Lightyear toys. *Toy Story* put Chan's company on the map and changed the trajectory of his company.

For Disney, it was a lesson learned. Never again would it be caught with its merchandising and licensing pants down. Subsequently, no major movie would be released without first planning for *all* the potential revenue-generating marketing and merchandising opportunities. Strategically planning for maximum leverage of all the assets, and—most importantly—following through on implementing these plans, became part of Disney's DNA. In that shift, Disney went from missing out on a huge opportunity with *Toy Story* to experiencing the benefits of HyperLeverage as a result of a planning system that maximized merchandising revenue. The result? Merchandise, like toy sales, now often far exceeds the revenue generated by ticket sales. Look at Figure 1 for some mind-blowing data.

It can take upwards of three years and even longer to get a global merchandising supply chain that can be leveraged in place, but for Disney, it's worth the time and effort. Why? Because the return on this HyperLeverage is exceptional. Movie tie-ins are now considered essential, even more important to the bottom line and brand equity of movie companies like Disney than ever before. Disney can HyperLeverage its gigantic war chest of cash and financing options to play the "long game" and fully capitalize on its resources. Figure 1: "Toy and Movie Sales Data" illustrates this point:

As mentioned earlier, tapping into HyperLeverage requires a change in thinking, planning, and execution. To leverage all the assets associated with the release of a new feature-length animated children's film, Disney decided to take a backwards approach to strategic planning, leveraging assets every step of the way. In other words, it reverse-engineered its desired outcome by starting with what it wanted to achieve at the end of the process—around the film's

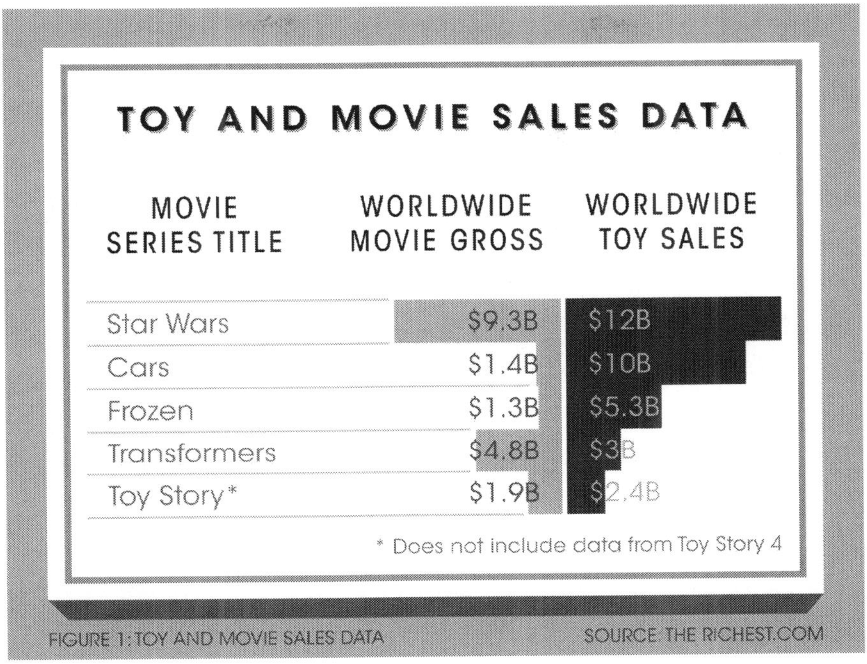

TOY AND MOVIE SALES DATA

MOVIE SERIES TITLE	WORLDWIDE MOVIE GROSS	WORLDWIDE TOY SALES
Star Wars	$9.3B	$12B
Cars	$1.4B	$10B
Frozen	$1.3B	$5.3B
Transformers	$4.8B	$3B
Toy Story*	$1.9B	$2.4B

* Does not include data from Toy Story 4

FIGURE 1: TOY AND MOVIE SALES DATA   SOURCE: THE RICHEST.COM

release—and then going back through the planning process to lay a foundation for maximum return on the time and money invested in the release of the film.

Here's what that looks like: first, executives at Disney knew that they would need merchandise on the store shelves ready to sell before the movie was released. Since the toy manufacturers needed to produce the merchandised products, Disney had to give them plenty of time to build the tools necessary to produce enough inventory with enough time to get it to the distributors in advance of the movie's launch. Additionally, Disney needed to finance this investment in equipment and inventory for the three years leading up to the movie's pre-marketing, when the first products would be sold.

Taking the next step backwards, the toy manufacturers needed to have their questions answered. What would be in demand? What would their margins look like? What would Disney allow as the licensee? They needed time to plan for this and make presentations to Disney executives to get their signoffs and approvals.

The leadership team learned from its mistakes with *Toy Story*. As they moved forward, they decided that Disney's success would be leveraged through merchandising. They actively sought to deploy meaningful assets (like the money to finance the equipment and inventory investments for three years) to leverage the merchandising opportunities around their movies. It was a business strategy that would ensure optimal returns. They actively identified leverage opportunities during every phase of the creation, strategic planning, and execution of the film's development and release. It's a system that Disney has used repeatedly—and it's why it remains a giant in the industry.

Now that HyperLeverage is part of Disney's DNA, the results the company sees around licensing and merchandising continue to expand its bottom line and brand equity. The merchandising and licensing around the latest movie in the *Toy Story* franchise, *Toy Story 4*, which was released in June 2019, was planned down to the minutest detail. Even Mattel Toys, which missed out big time on the original *Toy Story* opportunity, is connecting its all-time top toy brand, Barbie, to the *Toy Story* brand. Because Disney fully understands how to maximize its outcomes around merchandising, it actively identifies assets—both inside and outside the organization— to leverage. That's what HyperLeverage looks like in action.

Consider the Disney franchise, *Star Wars*. The first film in the franchise, *A New Hope*, was released in May 1977. Disney purchased Lucas Films, the developer and owner of the Star Wars franchise, in 2012, for $4 billion. The four Star Wars movies produced since have added another $5 billion to the total movie series total. That number doesn't reflect the hundreds of millions in licensing fees from tie-ins and toys that Disney took in. Star Wars is the all-time number one licensed toy franchise. And now Disney is leveraging its vast library of evergreen content and powerful, globally recognized movie and TV brands through its streaming video service to compete with competitors such as Netflix. It's a proactive move to defend its turf and reach its audience in new ways. It's the power of HyperLeverage at work again.

The HyperLeverage Advantage

"Give me a lever long enough and a fulcrum on
which to place it, and I shall move the world."
~Archimedes

Archimedes, the Greek mathematician, physicist, and engineer, was
perhaps the first individual in recorded history to refer to leverage as
a tool to solve problems and make things happen. His famous quote,

which appears on the opening page of this section, says it all. It's a manifesto for using leverage to magnify the results of one's efforts. He believed in taking action to initiate positive change. And it wasn't only rocks and boulders he was thinking of moving. He saw the advantages of leverage in its holistic context and how the potential for leverage existed in a multitude of situations.

CHAPTER 1

Looking for Leverage

everage is all around us every day, but it goes mostly unnoticed, except by those few who tune into it or actively look for it. Nature provides a great model for HyperLeverage in action. Mother Nature has a system in place to constantly leverage her assets: it's called evolution. *Popular Science* offered a fascinating article back in 2011 called, "Ten Astounding Cases of Modern Evolution and Adaptation." Among the truly amazing natural adaptations spotlighted were an Algerian mouse species that had learned how to survive human-kind's deadliest rodenticide, Warfarin, and a bedbug that had evolved a new thick, wax-like exoskeleton that repels pesticides, making it much more difficult to eradicate. The article even described how man continues to adapt to modern challenges. A study by scientists at the Italian National Research Council documented that the bodies of a group of cardiologists, who are exposed to dangerous x-rays during their work, appear to be actively developing protection against this job hazard. Isn't that amazing!

Mother Nature is always on the lookout for opportunities to leverage information from her environment. She has a truly awe-inspiring genetic system that actively learns, interprets, and passes on that information to the current and next generation. The phrase "survival of the fittest" emanates from the idea that a species' chances of surviving and thriving rely on its ability to adapt and evolve quickly to our world's ever-changing environment. That sounds like the same environment in which businesses operate, and evolution is the very definition of HyperLeverage. It's a jungle out there! So why not embrace the tried-and-true system that is running the planet—HyperLeverage?

Leverage Versus HyperLeverage

Without action, leverage only represents a potential utilization of resources that affect a positive and deliberate outcome. Without action, leverage is like money in the bank, only manifesting real value when it's deployed for additional gain. On the other hand, HyperLeverage is proactive exploitation of the potential that leverage represents. It requires intentional action.

As Figure 2 shows, HyperLeverage is leverage on steroids. It means systematically identifying and acting upon leverage opportunities to drive maximum growth. What does it look like when a company starts actively seeking and exploiting leverage? The story of the Play-Doh® brand, now owned by Hasbro, is a hundred-year journey from leverage to HyperLeverage. There's a much faster way to achieve HyperLeverage than what you'll see in this story. The Play-Doh® story drives home the difference between leverage and HyperLeverage and makes it crystal clear why the latter is preferable.

Play-Doh® is a household name today. This unique, hands-on toy is enjoyed by millions of children around the world. John Kell, writing in Fortune magazine in February 2016, relates that since the debut of this now-famous yellow-canned toy, more than 3 billion units have been sold. Even after decades on the market, the

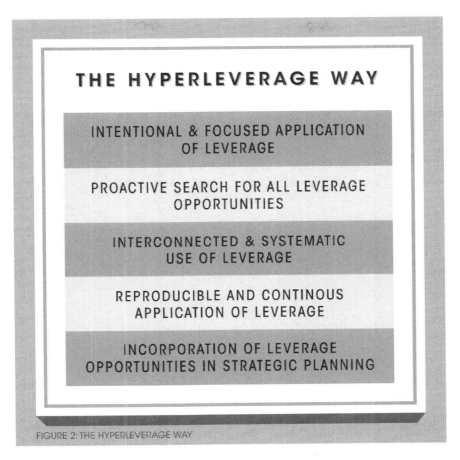

FIGURE 2: THE HYPERLEVERAGE WAY

Play-Doh® brand continues to grow, posting double-digit revenue growth, even in the 21st Century.

Davin Hiskey, in an article published in Insider Magazine in 2015, further details the story of Play-Doh®'s unusual beginning. All the way back in the 1920s, Kutol Products, a Cincinnati-based soap company run by the McVicker family, was about to go belly up. At the time, 21-year-old Cleo McVicker was charged with selling off Kutol's remaining assets, mainly powdered hand soaps. He managed to turn a nice profit on these assets and kept the company afloat, but just barely. A few years later, Cleo was in a meeting with Kroger grocery store when the rep asked if Kutol made wallpaper cleaner, a hot commodity at the time due to the layer of soot homeowners had to deal with in their coal-heated homes. In a bold stroke, Cleo told the Kroger rep that he could make the wallpaper cleaner for them, even though no one at Kutol knew how. Kroger ordered 15,000 cases. Luckily, Cleo's brother, Noah, figured out how to make the wallpaper cleaner and the company grew through the income from this new product for more than a decade. It's a perfect example of leverage in action. They made the most out of what they had and knew.

In the 1950s, however, oil and gas furnaces began replacing coal furnaces, and vinyl wallpaper came along. Kutol's staple product was slowly becoming obsolete, and sales were dwindling. By that time, Joe McVicker, Noah's nephew, had joined Kutol, which was again struggling financially.

Through a stroke of good luck and the help of Joe's sister-in-law, Kay Zufall, it was discovered that Kutol's wallpaper cleaner also worked wonderfully as a clay-like toy for kids. "Kutol's Rainbow Modeling Compound" was invented and quickly renamed Play-Doh®. Almost immediately, the new product started selling well across Ohio. Unfortunately, there was no budget for national advertising. What did Joe do? He leveraged his sales skills and talked his way into an audience with Bob Keeshan, better known as Captain Kangaroo. With a deal to give the Captain Kangaroo production company two percent of the sales generated, Play-Doh® was brought to a national audience and became an instant hit—all with no advertising budget! It was another example of leverage: Joe leveraged the talents he had to create a partnership that he could leverage for national exposure. I'm sure you're noticing that this company has walked to the edge of the precipice several times before discovering an asset or skill to leverage and save the company. It's a stressful and inefficient way to survive and certainly not an optimal way to thrive.

In 1958, sales of Play-Doh® reached nearly $3 million, and by 1964 it was being exported to Britain, France, and Italy. A year later, General Mills purchased Rainbow Crafts, the company the McVickers had created to produce Play-Doh®. The purchase price was $3 million—an unbelievable bargain, considering what would happen to the brand moving forward. It was a clear indication that the McVickers understood leverage, but not HyperLeverage. Joe and his team had no strategic plan in place to fully capitalize on the asset they had created.

In 1991, Hasbro became the owner of Play-Doh® through a series of acquisitions. This is where the McVickers' leverage-on-the-fly approach ends, and Hasbro's HyperLeverage of the Play-Doh® brand begins. Hasbro would transform Play-Doh® into one of its most popular and successful brands.

What Hasbro recognized—and the McVickers did not—was that Play-Doh® was the basis for an entire product line of associated accessories and toys that would be used to mold it into different shapes. This expanded the possibilities for kids to play with it and turned Play-Doh® into a true consumable revenue machine. In 2017 alone, Hasbro produced more than 500 million cans of Play-Doh®.

In the early 2000s, according to John Kell in Fortune magazine, the Play-Doh® brand reported "double-digit revenue growth, including a 32 percent increase in 2015." Though not the shiniest new toy on the block—Play-Doh® turned 60 in 2016—Hasbro's ability to capitalize on the enduring appeal of this toy has positioned it as a consistent sales driver for the company. It has turned out to be a true consumable toy that has spanned five generations and is still going strong.

Like Disney, Hasbro has created a system to actively identify, acquire, refine, and deploy assets that create added value and realize an optimal return. First, it acquired the Play-Doh® brand, and then maximized its value. In a HyperLeverage culture, this is done methodically. Nothing is done on the fly, as it was when the McVickers owned the brand. Everything is done with intention.

Despite the big financial hits that Hasbro suffered in 2018 with the bankruptcy and closure of Toys R Us, its largest retail distributor, Hasbro was set up to leverage its core brands. It adapted. It increased its online sales and leveraged its other distribution partners. Play-Doh® is distributed to thousands of retail outlets, supermarkets, pharmacies, convenience stores, and toy stores. The lesson is clear—the combination of a trusted brand, phenomenal distribution, consistent quality, and a relationship with the consumer that has spanned generations were all leveraged successfully to weather the financial storm.

Failure to Leverage

Barnes & Noble dominated the book retail market in the 1980s. At the beginning of the 21st century, it had it all and was the largest and most dominant chain of brick and mortar bookstores in the country. It had locations in all the major urban areas close to its target middle to upper middle-class population centers, a strong brand, and an online e-commerce store. When Amazon began dominating the book marketplace with online sales, Barnes & Noble started to struggle. In 2019, the company was sold to the Hedge Fund Elliott Advisors for a mere $638 million, having lost $1 billion of its value over the past five years.

What happened?

The real problem, wrote journalist Gracie Olmstead in a 2018 article for *The American Conservative*, is that Barnes and Noble, "… never seemed to prize their own distinctive beauty, and always sought to make themselves more like technology stores rather than emulating the success of their smaller, indie-bookstore counterparts." The bookstore failed to leverage its unique environment and shopping experience. It failed to leverage its staff of knowledgeable people who could interact face-to-face with customers and guide them to books they would otherwise not be aware of. It failed to leverage its unique position as a company that had an e-reader (The NOOK), an online store, and a physical story—a combination that Amazon did not have. Now that Barnes and Noble has been taken over by the private equity group, Elliott Advisors (who also own the British book chain, Waterstones), Barnes and Noble will begin to leverage and incorporate the lessons from its sister company's turnaround.

Perhaps a glaring example of a business that failed to leverage its assets is Sears. The sad, slow demise of this iconic American company is the story of a modest mail-order company started in Illinois in 1896 that went on to become the greatest retail and mail-order company that ever existed...only to lose it all. Six generations came to know it as one of the greatest retail mail order and retail companies to have ever existed. The story of Sears provides a multitude of examples and lessons on the power of leverage in business, how to acquire it, use it and ultimately lose it.

In the 1880s, Richard W. Sears and Alvah C. Roebuck recognized that the population centers of the country were moving west. They understood that with the advent of the industrial revolution, there was pent-up demand for both household goods and what was perceived at the time as luxury items. So, they responded by founding a modest mail-order company to sell watches.

Sears and Roebuck and especially Julius Rosenwald, a Chicago clothing merchant who joined as a partner in 1895, understood that people needed an access for purchasing essential goods. We take for granted the ease of e-commerce or even shopping in a retail mall or shopping center, when in fact they are quite modern conveniences.

Sears was far ahead of the game and pioneered the use of essential business skills of marketing and business intelligence, planning, and understanding demographic trends, and leveraged them to build a mail-order and retail brand and empire the likes of which were unknown at the time and which dominated the consumer goods landscape for decades and generations.

The company was also amongst the first to recognize that controlling distribution was a powerful leverage tool. It took advantage of the nascent growing national infrastructure of railroads and other delivery services to provide their goods to a far-reaching population. By the turn of the 20th century, Sears was already a household name and brand known for the breadth of consumer products of all kinds. It dominated the retail arena through its print catalog and subsequent national chain of stores.

Sears also understood the power of quality and consistency. By building brands such as Craftsman® tools and Kenmore® appliances, it not only promised but delivered value that transcended these actual products. It leveraged these brands and the goodwill they represented as magnets to attract customers to purchase other items as well.

This strategy is taken for granted today as standard brand marketing by most consumer-facing companies. They can point to Sears as leading the way decades before.

Sears eventually lost its way, became complacent, bloated, and unable to recognize and react in time to the changing forces of discount retailers like Wal-Mart and the emerging world of e-commerce.

In a consumer retail world controlled by technology, speed, and ability to adapt and change quickly and continuously, the generations-old business culture of Sears was left in the dust, unable to leverage any of its once-perceived advantages into sustainable revenue and growth.

HyperLeverage starts with having a HyperLeverage Mindset, a desire to do and get more from what you already have and a willingness to look at every situation with open eyes (and an acceptance that there are multiple views and viewpoints). Here's a case in point: when asked how many walls are in a room, most people will instinctively respond with the answer, four. Some will be more creative and say six, as they include the ceiling and the floor. Rarely, though, does anyone say eight or ten, thereby including the outside wall that was supporting the four walls that they could see. It's that kind of "see beyond what's right in front of your nose" thinking that is required for a HyperLeverage Mindset. If you're training yourself to have a HyperLeverage Mindset, you have to stop and remind yourself of what you see in front of you.

In business, this is a crucial concept to grasp. Why? Because you are trying to sell something to someone else and get a return (profit). Consider that customers' and clients' views are fundamental to being able to leverage your products, services, and value add. Therefore, your HyperLeverage journey begins by introducing a very simple tool, the Leverage Prism.

CHAPTER 2

The Leverage Prism

After seven years of toiling night and day, 365 days a year in my first startup, Colorations® Inc., I was ready to quit. Colorations® was a children's arts and craft development, manufacturing, and marketing company that I founded in 1990. From the beginning, my plan was always to sell my business to a large competitor after successfully grabbing a significant portion of its market share. It was part of my seven-year business plan.

My exit was taking place during the first "dot.com" boom, a period of extreme growth in the usage and adoption of the Internet. At the time, most companies were setting up the online portion of their businesses, and those that had a presence online were selling like hotcakes. Colorations®' products were sold at major school supply distributors, toy and gift distributors, and mass-market retailers such as Sam's Club, Costco, TJ Maxx, Kmart, and others. Our products were available in more than a thousand outlets in almost every state in the country, including Hawaii, Alaska, Puerto Rico, and even Guam. I had grown the company year after year by an average of more than 50 percent per year and Colorations® had become a recognized brand in my industry. In an era before social media and the Internet, I had leveraged my rags-to-riches story and pitched it to every print outlet

I could. Being written up in local newspapers, the *Christian Science Monitor*, *Entrepreneur* magazine, *Nations Business,* and *Inc.*, I utilized whatever print, radio and even local TV opportunity I had to talk about my products, my company, and my journey. My company and I even made it into a cover article in *Money* magazine in 1998!

As I began executing on my exit strategy, I believed that my market share and network of retail and catalog outlets would give me significant leverage in the negotiations. I put out feelers to my target companies, including Crayola and Rose Art, both market leaders. We had a series of discussions and meetings, and their response was tepid. They didn't seem to see the value in my company that I saw. I had established distribution in more than a thousand stores nationwide, and more importantly, our products were included in all the major school supply catalogs that were in print at the time.

With all the enthusiasm and optimism about the Internet in the late 1990s, it was still difficult for existing companies mired in the brick-and-mortar mentality and tradition to embrace it. These companies were scared by the uncertainty of the "dot.com bubble." The business press was reporting that companies were overpaying amid the feeding frenzy of acquisitions, and the bubble was going to pop any day. I was almost ready to accept a low-ball offer when out of the blue, I got a call from the CEO of one of my smallest customers, QTL Corporation, which would later become Excelligence Learning Corp, a school supply distributor in California. The CEO called to inquire whether he was too late to the party. He wanted to talk about a possible acquisition of my company. I told the owner of the company that I had an offer on the table, which I was thinking about accepting. He begged me to wait a day and took a red eye to Atlanta so we could meet the next morning.

He knew my story, had read the *Money* magazine article, and done his homework. He also knew where the market was moving in the dot.com era and the enormous potential it represented and felt he could leverage the Colorations® brand and products I had built. Rather than the distribution network and balance sheet that I thought reflected my company's value, he pointed to the company's intangibles. It was the creativity, innovation, and ability to come up with new products and new packaging that Colorations® represented to him. To him, buying Colorations® would take "me" off the market and away from the competitors as he developed Colorations® for himself. It was a huge lesson for me. I had never looked at myself as a business asset. I was completely blind to my company's real value and what I had to leverage in the negotiations with potential buyers.

We were looking at the same company but from completely different perspectives, as shown in Figure 3. I was looking at value as an owner, and he was looking at it as a potential buyer. I was thinking of old school balance sheets, profit and loss, earnings before interest, taxes, depreciation and amortization(EBITDA). He was thinking of something completely different.

In the end, we negotiated through the night and into the morning. QTL's CEO was quite savvy and understood that he could not offer me the career opportunities that I might have found merging with a major company like Crayola. Rather, he knew what he was "buying" and how to leverage it to create HyperLeverage. Offering me a royalty on my products spanning 25 years, he unlocked the innovation, creativity, and product development expertise that I possessed.

The business marriage was a success, and over four years after being absorbed by QTL, I had developed over 12 new product lines and more than 100 stock keeping units (SKUs), established two world-class manufacturing facilities that rivaled those of Crayola, and increased revenue from these and the existing Colorations® products by

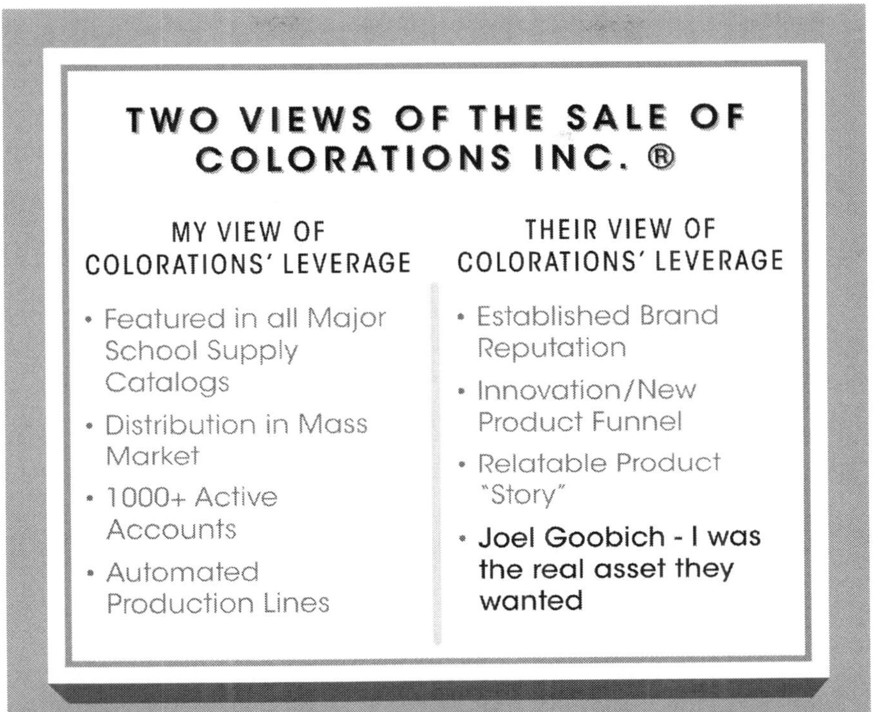

TWO VIEWS OF THE SALE OF COLORATIONS INC. ®

MY VIEW OF COLORATIONS' LEVERAGE	THEIR VIEW OF COLORATIONS' LEVERAGE
• Featured in all Major School Supply Catalogs	• Established Brand Reputation
• Distribution in Mass Market	• Innovation/New Product Funnel
• 1000+ Active Accounts	• Relatable Product "Story"
• Automated Production Lines	• **Joel Goobich - I was the real asset they wanted**

FIGURE 3: TWO VIEWS OF THE SALE OF COLORATIONS ® INC.

a factor of five. All because the buyer was looking at the opportunity through a different prism.

As a result of my experience as a business owner with Colorations®, I developed a new way of assessing value to help other business owners and executive teams. I call it the Leverage Prism, and today, through my business consultancy, I use it to help companies with their strategic planning, business growth initiatives, and exit strategies. You remember studying prisms in school. Those glass triangles that allow white light to enter on one side, bend it at an acute angle, and separate into a full spectrum of colors—a rainbow. Without looking through a prism, who would know that all those colors were inside white light? They are, and that's the value of a prism. It deconstructs the light so you can see components of that light, which would otherwise be invisible to the naked eye. My colleague was using a prism to look at the assets I'd created in building Colorations. He saw things that I hadn't seen.

In my work with business owners, I have found that rarely do they understand the true value of their business. Look at the McVickers and their sale of Play-Doh. In hindsight, they could have made more on the sale of their company. Most of the companies I work with either overestimate their company's value based on their emotional attachment or underestimate it because they don't fully comprehend the potential value of the assets they have created. Additionally, most owners look at their performance to date for perceived value, rather than future potential.

Leadership teams, executives, and business owners need a Leverage Prism on an ongoing basis to uncover and utilize the hidden pockets of value in their company. It is how businesses turn potential into the reality of profits and growth.

The story of the sale of my company, Colorations®, is not unique. Buyers and sellers often come from opposite perspectives. The same holds true in almost all business negotiations, transactions, and people-to-people interactions. The point is that being able to see things through the eyes of your vendors, customers, and competitors provides the perspective necessary to leverage your position more advantageously.

When I use the Leverage Prism for actionable strategic planning as part of a holistic big-picture approach, I deconstruct their business into its core components and evaluate each for its real and future value. It is often an eye-opening experience for business owners.

They are not interested in the past as much as the company's potential to deliver a strong return in the future. They're looking at the company's assets that will drive that value. Getting business owners to look through the eyes of their potential buyers can be a challenge, but it helps them get more money for their businesses.

Business leaders need prisms to reveal hidden characteristics and attributes that are not readily seen. The Leverage Prism is the first step toward HyperLeverage. It is an evaluation and analysis tool that allows us to comprehend what we already have. Without this, we chase our tails or waste time, money and effort doing things that won't get the results we desire or even worse, acquiring more assets when we already have the ones we need.

If we take the proverbial 20,000-foot view of the issues that we are dealing with in our business life, whether it's employee issues, marketing, operations, sales or finance, we often just see a singular view. This view is mostly colored by our direct experience, training, prejudice, and perception. Using the Leverage Prism tool, we can deconstruct this view and perception in the separate components of which it is constructed.

The Leverage Prism can highlight aspects of a business that are not being fully utilized or are resource hogs that don't return a worthwhile return on the underlying investment. The Leverage Prism is an evaluation and analysis tool that allows business owners to fully comprehend the value of their assets as a potential buyer sees them.

The Leverage Prism can also be used for other use cases like discovering resources and assets that are not being fully utilized in a company. We need tools to uncover the leverage we have and assess how to maximize the return on those assets. The Leverage Prism can also guide additional resources that a company might need to acquire to realize its full potential or identify areas for improvement. The key is that the Leverage Prism gives us a methodology to unlock HyperLeverage, something that can't be achieved unless we can deconstruct and analyze all potential opportunities. With the building blocks laid out in front of us, we can begin to construct a different and better engine to extract all the "nectar" from our resources.

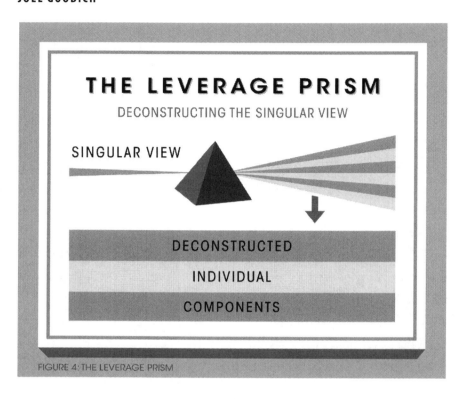

FIGURE 4: THE LEVERAGE PRISM

The advantages of utilizing this mental embodiment of a glass prism are manifold. To begin, it forces one to take off the blinders and preconceived notions that we all have to some degree and get to the core issues. Like starting to construct a jigsaw puzzle, we lay out all the pieces in front of us and look for those that build the framework. The prism approach lays bare those areas of fundamental value.

Wal-Mart, unlike Sears, adapts and harnesses its massive arsenal of leverageable assets. As an observer from the outside, one can detect how Wal-Mart has taken apart the pieces of the new economic reality of e-commerce and the existential threat that Amazon posed to its hegemony. 2018 was the year Wal-Mart finally found its stride in its fight against Amazon.

The annual Fortune 500 list published in June 2019 describes some of how Wal-Mart leveraged its retail footprint by, "Equipping thousands of stores for grocery pickup, resulting in an increase of its U.S. online revenue by 40 percent. Wal-Mart was also deft in capitalizing on many rivals' problems (Sears) or demise (Toys 'R' Us to name just one), leading it to its best holiday season in years. The company is now innovating with things like a personal shopping service and self-driving delivery vans. Wal-Mart's success extended to its resurgent Sam's Club business, as well as internationally, where it has decided to focus on a few key markets, all propelling company sales to 3 percent growth—and well past the $500 billion mark."

This impressive growth didn't happen by chance or in the blink of an eye. The executive team at Wal-Mart utilized the fundamental first step of the HyperLeverage system—the use of a leverage prism technique to deconstruct their view of themselves and the market and carefully examine those areas they could take more advantage of. From this, they clearly recognized they could utilize the location and inventory of their existing stores, not just for walk-in retail traffic, but to supercharge the growth of their online sales by providing an easily accessible place to pick up products without having to wait for or pay for delivery.

CHAPTER 3

Mastering HyperLeverage

The pressure to achieve results quickly in today's competitive, fast-changing marketplace is enormous. Too often, companies, teams, and professionals get caught up in the madness of this race and forget where they're going and how best to get there. There's no time to step out of the rat race and look at the big picture. The pressure is on. This short-term, happenstance approach is a huge mistake and one that could cost your company millions of dollars in inefficiency and unrealized potential.

When everyone is focused on the next quarter's sales target or next month's revenue goals, the leverage that could take your company to the next level goes undiscovered and the opportunity for HyperLeverage, with all its benefits and growth potential, goes unrealized. Your company might luck out, stumble on a few leverage opportunities, and realize a short-term advantage (think back to the McVickers' story), but the consistently exceptional outcomes made possible by HyperLeverage will elude you. Over time, the opportunity cost will take its toll, and your company will slowly lose its competitive advantage, even as you continue to work harder and longer to achieve the same or slightly better results. Don't make this mistake.

HyperLeverage and its holistic approach to proactively and intentionally taking full advantage of all resources and opportunities is essential in today's business world, and it can only exist within an environment that is structured to nurture it. Having tools and a system to unlock leverage is crucial.

The DOIT Leverage Method Combines Analysis And Action

Throughout my career, both as an entrepreneur, consultant, and business strategist, I've honed a business approach of taking a step back to take in the entire business canvas. That has become my go-to tool for discovering and unlocking the potential leverage in any business situation. This wide-angled view is the genesis of the DOIT Leverage Method and evaluation system I developed. It combines the "what's behind the curtain" Leverage Prism technique with an analysis of how each essential component can be organized and improved to reach more impactful results through the utilization of existing assets and resources. What sets the DOIT Leverage Method apart from other simple business evaluation methodologies such as a SWOT analysis is the emphasis on **taking action**, not just analyzing and planning. As I discussed earlier and depicted previously in Figure 2, HyperLeverage mandates that you take charge with a clear intent to exploit the potential of every leverage situation that exists. HyperLeverage doesn't happen by chance. It requires an investment of effort and resources.

The DOIT Leverage Method is a disciplinary approach to making sure that you understand the core leverage issues and can identify all leverage opportunities. The power of the DOIT Leverage Method lies in its combination of analysis, critical thinking, planning, and implementation. Without action, actual leverage can't be realized. Figure 5 depicts the four activities that make up the DOIT Leverage Method.

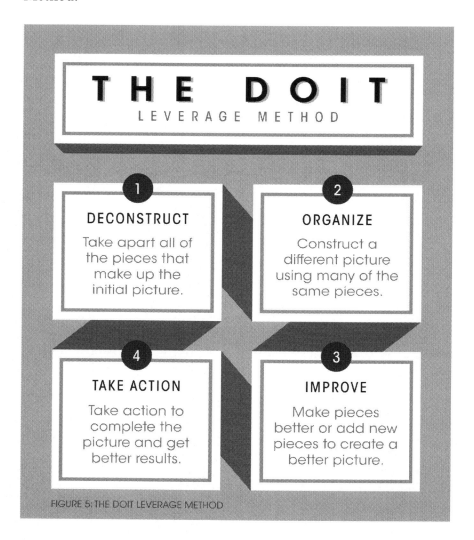

FIGURE 5: THE DOIT LEVERAGE METHOD

Deconstruct

The DOIT Leverage Method starts by utilizing the Leverage Prism tool to deconstruct the underlying components of specific business issues. This foundation then allows for a deeper examination of the individual parts to see if every advantage is being squeezed out of them and how they can be better utilized and organized.

Think of this stage like building a house with a box of Lego® pieces. The individual pieces come in a box with a picture of different objects you can build with them when they are put together. However, when you open the box, all you see is a big pile of connected, individual pieces. How are you going to get this pile of pieces to look anything like the picture on the front of the box? Perhaps you can build a different, better structure.

You start by deconstructing how a building is put together. It has a foundation, supporting walls, windows, doors and a roof. You discover and count all of the construction pieces that you have at your disposal. The Leverage Prism tool allows you to do this deconstruction for your business. It allows you to break up your established viewpoint (the big picture) of a specific business situation and see its components. Once you've deconstructed the situation, you can start to organize those components for reconstruction.

Organize

When you begin to organize, you become a treasure hunter, peeking under rocks, squeezing through tunnels, taking risks, thinking differently. The DOIT Leverage Method is only as effective as the inputs (such as data, intelligence, and market research) that go into it and the brutal "look in the mirror" honesty that comes from true critical thinking.

Remember when you built a structure using building blocks such as Lego®? Almost all start by sorting out the corner and edge pieces to create the frame. It gives you a manageable place to start and helps to orient you. It's a sort of framework to tackle a big and confusing undertaking. After the frame is in place, you can complete the rest of the building. It's much the same in business. The DOIT Leverage Method is a framework for assessing problems and opportunities. You are not looking to build the same picture of your business that you deconstructed. You are looking to develop a new canvas, a new viewpoint using the same components, or determine which pieces need replacement, improvement, or what additional pieces are required.

The area that is perhaps the most important when it comes to HyperLeverage is thinking about how to organize and reconstruct the components of the business "building blocks" in a way that creates additional value. Stepping outside the box of conventional thinking is so important at this point. Think back to the example of Colorations® earlier in this chapter. The leverageable opportunities may not be so apparent or directly "in your face." This is where taking a "bigger picture" stance allows other ideas to come to the forefront. For example, using the Lego® analogy, you could start by grouping the pieces by length, then by color, and then look at the picture on the box and the way they were used. This will give you a starting point to see where to start.

When organizing a new "picture," we all have the tendency to overvalue the leverage potential of certain assets and undervalue the opportunities of others. We overlook or diminish the weaknesses in our skills and our organizations. Because our focus is more "present tense," we ignore or downplay threats that loom on the horizon. This impedes our ability to mine the golden nuggets of leverage.

Improve

Now it's time to decide what you can and will do to make improvements. Have you determined that you are missing a necessary building block?

Perhaps you identified missing skills and experience in your workforce. Maybe your current systems could be improved with the addition of the latest technology. Or perhaps you require an investment in certain equipment and infrastructure so your business "building blocks" you've organized and identified can support additional business growth. This is the time to evaluate what you can and should make better and how to accomplish it.

Implicit in this stage is a recognition that things must change. You need to recognize what can be changed and at what rate your organization can handle that change. In the final stage of the DOIT Leverage Method—the Take Action phase—you will identify how this change will be managed and by whom. You'll also identify milestones and measurements that will be used to measure success.

Take Action

As I stated previously, implementation and taking comprehensive and focused action is the connective glue in the HyperLeverage ecosystem. To turn leverage and its potential advantages into reality, you must go beyond the talk, beyond the theoretical evaluations, beyond the data and numbers. You must get your hands dirty and move things. Those business building blocks will not come together into a cohesive structure if you don't apply the lessons learned from the Deconstruct, Organize, and Improve stages. By not acting on the work you did in the previous three phases of the DOIT Leverage Method, you are essentially like the too eager negotiator or salesman who leaves money on the table.

You are at the point in the DOIT Leverage Method where it all comes together again. Only this time, you've developed a different vantage point. You are not constructing the same structure as before. You are building something better, stronger, and longer lasting. It's time to put a detailed comprehensive plan into place, including how you will manage the project. Have you prioritized the key leverage activities, whether it's training, hiring, or introducing new technology and systems? Who has the responsibility and the authority to implement? How will you communicate the new picture, objectives, and action plans to vested parties?

Have you pushed the envelope and comfort level enough to affect the necessary sense of purpose and urgency? Remember, this is an exercise in change, which brings with it the necessity to be mindful of how team members, vendors, and even clients might react.

Finally, with everything in place, it's time to hit the gas pedal and get going. It's all too easy to hold back and give it another go-around of analysis and planning. I caution you to squelch those urges. That is why you need to plan for an appropriate and adequate measurement process for any plan of action you take. The DOIT Leverage Method by definition is a closed loop of continuous measurement, refinement and implementation.

CHAPTER 4

The 4 Ps of HyperLeverage

All organizations, especially for-profit businesses, need to adopt the mindset that all of their assets have leverage potential. No settling for those mediocre return on investments. The answer lies in four core areas of business activity—people, planning, performance, and progress and the relationships between them.

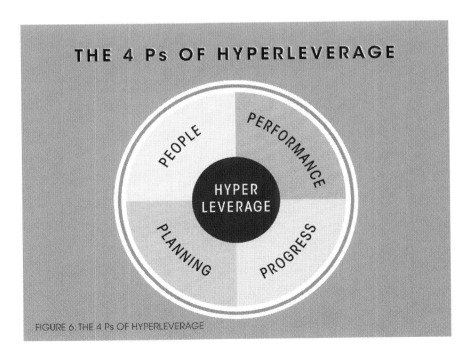

FIGURE 6: THE 4 Ps OF HYPERLEVERAGE

Taking action is the "Performance" component of the 4 Ps. However, before you can take the appropriate and most advantageous action, you need to know what actions to take, when to take action, and how to take action. That's the "Planning" component.

People are indeed the integral glue of any organization. They make the decisions. They control the levers of leverage. Whether individually or as members of teams, they are the ones that plan what needs to be done to meet business objectives and then create the plans and finally implement them. It's the combination of these activities that make "People" a critical element in the HyperLeverage system.

To plan, perform, and progress productively, you need to have the right human resources, work conditions, vendors, or partners in place. It would be best if you had the right planning, strategies, roadmap, and plans of action. I turn to sports for inspiration to make my second point about HyperLeveraging planning. One needs to look no further than team sports, even the highest level of college sports, to see that an organization does not need to rely on one or two superstars to succeed. It's those teams that have planned for and created robust, reproducible and comprehensive systems, like the New England Patriots or the University of Alabama football teams, that can achieve HyperLeverage.

Isn't that what would work in your business? Instead of relying on a "superstar" employee mentality, you create a culture and develop the framework and systems in which you allow "ordinary" people to reach their potential. For many organizations, the differentiating factor separating good from great is their ability to perform at a consistently high level. That's what Marc Benioff envisioned as he built Salesforce into the largest CRM service company on the planet. It's the consistent high level of performance and implementation that creates the structural bridge to achieving HyperLeverage.

Finally, to achieve and maintain HyperLeverage, a business needs to have a systematic approach to progress. The nature of free trade and an open economic system guarantees that new ideas will turn into innovations and technologies that will change the business landscape. Companies that systematically encourage innovation and adopt new technologies will become industry leaders. Organizations such as IBM, which has reinvented itself time and again, understand this underlying factor of the modern business environment and learn to embrace and leverage change, and stand the best chance to HyperLeverage Progress.

Now, let's take a deeper dive into each of the 4 Ps—People, Planning, Performance, and Progress—since they are the keys to identifying and exploiting business leverage.

HyperLeverage and People

"Great things in business are never done by one person. They're done by a team of people."
~Steve Jobs

DEFINITION: HYPERLEVERAGE AND PEOPLE

1. Leveraging employees by providing the right work conditions, incentives, tools, training and opportunities for them to fully develop their skills and exploit their experience, talents and professional connections to achieve exceptional and impactful results.

2. Actively identifying and utilizing all professional business and vendor relationships to advance the objectives of an organization for maximum benefit.

3. Maximizing all avenues of communication with employees, vendors, partners, clients and prospective customers in order to have them take positive action that directly benefits your organization.

People are the foundation of every business and organization. They are the workforce, the vendors and suppliers, clients, and customers. Simply put, without people, there is no business. Understanding how to HyperLeverage the human side of your business is mandatory for success. That's why people are the first of the 4 Ps we're going to break down.

Workforce is a terrible word. It sounds like the desks at every company in America are filled with drones or minions. Slowly, the lexicon we use to talk about "the workforce" is changing, as it should. People who feel like drones and minions, work like drones and minions. The opportunity to change the culture of your company and truly leverage your most important asset—your people—starts with the words you use when you are talking with them. That's right, you can HyperLeverage your words, your lexicon. It's a powerful tool.

In this section, we'll look at how and why to HyperLeverage people within your organization—individuals, groups, teams, and even the entire corporate community. We'll also look at the reasons why you should HyperLeverage processes, environments, and systems to attract, hire, develop, train, and retain the best people for your organization. We'll examine how vital it is to HyperLeverage communication, both internally and externally, to nurture a healthy corporate culture and to inform the world of the virtues of your brand, products, and services.

Finally, we'll discuss and point out the ins and outs of attaining HyperLeverage through your clients, vendors and partnerships. These are the people outside an organization that are integral to supporting a brand, improving operational performance, and developing new business opportunities. In short, how these external people can be proactively leveraged to achieve exceptional results. Ready to dive in? Let's do it. Head first!

CHAPTER 5

Hiring & Talent

n today's competitive job market, finding and hiring the right talent with a HyperLeverage Mindset of being cognizant of all leverage opportunities is the only way to build a strong foundation for your company's growth. Netflix is that kind of company. Disrupting the video-store model built by Blockbuster, Netflix introduced the world to streaming and on-demand TV shows and movies. The 21-year-old company has grown to more than 120 million subscribers across the globe and employs more than 5,500 people. Netflix is now a household name and a top media and technology company that continues to innovate and grow.

The Netflix team has been breaking the rules since they were a startup and continue to question the status quo with an eye on how to do things better. They use a DOIT-like methodology of methodically breaking apart the existing view into its components, organizing and rearrange the parts, and discarding unnecessary steps and roadblocks. Their goal is always to construct a better mousetrap. This process is what they used in 2009, when they decided to revamp the way they went about finding and hiring new talent. They wanted to build a hiring system to identify, hire, and retain the precise type of talent they needed to take the company to the next level. The hiring system they built didn't happen by chance. It was built in a proactive, meaningful, and certainly intentional way—the very description of HyperLeverage.

Recognizing that hiring the "old fashioned" way was not congruent with its company's values, Netflix set out to reengineer the hiring process. The company was intent on finding individuals who possessed nine core traits that embodied the company's values: good judgment, good communication, impact, curiosity, innovation, honesty, selflessness, courage, and passion. They wanted to create a more holistic approach to hiring and get rid of the "round peg for a round hole" method that many, if not most, other companies in the industry were using.

The team at Netflix eschewed the accepted mindset of hiring people for a specific skill set to fill a specific job. Instead, they decided to describe their ideal candidate as someone who could focus on great results. In other words, they only sought professionals who were eager and able to learn rapidly. Additionally, they sought out individuals who could contribute and collaborate effectively outside their areas of specialization. In short, Netflix decided to stop filling immediate gaps to build a company filled with talented people who wanted to leverage *all* their talents for years to come.

As Patty McCord, then Chief Talent Office, explained in a *Harvard Business Review* article in January 2014, Netflix strived to hire, reward, and tolerate only, "...fully formed adults." After all, Netflix had a business to run and a market to disrupt, and they didn't want to waste endless time and money on writing and enforcing HR policies to deal with the small sampling of their workforce that might cause problems. It was the "adults in the room" that deserved the attention; the others didn't belong.

I like this story because it embodies the principles of HyperLeverage. That is, to search out and exploit existing leverage opportunities and bend them to your advantage. So, how did Netflix do this? It did its homework and created a comprehensive document that essentially used the *Start with Why* system espoused by leadership guru Simon Sinek. Netflix developed a 125-page slide deck that laid out the seven aspects of its culture for both current and potential employees. It was looking for people with a strong work ethic who didn't need handholding. It was looking for people who would make the company's interests a priority. It wanted to hire people who understood what a high-performance workplace looked like and required. It didn't want to waste time on writing and enforcing HR policies to police its people. It was after job applicants who were motivated to work for Netflix and had done their homework on the company before interviewing. This later requirement is something that would come up often during the interview process as the company probed how a candidate would fit into the existing culture and workplace environment.

With regard to talent, HyperLeverage is not a one-time event. It is an ongoing activity at any organization. Because every business or business marketplace is dynamic, the talent and performance needs will change. It's not out of the ordinary for a workforce to need to change as well. Netflix recognized that its approach to building a strong team did not end with the hiring process. In what appears to be an adaptation of the highly respected management concepts of Jack Welch a generation earlier at GE, Netflix uses something called a "keeper test" to inform a manager of the effectiveness of a team member. Simply put, a manager is tasked with answering this question: "If one of my team members were thinking of leaving for another firm, would I try hard to keep them?" If the answer was "no," then it was time to find a replacement.

On the surface, this may seem harsh, ruthless, and even counterproductive to maintaining a positive corporate culture. However, together with the more recent HR tool called 360, which allows everyone at the company to review their peers, Netflix intentionally provides context to everyone in the company on why someone was let go. The result is more transparency and objectivity in the service of cementing the corporate culture as defined by its strong-willed leader, Reed Hastings. The actions of the company are therefore clearly communicated for all to understand, allowing for a more productive work environment and paving the road to HyperLeverage of people's talents.

The cost of hiring churn can wreak havoc on organizations. In an environment of extreme competitiveness for high tech talent, the company's adherence to a different talent acquisition process has borne fruit in the hyper-competitive, high-tech Silicon Valley environment. Netflix has been able to maintain a much higher level of retention with an average tenure of 3.1 years, which is more than 20 percent higher than Airbnb or Facebook and a whopping 70 percent higher than Uber.

For those thinking of running out to benchmark or even emulate the Netflix system, I say, "Hold your horses." The story of Netflix and its ability to HyperLeverage its talent pool is indeed instructive. However, it should not be copied verbatim. Every organization has a different culture, a different flavor. Thus, a company's system for hiring and retaining high-skilled talent must be meaningful to the specifics of each organization.

Netflix has an enviable position of being able to be more selective and therefore approach its workforce as expendable to some degree. Smaller and less well-established companies do not always have this luxury. However, this doesn't mean they shouldn't develop a talent acquisition and retention method that dovetails with their core values. In fact, the opposite is true. Smaller and less well-established companies absolutely must develop this type of talent acquisition system, if they want to leverage their talent effectively. Use the DOIT Leverage Methodology to discover leverage opportunities as described in Chapter 3 to create a system that works for you and your company. Then, put it into action.

Today's "Kitchen Sink" Approach to Hiring

Today's hiring process at most companies looks nothing like the Netflix approach. In the name of efficiency, premium paper resumes delivered by "snail mail" have been replaced by online submissions through job boards, recruiting sites, and social platforms like LinkedIn. Software systems sort through the avalanche of online resume submissions in search of predetermined keywords hoping to uncover a pool of promising candidates while not overlooking great people whose resumes don't match up. The process has become a numbers game for companies and a keyword-stuffing game for job candidates.

This has opened a Pandora's box when it comes to hiring. How can anyone possibly sift through the avalanche of emails and documents that hit a company's inboxes as a result of this process? No one can, and no one should have to. In most cases, keyword matching helps plug a hole at a company, not discover its next great leaders. The supposed efficiencies gained by most companies through these new technologies require a growing expenditure of precious time with diminishing results. It's time to start thinking like the team at Netflix. It's time to start questioning the status quo. While technology has its place in the hiring process, relying too heavily on it can squander a golden opportunity to discover HyperLeverage in the hiring process and increase the pool and potential of human talent at your company.

The short- and long-term costs of an ineffective hiring process are substantial. Lost time and productivity, missed opportunities, or internal morale issues can arise as a result of an ineffective hiring process. The negative consequences that reveal themselves rarely compare to the losses that are more difficult to detect but often have the biggest impact over time. Slow erosion of innovation and growth can cause a once successful company to stall out and stagnate.

Viewed through the Leverage Prism hiring is like choosing the right equipment to get the job done in that it's a direct investment. According to a 2015 Leadership IQ Study, 46 percent of hires were considered failures within 18 months of their hire. Therefore, the HyperLeverage move is to proactively put a continuous talent acquisition and retention system in place. Be proactive—not reactive.

Making a poor decision still leaves one with a cash outlay and soft costs of time expended with little or even a negative return. A Career Builder study released in December 2017 suggested, "The average cost of making the wrong choice is $14,900, and losing a good employee costs $29,600."

There are sunk costs that take time to recoup, like the disruption of workflows, potential team or company morale issues, and delays or errors in product or service deliverables. If you must go through it repeatedly, then the expenses add up quickly.

The hiring process should start by identifying candidates who not only meet a company's current needs but will enrich its culture and advance its values as well. As Netflix demonstrated, the emphasis of the interview process should not be solely about the candidates selling themselves to the company. Rather, the company should leverage its unique blend of culture, opportunity, products, and brand to attract candidates who are closely aligned with those characteristics and eager to support them.

The mindset and process to achieve this looks very different than the current hiring process at most companies. Unfortunately, at many companies, a hiring manager works off a boilerplate job description.

Rarely does the manager gather input from the team with whom the new hire will work. At most companies, the strategic work described above has not been done. There is no "why" in place and, as a result, there is no process in place to find, attract, or hire the ideal candidate to fit that "why." If a company wants to HyperLeverage its hiring and reap the benefits for years to come, the leadership team must think and do things differently. Detailing how the company will leverage the position and the person that fills it for the betterment and growth of the company is the better starting point and will require a different approach.

At a minimum, this evaluation should be documented and shared internally. For example, a marketing job may be tasked with attaining certain performance metrics such as reaching a specific number of downloads or inbound marketing leads in a particular time frame. These goals may be directly correlated to a new product launch, which will rely on meeting or exceeding this milestone. This approach will demonstrate to the hiring team and the new hire a tangible and meaningful result of their efforts.

As much as the objective is to hire someone whose talents can be leveraged over time, it is incumbent on the company to shorten the "hit the ground running" time frame for a new hire. This strategy works for the benefit of the company and the new hire, who will feel energized knowing what is expected from day one.

HyperLeverage in the Hiring Process

With a Netflix-style approach to hiring, the kitchen sink list of requirements and one-size-fits-all "check-box" approach gets thrown out. Hiring becomes focused, streamlined, and aligned with the company's most important values and goals. As Netflix has shown us, it is a much more productive approach and one that ultimately has a positive impact on the bottom line.

This approach begins with a deeper internal conversation at the leadership level and requires collaboration with stakeholders who are often outside the department that is doing the actual hiring. At first, it might seem daunting to reconfigure your hiring process, but the long-term benefits are worth it. Netflix developed an internal process to hire the right people, and you can, too. When I am called in as a consultant, I use the Leverage Prism, which allows me to help hiring managers break down the position the company needs filled. Figure 7 deconstructs the hiring process components using this tool.

You probably have a defined process in place for hiring—like developing a job description with the necessary skills, experience and educational requirements—but where's the leverage in your current process? Is your current hiring process helping you find and hire the type of talent that can take your company to the next level? If you're not happy with the answers to these questions, it's time to step back and assess your hiring process at the 20,000-foot level. As we see from Figure 7, having a more holistic approach will yield a new hire who can be HyperLeveraged to achieve substantially more.

What is your hiring process for helping your company achieve? Where could a more strategic hiring mindset and process take your company? If you look at some of the growth challenges you face or hurdles your company has been unable to overcome, you are likely to find that hiring is a whole lot more important than just plugging someone into a position. It's foundational if you want to HyperLeverage your people.

Today, an effective hiring process must be driven by long-term goals. Since we know that people are a company's most important asset, it is critical to understand at a very granular level which hire will help your company achieve its most important strategic goals.

DECONSTRUCTING THE HIRING PROCESS

HIRING

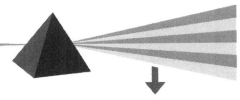

DETERMINE THE OBJECTIVE OF THE POSITION

GET INPUT FROM ALL STAKEHOLDERS

CULTURE & PERSONALITY FIT

CRITICAL THINKING & CREATIVITY SKILLS

DIRECT EXPERIENCE & SKILL SET

REFERENCES/PROFESSIONAL NETWORK

ADAPTABILITY TO CHANGE

GROWTH POTENTIAL/CAREER GOALS

WORK HABITS

TEAM WORK EXPERIENCE

FIGURE 7: DECONSTRUCTING THE HIRING PROCESS

In addition, you should identify what a more effective hiring process would mean to your company's growth and bottom line if it were aligned with those goals. Here's a blueprint that I suggest, utilizing elements of the DOIT Leverage Methodology.

> Start in the right place by defining your culture and long-term goals and including all the necessary stakeholders in the conversation. Determine how the open position will be instrumental in reaching important cultural and strategic considerations. When a company can clearly state its "why" (context/culture/business objectives) at the beginning of the job description or interview and not just the "what" (skills/experience/training), there's a foundation for hiring success. It's a much better prism through which to view and manage the hiring process.

> Deconstruct the old hiring process and evaluate what parts of it are working well and which are not. Use examples of recent hires that didn't work out and correlate this to any warning signs that might have been missed during the hiring process. Was it poor interview preparation, background checks, or perhaps the job description and requirements as written that didn't meet the actual challenges?

> Reconstruct a new hiring process that incorporates the best parts of your previous process and a more holistic approach that dovetails with both short-term and long-term needs. Look to incorporate new technologies that can screen candidates while being extremely cognizant that keywords and job experience listed on a resume are in most instances mimicking what you have already written in your job description. Develop key performance indicators for the position that you will use and can measure.

> ➢ Put it in action and put it to the test by monitoring the effectiveness of your hiring process by back-testing 6, 12, and even 24-months after a new hire has started. Don't be static and continue to refine the entire process—from start to finish.

With a more intentional process in place, you now have a strong foundation to experience HyperLeverage in your hiring process and reap the benefits for years to come. Think of this as investing in infrastructure, like purchasing an industrial plant and filling it with the right equipment. You have proactively built or added additional components to your team, who are already aligned with your mission and your culture, and they have been given a roadmap for success that dovetails with the company's same path.

Getting the Most Out of Talent

When you've finally got the right people in the right jobs, you will start to see the benefits. It's the first step in reaching the goal of being able to HyperLeverage the collective power of your people. There are a few more building blocks to get there. It starts with recognizing and capitalizing on the talent you already have in-house, like the story of my friend Everett and how his skills and experience were taken for granted.

Everett had taught himself IT programming in night school in his mid-thirties while working full time in the accounting department at a distribution company in the Silicon Valley. It was not a very "techy" company, and he realized that he could "buy" himself some job security by being able to tackle the small and increasingly more sophisticated IT tasks the company would have to solve. Over the next 18 years, he became the in-house "IT Guy" and was enjoying the fruits of his educational investment. He liked that his job was all about fixing problems and putting out fires, but he especially enjoyed being presented with a challenge or offered the opportunity to learn something new. For many years, challenges and opportunities to learn were a constant part of his workday. These opportunities made him happy about his career decisions, but things had changed recently.

Everett's work assignments became increasingly routine. Nothing new seemed to cross his plate. New management had taken over the firm when the original owner had retired and sold it. The new team was quite content with the same old-same old. They espoused a "don't rock the boat" philosophy. The new leadership felt they had a good thing going at the firm, and there was no need to make changes, implement new technology, or modernize. Other firms could spend time on those distractions. Instead, the new management team focused on squeezing out extra profits and minimizing investments of time and money in new business practices and technologies. Everett was stuck and no longer happy in his position. To him, the new owners were just running the place on autopilot. He wasn't the only one who felt this way. His colleagues were talking about it amongst themselves as well.

Everett knew he was no longer going to learn anything new that he could leverage later in his career. He was frustrated that the firm's new owners weren't leveraging the gold mine of talent that he and his colleagues represented. When the firm decided to downsize Everett's department, they offered him an early retirement package. He jumped on it. He wasn't concerned about what would come next. He was still too young to consider retirement, collect social security, or hang around in a dead-end job. He still had pepper in his blood and had full confidence in his ability to earn a living doing something with passion, even if it was something he had never done before. Everett leveraged the severance package at his company to extricate himself from a situation where he had become deleveraged.

If Everett's company had made an effort to speak with him and explore his many talents, perhaps they would have found he possessed a superior aptitude for communicating and imparting knowledge to others and tapped him as an internal trainer or even for a position where he could interact with clients and potential customers. They would have found that he was a "fixer," the go-to person you want on your team when things get bad.

You're probably not surprised to hear that Everett landed on his feet. The next stage of his career was not one he had contemplated before the new leadership had taken over. In what I would describe it as putting HyperLeverage into action, Everett took the time after his layoff to deconstruct his past career, his talents, and skills. He came to a momentous decision. He wasn't washed up, and he was not going to put himself in a position like this again. Together with two other coworkers who followed him out the door, he started his own company focusing on improving the IT systems of small to medium-sized accounting companies, like the one he just left. As an entrepreneur and now CEO, he tapped into skills such as business strategy, business development, and client management that he was never allowed to pursue. His former company managed to survive for a few more years, but after losing customers to more technology-oriented competitors, it was sold at a major discount.

The story of Everett's deleveraging and missed potential is one that is frequently repeated. Sometimes the deleveraged employee stays but stops performing at peak levels. Other times, he or she leaves in search of something new and more interesting. Sadly, corporate leaders who are not focused on the potential of their people, fail to see the value in reengaging, retraining, or redirecting a deleveraged employee. All too often, it's easier for management to say that the employee is "too expensive" or "interested in moving on." Maybe that is the case sometimes, but in my experience, most of the time it's a failure of the leadership team to understand the true cost of losing out on the potential of a deleveraged employee. A core responsibility of upper management is to transcend the present day and near-term issues and keep an eye on the long term. Companies with higher employee turnover rates than others have a fundamental problem in the present tense that belies other fundamental issues.

Loyal, talented individuals—who represent a treasure trove of knowledge, experience, and untapped potential—are all too often dismissed or offered early retirement simply because the company for which they work has no vision or plan to leverage the employee's talents or potential. The leadership team hasn't developed an infra-structure to adapt, repurpose, or re-engage employees who are in a rut, often through no fault of their own. The inefficiencies of this scenario, multiplied across an entire corporate community, can be a significant drag on productivity, and even a company's bottom line. If unaddressed and widespread, this practice can ultimately lead to a company's slow, painful death.

What is the untapped potential of your people costing your company? The answer might be more quantifiable than you care to admit. A relatively simple way is to take a random sample of those that have left your company and what they did with their careers afterward. Did they leave and start a new company? That would point to your company not realizing and leveraging that potential when you had the opportunity. Did people who left your company advance their careers in ways that could have benefited your company had they stayed and done the same work for you? These questions may seem like an exercise in futility, but they aren't. Rather, they will serve to remind you to look at the potential of your talent pool.

The bigger question is: how did the company for which Everett had worked for 18 years fail to take full advantage of his skill set, his aptitude, his desire to learn, and his ability to apply new skills for the betterment of the company? It didn't understand the value of discovering his potential because it was happy with the status quo and not focused on being the best. Cutting costs and "not rocking the boat" was its short-sighted philosophy. The company incorrectly assumed that Everett's job skills were the extent of his potential. It failed to see Everett's broader talents because it had no system in place to explore that potential. As a result, it was unable to leverage Everett's ability to contribute to even more productive ways.

Unfortunately, corporations failing to capitalize on their "people-potential," as the firm did in Everett's story, is commonplace, perhaps even the norm. The underutilization of talent and failure to cultivate employees' full potential for the benefit of both the individual *and* the company—well, that's how business is done these days. Unfortunately, what too many leadership teams fail to consider is that in today's changing world, this problem can become life-threatening for a company.

In the mid-to-late 2000s, I worked with a team of highly skilled and motivated professionals at a company in Charleston, South Carolina that developed and sold specialty inks and printers. The company had an enviable and unique position in the market, as it owned very strong patents that afforded them protection for another 10 years from any significant competition.

The problem was that the company's owners and executive management had more "love" for their technology at the expense of its employees and even its clients. Both were treated with a sense of arrogance and even disdain. The top-down hierarchical management employed a rigid work environment even among its salaried professional-level employees, including "spying" on employees by checking their emails, Internet usage, and employing a punch in-punch out time clock.

Unlike Netflix, the company did not treat its employees as adults nor provide them an avenue to maximize their skills. Morale issues were rampant. Turnover reached over 50 percent annually in the professional, middle, and even upper-management ranks. For a small company of only around 130 employees, this meant that projects ended up taking twice as long to complete, new products were delayed by months, and revenue could not keep up with anticipated sales-budget projections. The bottom line was that revenues began to suffer because of the company's high employee turnover. Every time it had to hire a replacement, it ate further into its dwindling profits. This is a reverse example of HyperLeverage.

According to the *2018 Retention Report* published by the Work Institute, "Workplace turnover is increasing. Work Institute estimates that 42 million, or one in four, employees will leave their jobs in 2018 and that nearly 77 percent of that turnover could be prevented by employers. Employers will pay $600 billion in turnover costs in 2018 and can expect that number to increase to $680 billion by 2020. 'Employees have career options, and our study shows they are not hesitant to leave their current positions for jobs that better fit their preferences and expectations,' said Danny Nelms, president of Work Institute."

Here is the reality today: most companies don't hold on to their talented people long enough to realize their full potential. This happens for a variety of reasons, but the observation above articulates the problem clearly: there is not an alignment of "preferences and expectations." In part, this points back to the shortcomings of both the current hiring process and the experience too many employees have once they have joined a company. When corporate leadership teams decide to build a hiring system that encourages alignment *and* a corporate culture that fosters personal and career growth, they have an opportunity not only to stop the madness described above but to begin experiencing the many benefits that will come out of the HyperLeverage their new system will create.

Gone are the days when companies could keep hiring new employees as turnover happened—even though this was the norm back in the 1980s and '90s. In fact, during the famous tenure of Jack Welch at General Electric (GE), turnover was *forced*. Considered at the time to be the world's best executive manager, Welch had a big idea when he became the youngest CEO of GE at the age of 46. He was going to leverage his workforce by instituting a management practice called the "Vitality Curve," also known as Stack Ranking. This is a leadership construct where a workforce is graded and ranked according to their performance. Borrowing from the Pareto Principle, which is the famous 80/20 rule stating that 80 percent of results come from 20 percent of efforts, the GE team would cull out the lowest producers and replace them with new blood.

Welch achieved extraordinary results with this approach. Leveraging his "rank and yank" system, as it was called, Welch was able to increase earnings 28-fold and revenue 5-fold during his tenure as CEO from 1981 to 2001. Welch posited that the cost of having underperformers and not being able to fully leverage their positions was costing GE much more than it would cost to hire new blood.

The downside of this approach is that it creates a scenario where people are very hesitant to help others and work as functional teams, especially if employees are fearful of losing their job or continually looking over their shoulders. This type of environment breeds mistrust and narrow-minded decision-making. For Welch's system to work, he assumed that it was cheaper and more efficient for GE to hire somebody new, train him or her, and bring the individual up to speed rather than try to "train up" the individuals ranked in the bottom 10 percent.

Using Welch's approach to leverage a workforce these days could be risky. As I wrote earlier in this chapter, if you don't know exactly how to hire the right talent, you could be hurting your organization. An approach that relies on ranking and rating employees to separate the high performers from others presupposes that a company has its "shit" together. Meaning that it has provided the necessary support, opportunities for success, resources, training, and guidance for all its employees to succeed.

In my experience as both a business owner, executive manager, and business consultant, rarely have I found that people's skills and contributions cannot be improved when an organization's leadership takes a hard look in the mirror to examine its deficiencies. How can a company realize and fairly rank its employees if it doesn't evaluate itself first? It takes employing the three principles of HyperLeverage— proactiveness, intention, and meaningfulness—to provide the framework for people's success. Even employees that are considered self-starters need direction, encouragement, and training. That's the essence of this book. It is the mechanism to untapped potential. When I read of companies, even successful ones such as Netflix that have adopted a systematic rating approach, I immediately question the management first, starting at the top.

Does that describe your company? Is there a misplaced expectation of upper management of its workforce? It is their responsibility to set clear objectives, milestones, and build the path to success.

There are also strong benefits of "training up" your employees. We'll discuss those benefits later in the chapter. This isn't to say managers should never let anyone go. Replacing non-productive employees is necessary. In some cases, there comes a time when the ability to leverage an existing employee's potential yields diminishing returns. GE's success using this draconian technique did not stand the test of time, nor is it currently emulated by many other companies. In today's tight job market for many skills, it could be a recipe for disaster.

In my estimation, HyperLeverage could be achieved if a company can stock up on talent based on the workforce needs necessary to support future growth or changes in technology. In an ideal setting, where HyperLeverage is at work, these hiring decisions could be made well in advance of the actual need. Think of it like a pro basketball or football team that drafts or trades for highly skilled, yet unproven talent, so that they can get them inculcated into the team's culture and system. It's an investment in the future, like a manufacturer building a plant that has more capacity than required until a later date.

And this doesn't have to be limited to big companies with huge HR budgets. Take the example of Landmark, an accounting firm with just over 100 employees in Fort Smith, Arkansas. Using this approach, it padded its team with new college graduates as well as an experienced tax manager. Katie Lejong, a partner in the firm, was recently quoted as saying, "It does tend to add costs since newcomers handle work that could be done by existing staff. But, there's a balance. We want to create capacity for the future." Now that's an example of how HyperLeverage can be found through a company's talent. It's proactive. It's intentional. It has significant meaning to the future success of the business.

It's time to do the hard work and start creating people-first systems that encourage alignment, retention, and growth for companies and the people who make them possible. A classic example of a missed opportunity is an HR process stuck in time and rarely leveraged to anyone's advantage—the annual review. Instead of using the review process as an opportunity for change and growth, it's a static, backwards-looking exercise that assesses performance—not potential. As a result, the gains are short-term. If a manager is lucky, he or she might see a few months of increased output from an employee until the next review period. The annual review is also a time of high stress on both sides of the desk, which is not a recipe for strong productivity. How can companies leverage the review process? Should there even be a formal review process these days? What kind of leverage can be uncovered and capitalized upon in this process?

Using performance reviews to HyperLeverage talent means defining key performance metrics. These quantified goals must be clearly communicated and, in some cases, even built into employee agreements. Good sports coaches use key performance metrics all the time. They create a measurement tool with their players to help them recognize their potential and push to reaching it every game.

HyperLeveraging Training and Education

Carol Meyrowitz, CEO of TJ Maxx from 2007 through 2016, wrote an article in the May 2014 issue of *Harvard Business Review* about how the $28 billion retailer relies on hiring buyers who can be flexible and spot opportunities. After all, retail buyers must have a keen eye for what people want and must search for and nurture vendors who can deliver the goods that are right to buy. They must understand market trends and know how to strike when the iron is hot. They also must negotiate the best terms. In the end, the quality of their product choices and the prices they can procure them for determine the profits that will be realized.

TJ Maxx's leadership is committed to continual employee teaching and talent development throughout the organization, especially in the buying and merchandising areas, which have the most direct link to their customers. Becoming an outstanding buyer demands curiosity and frequent training. Buyers must become both opportunistic and extremely flexible. They must develop relationships with the company's vendors. The skills TJ Maxx needs from its buyers also aren't skills taught in business schools. It takes time to train someone for this type of job. The company must make a substantial up-front investment of time and money in its new employees. That means the right hire is key. Since Meyrowitz understood that the buyers were the heart and soul of her organization, she was more than willing to make the commitment and investment. Who would train these new hires? Did Meyrowitz choose to go outside her organization and bring in expensive consultants? No, she didn't. Rather, she recognized that the ultimate leverage she and her management team had was to play the role of teacher and foster a culture of learning.

Whenever Meyrowitz walked into a meeting during her tenure at TJ Maxx, she would ask herself, "What can I teach this team during this meeting?" Her upper management was tasked with creating and encouraging an open culture in which mentorships between senior executives and buyers was a daily activity. It was an extremely cost-effective, long-term investment that paid off handsomely for TJ Maxx.

In the past decade or so, the size of the buying organization more than doubled and, with it, the depth and breadth of the buyer's knowledge expanded. Buyers have the authority to make decisions that can shift buying dollars to hot categories and latest fashion trends. By the end of 2017, revenues had reached a record $35 billion and the store count had exceeded 4000, in large part to the effectiveness of the 1000 or so retail buyers and associates.

A well-educated corporate community is knowledgeable about the latest techniques and information and can make wise decisions. They work together collaboratively. They are more motivated and able to more readily handle the ever-changing dynamics of business in a global economy.

According to Liz Wiseman, internationally recognized expert on corporate talent and author of the bestselling book Multipliers,

"When leaders teach, they invest in their people's ability to solve and avoid problems in the future."

An expansive report from the Gallup organization in 2016 titled, *How Millennials Want to Work and Live,* researched extensively what the authors called the "Big Six" functional changes that organizations will need to adopt regarding the changing and younger workforce. Two of these functional changes exposed the need for companies to develop employee skill sets and the desire of the younger workforce for coaches and mentors versus the more rigid and classical command and control management approach. The latter requires managers to take on a role more akin to a teacher rather than a delegator. The report also found that younger workers were more apt to be disengaged and on a continual lookout for new jobs, leading to the skyrocketing turnover rates mentioned earlier in this chapter.

These changes spotlight the need for businesses to leverage relevant and continuous education and training to retain, engage, and inspire the next wave of employees who will become the company's future. According to *Entrepreneur* magazine, 87 percent of millennials say that professional development is an important and core component of any job. As the TJ Maxx story demonstrates, there's an opportunity in this shift to HyperLeverage. TJ Maxx's people were trained to become future teachers. Upper management modeled what this teacher role should look like. The leverage comes in the training. The HyperLeverage comes in making training and mentoring part of the company's very DNA.

Generally, companies promote people into management positions based on either their previous experience in a similar role, their seniority (less so these days), or because of their specific skills in a business area. Rarely do companies hire managers based on direct educational experience in the field of management. A well-trained manager would have been exposed to a variety of managerial theories, been educated in some degree of psychology, and learned about advanced communication skills. These experiences can all be transferred and honed. An organization that wants to leverage and elevate its people would put a premium on providing this formal education to key employees it has identified as having long-term potential as trainers or mentors and the ability to create successful learning environments.

A smart organization can unlock HyperLeverage in its training process through an intentional, well designed, and thoughtful program that includes:

➤ Providing new and existing employees with training on "soft skills" like communication, team building, and problem-solving. Getting everyone on the same page and with the same expectations.

➤ Focusing on training new employees to mentor each other and assign them to higher-level mentors from the management team to provide a bigger picture perspective that coincides with the strategic goals of the company.

➤ For leaders, recognizing those who take advantage of optional training, showing the whole community that this is something its organization values, and making sure that opportunities are available for all who desire and are willing to invest.

➤ Proactively scouting for and promoting individuals who embody the type of mentors desired to lead the company in the future. This would include developing a "pay it forward" mentality of the "more you give, the more you get," which enhances collaboration, trust, and, ultimately, productivity.

A leadership team that wants to learn how to unlock HyperLeverage within its human resources has spent time defining its strategic priorities around training and mentoring. It has gathered ideas from individuals throughout all levels of its organization and understands what it needs to do to create a successful culture that embraces the values it has set forth. The leadership team also inspires a sense of responsibility and ownership among its people. In doing so, it fosters employee satisfaction. Empowered employees tend to stay with companies longer and are more willing to go the extra mile to achieve the company's goals.

The bottom line here is not some complex scientific equation taken from a Rocket Scientist's book. It's quite simple. A company cannot survive long-term through the work of just a few champions. It needs to elevate the mean skill level and intelligence of all in a meaningful way. The most efficient manner is by developing an infrastructure of training, shared learning, and transference of knowledge and judgment that mentorships can provide.

Takeaways

⚠ Hiring and nurturing talent is an ongoing HyperLeverage activity. It must be congruent and aligned with a company's values, culture, and objectives and conducted with an emphasis on holistic and long-term benefits.

⚠ Organizations that commit to continual employee training and talent development can more effectively leverage their workforce and reduce turnover.

⚠ Business leaders should leverage their experience to act as both teachers and mentors to others in their organization, using a "filter-down" approach. Encouraging mentorship throughout a company not only increases skill transfer but supports a positive business culture.

⚠ Performing ongoing reviews throughout the year, rather than annually, leads to better utilization of employee skills and can reveal untapped human asset potential that can be leveraged.

CHAPTER 6

The Work Environment

As we have discussed, the success of any company or organization starts with the right people. The ability to identify, attract, and retain great people has long been a necessary core competency for any leadership team that wants to be highly successful. Few companies thrive, or even survive, without the right people in the right positions.

There is, however, an additional concept that should be added to the core-competency list: empowerment. For exceptional results, leadership teams must learn to empower their people not only as individuals but as communities. If you have all the right people working for you, but don't give them the tools, resources, and knowledge to contribute to your company's growth through collaboration and innovation with their colleagues, then you have failed to unlock the HyperLeverage of your culture or people. This means you have neglected to unlock the human potential of your company. Being able to identify, attract, and retain the right people gives your company leverage. Being able to empower those people as individuals and communities gives your company HyperLeverage.

With unemployment at record levels and the demand for highly trained professionals in certain disciplines continuing to explode, it is no surprise that hiring and retaining talent has become the number one differentiator between successful companies and those that lag.

It is imperative to have a HyperLeverage Mindset and actively search for individuals who can solve short-term hiring needs, and that can blossom into world-class talent. Even keeping a team of professionals together for one more year than the industry average can make a major difference. The world of team sports is such an easy guide to this. Sports dynasties happen when a core group of players learn to perform as a team year after year.

Empowering individuals in your organization is a strong foundation for the next level of HyperLeverage: Community. Though empowered individuals can make stellar contributions, the efforts of one individual, or a handful, is rarely enough to achieve the exponential growth a company can experience when it finds HyperLeverage across its entire community. Shaping community work environments that stimulate collaboration, creativity, and innovation as well as motivate people to grow and reach their full potential—*this* is the holy grail of highly successful companies. *This* is the path to HyperLeverage. It embeds "people power" into the very DNA of your company.

Gone are the days when a business could look at its workforce as a collection of singular contributors, pigeonholed into jobs that are limited in their scope, and fail to take advantage of the collective pool of skills, talents, and experience. In smaller companies and start-ups—where innovation thrives—people must wear multiple "hats" and juggle a wide range of responsibilities. Larger organizations can tap this same entrepreneurial energy if they learn to create systems and environments that foster community-wide collaboration and innovation. It is in these types of environments that people, communities, and companies thrive and grow.

Perhaps the most famous example of this is the development and promotion of the sticky note or post-it note, as it is often called. Long before personal computers, cellphones, and other mobile devices, it became the solution for jotting down simple notes or reminders. The story goes that Dr. Spencer Silver, a scientist at 3M, accidentally created a low-tack, removable adhesive when he was looking for the exact opposite effect. Five years later, after failing to get traction for this technology as the basis for a new product area, his colleague Art Fry used 3M's officially sanctioned internal "bootlegging" policy to develop this technology into what it has become today, a $2.2 billion worldwide market.

What did 3M know then and to this day? It recognized the untapped potential of its talent pool. In my mind, that is talent HyperLeverage on a pedestal. Even with the formal intrapreneurial grants such as the Genesis Grant that can award upwards of $100,000 for an individual internal research project, the important point is that intrapreneurship is proactively and intentionally pursued. It's part of the company culture.

Meredith Gonsalves, a global manager of digital and social media strategy at Deloitte, a multinational professional services network, had a small team and a big problem. She had been tasked with attracting younger, millennial-aged professionals to work for what many considered a stodgy, "your father's type" of company. She understood that social media was the best way to reach her target demographic—millennials are the most active users of social media—but she wasn't sure what story she should tell them, or which social network was the best channel to reach them. How could she convey Deloitte's unique benefits in the company's classic voice while making Deloitte stand out in the sea of sexy, newer technology startups that were popping up like mushrooms across the country?

As head of digital and social media strategy, she also understood that her younger colleagues represented a vast untapped reservoir of talent and skills that she couldn't afford to go out and hire. Her team's research indicated that Instagram was the most effective social media method to reach her target audience, so she set out to find people within the Deloitte organization who knew and understood how to leverage Instagram. With a global workforce of more than 280,000 employees, Deloitte had a growing and large subset of professionals aged 25 to 35 who used Instagram daily for personal communication.

Gonsalves was finding HyperLeverage in her people. After deconstructing her problem, she looked around her organization for assets the company already possessed and saw a plethora of talent to meet her needs. Meredith and her team were given permission to task millennial-aged professionals at Deloitte—hired to do different jobs across diverse and unrelated departments and in different locations—to dedicate a few hours of their time in addition to their regular responsibilities to participate as part of a new Instagram team for Deloitte. Empowering these employees to become the "Face of Deloitte," these employees shared their Deloitte stories through Instagram. What's it like to work at Deloitte? These young, hip Instagramers were letting the world know what it was like to work at the company today. They provided a human face to the culture. The results have been quite impressive, with applications up by record levels. It's a perfect example of what it looks like to find HyperLeverage through community. Gonsalves' initiative succeeded because she was able to demonstrate to her upper management how her approach represented a meaningful exploitation of existing talent that would yield a plethora of positive results. This included excitement amongst the younger-aged employees about taking pride in the company and work they were doing and, of course, paving the way to enhance the talent pool.

It's clear that companies that recognize that the entirety of their organization is greater than the sum of its parts—especially when it comes to human talent—are positioned to leverage the full potential and investment in their organization, especially their people.

Even Thomas Edison, who had 1,093 patents to his name and is considered one of the world's greatest inventors, understood the power of community of peers. From the light bulb to the phonograph to the first electrical grid system, his fingerprint has been on so many of the household items used in the late 19th and early 20th centuries that it is difficult to imagine the modern world without his contributions. Did he do this by himself—toiling away in his small lab until the proverbial light bulb went on with a *eureka* moment? Far from it. Edison utilized HyperLeverage. He leveraged the community of inventors and scientists who mostly toiled by themselves by developing a team structure like no one before him had ever done in the pursuit of research and development.

Establishing an independent company and constructing a series of labs on a property called Menlo Park, Edison hired the smartest and most inspired engineers and inventors of his day and organized them into teams dedicated to churning out invention after invention. As the shrewd and even cut-throat businessman that he was, Edison took ownership of them and patented them under his name. Just like Silicon Valley beacons the best and the brightest in software development, the allure of working for Edison at Menlo Park reached across the globe, even ensnaring a young Nicolai Tesla, who joined the Edison Machine Works for a brief time in 1884. Edison demonstrated that by hiring smartly and placing people together in appropriate teams, he could leverage their skills more efficiently than trying to do it on his own.

I contend that Edison's greatest and most influential and lasting invention was the modern-day research laboratory. Not the light bulb. Not the phonograph. Not the electric grid. These have been influential and important; however, it's the dedicated research lab with a proactive and intentional objective of innovation that has changed the business worldwide in the most dramatic of ways. His research lab concept is a lasting example of HyperLeverage of people that intentionally exploited a pool of scientists to achieve truly exceptional results.

HyperLeveraging Work Conditions

There are many things over which an organization has little control. A company can't control its external marketplace. It can't control regulations that are placed on its industry. It can't control the weather. However, there is one important area that companies can control and leverage: the work conditions and physical surroundings in which it conducts business. When it comes to creating an environment for HyperLeverage to thrive, work conditions are crucial for companies that wish to inspire exceptional results from their people. The work environment is a physical manifestation of internal company culture.

Think about it—if you work in a dark office building with no natural sunlight, low ceilings, old moldy and disintegrating carpeting, you're not going to be as juiced about coming to work as you are if you're entering a modern, well-lit work environment with gobs of sunlight streaming in from windows overlooking a phenomenal view. However, it's not just the physical location or layout of the work environment that leads to a more energized and motivated employee community. Paying attention to and emphasizing positive work conditions represent a proactive search for and deployment of assets to add value. You're investing in something that directly influences how people respond to your company, including vendors and clients.

It's been cited repeatedly that salary and financial compensation are not the top considerations of employees when assessing a company. Of course, getting a fair compensation package is necessary to instill a sense of security and fairness, and a correlation between one's efforts, results, and the salary that is being paid. Issie Laposky, writing in *Inc. Magazine* in August 2010, cited additional job-setting characteristics that might be important to candidates and employees. After all, work is where most professionals spend 40 hours a week or more.

There is also evidence that the state of the physical surroundings in which a person works correlates directly with employee productivity levels. Contrary to the common belief that open workspaces lead to more collaboration, better communication, and therefore better teamwork, science does not support it. Today, close to 70 percent of companies have some degree of an open work environment and 10-15 percent have a completely open workspace. It is interesting to note that the perception that openness is good and leads to better productivity is not the reality.

As revealed in multiple studies conducted over the past decade, productivity increases when the ambient noise level decreases. Open office spaces, including half-wall cubicles, consistently lead to more noise distractions and loss of focus. Add to that the propensity for more interruptions. Openwork environments encourage face-to-face and unsolicited interruptions and can account for up to one third more than even email or phone calls.

In a world where we still believe that multitasking can defy the laws of physics, these interruptions and breaks in a worker's focus can lead to up to 3 hours or more of lost productivity. It is expensive and, in most cases, impossible and even unwise to create a closed office. Simply filling a space based on maximum use of space or even aesthetics is not the same as HyperLeverage. In my experience, rarely has proactive thought gone into this. Over time, as employees come and go, as teams are disbanded and reconfigured, the original intent is no longer valid.

HyperLeverage requires forethought and accurate information upon which to make work-environment decisions, including input from employees. For example, a software development team may need to work near each other in a more open environment, but a social-media marketing group could be made up individuals working remotely and gathering online once or twice a week.

Professor Jo Silvester and Dr. Efrosyni Konstantinou from the City University of London Center for Performance at Work found that "Worker controlled lighting and lighting solutions tailored to the individual needs of workers have considerable potential for enhancing employees' work satisfaction and enhancing retention. Optimal working conditions may be particularly important in the case of workers that employers would most like to attract and retain." Another study entitled "Lighting, Well-being and Performance at Work" recommended that "Companies should consider the need to invest in workplace lighting as a means to develop work environments that support well-being and performance, and reduce the likelihood of employee stress, absenteeism, and industrial accidents." You see, HyperLeverage can be found in something as small and simple as a well-lit office. With forethought and follow-through, those extra few hundred watts of power can unleash untapped potential, yielding far greater results.

In the early 2000s, the upper management at Lowes understood this concept and used lighting to attract a more female customer base and give its employees a more positive and invigorating work environment. The warehouse-style setup of its rival Home Depot, in the minds of Lowes executives, was a turnoff. The Lowes management team recognized that it would cost more in electrical bills, maintenance, and design costs, but felt the results would be worth it. Their investment paid off. Since implementing the plan, not only has Lowes increased its customer base, it has experienced a record growth of

20 percent over five years—more than double that of its rival Home Depot. With the explosive popularity of home improvement series like Joanna and Chip Gaines' Fixer Upper and the Magnolia brand they created, women are even more empowered and active in making home improvement buying decisions. A recent study showed that women represent over 65 percent of the online purchases at Wayfair and 47 percent of online purchases from Lowes.

It's not just the internal physical space that breeds a better work environment. For many, the location of the office or business is important for employee satisfaction and performance. The commute to work has become a huge factor in employee longevity. Being able to walk or bike or take affordable public transportation to work has become a tremendous advantage that companies are beginning to leverage, especially among the tech and startup communities. A company can leverage this in several ways:

> - Employees come to work refreshed and invigorated, not stressed from a long commute.
> - Employees don't have to spend money on car and transportation costs that take a big bite out of their monthly budget. This benefit leaves them with more money to do things that are important to them, like entertainment, eating out, or travel.
> - It encourages employees to live close to each other, leading to greater camaraderie.

The revitalization of inner cities, which started 20 years ago, has accelerated with the millennial generation, which is not in a rush to start families, buy homes and rush out to the suburbs like their parents. Companies are leveraging this by building and establishing businesses in urban environments developed specifically to leverage transportation and quality-of-life issues. In Austin, Texas, the

Domain, in the northern section of the city, has become a magnet for new technology companies. Apartments, shopping, entertainment, and employment opportunities are all within a couple of blocks, with plenty of walking or biking access. Downtown San Francisco took note of how many of its residents were commuting outside the city and decided to HyperLeverage its location as advantageous in an effort to court these high-tech companies and startups and their high salary structures. Within a short period, the city became a business nexus.

The daily commute in some metropolitan areas can be two or three hours of daily hell. Employees often cite their commute as a top reason for leaving an otherwise good company and job. A study by Robert Half, a job placement company, found that almost one in four people cited a long commute as a reason to quit or look for another job.

What is a company to do? Not every company has deep pockets to afford the top dollar office rates or can do a full or new build-out of its existing space to modify the physical layout. Figure 8, "Best Practices to Leverage a Workplace," presents some of the core ideas that almost any company can use to unlock HyperLeverage in its work environment. Extracted from the March 2019 Fortune article, "100 Best Companies to Work for," it reveals several common practices that lead to a hyper-productive workplace.

These companies are examples of how to do more with their workforce to achieve exceptional results. They view their employees from a holistic vantage point while recognizing the importance of aligning company culture with the personal and social values of the employees it wishes to attract. Companies understand this and create environments for happy hour and other social, out-of-office interactions that help to solidify the team spirit. Companies benefit from these public social interactions in other ways as well. A

FIGURE 8: BEST PRACTICES TO LEVERAGE A WORKPLACE   SOURCE: FORTUNE MAGAZINE

group of employees wearing company T-shirts and having a good time together at a restaurant can be witnessed by others. Having your workforce act as an "advertisement" can be powerful and even cost-effective.

Attracting and maintaining a vibrant professional workforce is critical, so your company needs to be situated where people want to live. Companies can leverage location to attract the type of workers they want and need. A company that produces software will look for a younger professional group...mostly male and not interested in living on the outskirts of town. They are looking to bike to work, use a scooter, or take an Uber. Though it is likely to cost more for a company to be in town, the soft benefits and ability to attract more of the right employees may outweigh the hard costs.

On the opposite end of the spectrum is another workplace trend that offers a different set of challenges and opportunities. According to Upwork's *Future Workforce Report*, "In the next ten years, hiring managers predict that 38 percent of their full-time, permanent employees will work predominantly remotely." With the expansion of the Internet, cloud storage, and advancements in communication and work tools, such as Slack, GoToMeeting, and others, it is no longer necessary to have all employees in one location under one roof. Many companies have a significant percentage of their employee base work virtually.

Take the example of Thinkmojo, a leading video marketing and production agency. The company was based in Silicon Valley but had employees located throughout the United States and Canada. To this day, the company does not have a central office. All communications are handled via shared cloud applications. Internal communication is via Slack, phone, and teleconference. Communications with clients are handled the same way.

The company has been able to HyperLeverage this virtual work environment to save on overhead, empower its employees through technology, and hire the best professionals for their skills and cultural fit rather than their geographic location. Another advantage is that Thinkmojo doesn't have to shell out Silicon Valley salaries to attract top talent. Nor does it have to invest in a physical workplace environment. Savings in this area are plugged back into better employee fringe benefits such as health insurance and vacation/PTO time and a kick-ass good annual companywide meeting. There's no doubt that for some types of companies, virtual offices can be effectively leveraged by companies to attract and retain the right people.

HyperLeveraging Corporate Culture

Corporate culture is an increasingly powerful "soft" asset that can be leveraged to yield exceptional results. The HyperLeverage in this opportunity means the organization's leadership team is intentionally and proactively molding a culture with select traits. According to *Inc.* magazine's online encyclopedia of business terminology, "Corporate culture refers to the shared values, attitudes, standards, and beliefs that characterize members of an organization and define its nature. Corporate culture is rooted in an organization's goals, strategies, structures, and approaches to labor, customers, investors, and the greater community. As such, it is an essential component of any business's ultimate success or failure."

The Story of REI

For outdoor enthusiasts, REI, a cooperative where profits benefit its member-owners, has long been the company to turn to for great gear. REI employees also agree that this is a place where greatness happens, even beyond the company's beloved camping and outdoor products. REI's mission is to equip both customers and employees for the outdoors, not just to have fun but also to promote stewardship of the environment.

REI says that its employees give "life to their purpose," firmly attributing company success to workers. The CEO of REI has acknowledged that employees can get benefits anywhere but allowing outdoors-oriented employees to immerse themselves in REI culture is what makes it unique. Employees can win equipment through "challenge grants" where they submit a proposal for an outdoor adventure that would be challenging. Regular townhall-style meetings are held where employees can submit questions anonymously to help management understand what's happening in the company.

As we've discussed before, leverage needs to be coupled with purposeful action to turn into HyperLeverage. REI understood that sharing its values with its employees, vendors, and customers was not enough. It had to turn its values into real, meaningful action. For the REI team, that action was sitting right in front of their noses. They needed to empower their employees to pursue outdoor life experiences that completely define the company, its products, and the causes it supports.

When your employees are completely immersed in the same interests as your company, like the REI example, the culture propels itself forward almost on its own. Culture that is owned and propelled by the same people puts value in their voices.

Flying High with Southwest

Forbes magazine, in an interview with Southwest Airlines CFO Tammy Romo at the end of 2018, demonstrated that being a discount and low-cost oriented company doesn't have to translate into a corporate culture that cuts corners. It's illustrative of how core values can inculcate a large and diverse workforce and how they are easily discerned by the public.

The airline industry is often mocked for grumpy employees and poor customer service, but Southwest Airlines bucks those trends. Customers loyal to Southwest often point to happy and friendly employees who try hard to help.

Southwest isn't new to the game. It's been in operation for 43 years. Somehow, the company has managed to communicate its goals and vision to employees in a way that makes them a part of a unified team. Southwest also gives employees "permission" to go that extra mile to make customers happy, empowering them to do what they need to do to meet that vision.

Ever been on a Southwest flight? The flight attendants can make everyone feel at ease with their enthusiasm and willingness to add some humor to the information they are required to communicate. It is evidence that they buy into the larger common goals of the airline and are excited to be part of it.

Culture is all about the people who create it, and with an attitude that people are its greatest asset—employees, vendors, *and* customers—Southwest has unlocked HyperLeverage in its "warrior spirit" culture. As a result, the Southwest brand shines bright in an airline marketplace that often treats its employees and customers more like cattle. Eschewing the "us versus them" model of some of its bigger competitors—that nitpick their customers on every little item, charging them for checked bags, flight changes, seat upgrades, etc.—Southwest thrives by leveraging a community-oriented "group think." This approach is present in everything from the way Southwest engages with and boards its passengers to how its flight and ground crew teams manage transition. The result of both is increased productivity, lower costs and happier and more loyal customers. The results of its approach are impressive: Southwest has experienced 45 years of consecutive profitability.

How can a management team begin to shape a powerful culture that can be leveraged, and what are some of the best practices that can be used? Let's revisit our Leverage Prism and deconstruct the elements of a corporate culture.

At first glance, there is a distinct overlap between the activities and mindset necessary to leverage a workforce and the components of corporate culture. That is no surprise. It would be hard to keep employees motivated or attract new hires or even support a brand if there was a large disconnect between the two. The website wishlistrewards.com shows a list of desired cultural traits in an organization. These mirror the same traits that one would also want from employees. The Supreme Court got it right with the Citizens United case; corporations are indeed like people.

Takeaways

⚠ A community forms when cultural and business objectives are transparent and reinforced through company activities, products, and services. Corporate culture is a powerful soft asset that can be leveraged for business success.

⚠ Work conditions are not just the physical environment or location of the business. They involve a holistic approach to how work is conducted. Any organization can control and leverage the quality of its work environment. It reflects its core values.

⚠ Empowering employees to work together as a community and not just singular contributors provides more utilization of individual skills and experience and paves the way to discover HyperLeverage among your workforce.

CHAPTER 7

Communications

Effective communication isn't about saying things. It has a much more important role. It's about connecting with people. "Connecting is the ability to identify with people and relate to them in a way that increases your influence with them," John Maxwell wrote in his book, *Everyone Communicates, Few Connect.* He's right. A connection is the goal of communication. It's not enough to work hard, do a great job, and spread the word. To be successful, you must learn how to communicate effectively to connect with others. This holds true for people, teams, communities, and companies.

The type of communication that truly connects us goes beyond simple words and gestures. It can be an act of gratitude or appreciation, making eye contact to drive home a point, smiling or using humor to diffuse a tough situation or even shrugging to signal you don't have all the answers. For many companies, the primary means of external communication is advertising, whether through traditional print and media avenues or the myriad of opportunities online and through social media. Other companies use content marketing as a method to communicate their authority and values and support their brand. No matter how and where it's done, finding HyperLeverage through communication requires energy, practice, and intent.

We assume that our ability to communicate well is natural; it's not. Strong communication is a skill that can be learned, practiced, and improved over time. To achieve build authority, become trusted enough to be handed true responsibility and to influence others, you must master strong communication skills. It is often the deciding factor in success. Communication is a leadership discipline. It is teachable, but it must be applied and maintained.

What does it mean to HyperLeverage communication to achieve exceptional results? It starts with a recognition that communication is a two-way street. You need someone to listen and process the information you are sharing. Just think of when you were a kid and your dad "lectured" you about something you may have done wrong. Was that communication? Not really. You tuned out. You didn't process the information being shared with you.

There are two types of business communication: internal and external. They share common attributes and share similar goals. However, they are executed differently and by different people. Truly iconic brands work hard to align their external and internal communications. Their messages are consistent, cogent, relevant, intentional, and build awareness and trust—both inside and outside the company. It sounds simple, but it's not easy.

HyperLeveraging External Communication

In the 1970s, "Mad Man" advertising executive Mitchell Epstein coined the slogan, "When EF Hutton talks, people listen." It became an iconic ad of its time and is a great example of HyperLeveraging business communication effectively. The message is very simple yet highly impactful. It piques our curiosity to know more. What was Epstein trying to communicate? In those mere five words, he managed to convey a powerful, emotional message, so let's unpack Epstein's slogan word for word:

> **When** denotes control over timing. It means that the person communicating can determine when the message is delivered. That's powerful. It's proactive.
>
> **EF Hutton** shows authority, influence, and status. After all, without this name, why would anyone listen? With a strong brand name, a company has something others covet or need. It could be information, a product or new service.
>
> **Talks** represents Hutton's form of communication. It's human and conjures images of a cocktail party or speech where EF Hutton is the center of attention because his words are important.
>
> **People** is plural and thus conveys clearly and succinctly that EF Hutton is respected by many; he's an influencer.
>
> **Listening** is the activity that the speaker desires to have happen. It's his call to action. The speaker wants to create a connection that leads the "listener" to doing something with EF Hutton.

With five simple words, Epstein managed to hit all the right notes for his client, EF Hutton. It was one of the most successful ad campaigns in history and helped propel the financial brokerage firm to the second largest in the country in the late 1970s and early 1980s. One does not reach that level of advertising success without a complete understanding of the EF Hutton brand—its core values and mission, its relationship with its clients, its brand voice, and how people perceive the company. Does this remind you of the type of work Netflix did to HyperLeverage its hiring process? It should, as it requires the same type of deep work by a leadership team. It's by doing that type of work that HyperLeverage is discovered.

Would Epstein's ad resonate today? It's hard to tell. Communication has changed completely. Barry Waldman, Professor of Communications at the College of Charleston and CEO of Big Fly Communications, has witnessed the changing landscape of business communication for three decades. He has seen how the Internet and the rise of social media have transformed it. "Today, people get information from multiple sources that are in their control. A company has to forget what's in it for them and communicate in a way that speaks directly to what's in it for the listener."

Today, consumers may *want* to hear what you have to say, but they don't *need* to hear it. Your customers are in control now. If they don't provide value, people won't listen for long. They will simply tune you out. "It's now all about building inbound bridges and superhighways to your company and brand," Waldman says. "It's about transparency, authenticity, and responsiveness. Rarely do old fashioned outbound communication techniques work, no matter the efficiency that might come from mass mailings and in-your-face advertisements."

Most likely, your company is already tweeting, posting, blogging, advertising, content marketing, pinning, and maybe even podcasting and doing webinars or streaming video events. There are a lot of communication channels these days. Are they effective for you? Are you fully HyperLeveraging your communications through these channels? Because if you don't have a system that was designed intentionally to provide a meaningful measure of success with specific performance metrics around a clear goal, then you are not practicing

HyperLeverage. According to Neil Patel, a world-renowned marketing expert, close to 60 percent of companies surveyed consider their content marketing less than effective. Obviously not a sufficient level to be considered HyperLeverage. Most companies treat communication in a haphazard and non-holistic manner. It happens piecemeal and randomly.

How do you start to turn this around? How do you exploit what you have and get exceptional and not plain vanilla results? It starts with the basics. Call it communication 101. Listen to your customers—every day, through multiple channels, and with the intention of gathering information, learning, and processing the information they share. That sounds a lot like connection, doesn't it? It is. Get on the phone and talk to your customers. What do they think about your company and your products? What are you doing right, and what are you doing wrong? Let's break down the components of external communication through our Leverage Prism, as shown in Figure 9, Deconstructing External Communications, so we can frame more questions to ask our customers.

We've already established that to HyperLeverage external communications, you must listen and provide your message in a variety of mediums and distribution methods that match your target audience's preferred manner of accessing information. I know that this can sound onerous and a waste of time, since there are so many different communication avenues available today.

I'm not saying you need to use all of these forms of external communication, or even most of them. What you must do is identify the ones that match your audience. It should not come as a surprise that different demographics demand a different communications approach. Get to know your audience. What is their persona? Do actual fieldwork and ask people how they prefer for you to communicate

DECONSTRUCTING EXTERNAL COMMUNICATIONS

EXTERNAL
COMMUNICATIONS

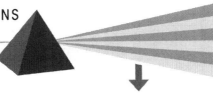

CONTENT MARKETING

ADVERTISING

SOCIAL MEDIA

BLOGS/NEWSLETTERS

EMAIL/TELEPHONE/TEXT MESSAGING

"SNAIL MAIL"/PRINTED MATERIALS

SIGNAGE

PODCASTING/VIDEOS

WEBINARS/SEMINARS/CONFERENCES

PRESS RELEASES

FIGURE 9: DECONSTRUCTING EXTERNAL COMMUNICATIONS

with them. Without real data, you will just be making assumptions. That can be okay, but it can also be risky if you are off the mark.

For example, a younger audience responds more to short and concise messages. They tend to make quick and snap decisions. Which is why communicating using imagery and video is an almost absolute must medium. On the other hand, if your market is the above 50+ crowd, this would be a colossal waste of time, effort, and money as this demographic tends to read and mull things over. There are few "one size fits all" modes of communication anymore. A strategy that employs a kitchen sink approach will ultimately sink and fail.

Once you've determined the right communication method to drive down, you've got to find a way to connect on a personal level. The more granular you can get, the more effective it becomes. Today, the opportunities to create personalized video at scale for marketing purposes continue to expand. Video Marketing hosting and analytics companies like Wistia (Soapbox video service) and Vidyard (GoVideo service) offer free Google Chrome extensions for creating and using personalized one-to-one business videos. These tools provide the ability and ease to leverage video for both internal and external communication, which has grown exponentially. Instead of sending emails or using social media, simple personal videos cut through the noise and deliver a message that invokes more emotion and yields faster responses.

I can personally attest to the phenomenal results of up to three times more conversions that video marketing customers of mine experienced when they got granular and personal. Vidyard cites statistics that show personalized videos are viewed more often and for longer than traditional marketing videos produced for a wider audience. It's not just large B2C enterprises with gigantic databases that are using it. Educational institutions leverage personalized videos to engage prospective students and organizations with large season ticket holders, such as sports teams, have discovered that customers want to be communicated with through a personal touch.

It's not just video, and it's not just personalization. It's also about what defines effective communication, which is giving and receiving. Talking and listening. An effective communication strategy must allow for an easy and real two-way street of information flow to achieve HyperLeverage. I have seen how the explosion of surveys and requests for ratings has turned into a new form of spam. What may have started as a way to "listen" to the customer, has become more of an annoyance and a cynical exercise in caring what the other side is saying, while being more intent on collecting marketing data.

Because it's the few and far between that apply the lessons of HyperLeverage and truly attain exceptional results. That's the essential lesson of this book.

External communications are about building a brand. Brands are increasingly more important to break through the din of market competition. That requires a very proactive and meaningful communication strategy that evokes a positive emotional reaction to the brand and the messaging used to support it.

HyperLeveraging Customer Service

Companies have dealt with the challenge of customer service and a customer interface for decades. Many of the solutions that are employed are not user-focused and showcase the lack of good communication. Many companies' customer service processes demonstrate disdain and lack of respect for a customer's time, money, and patience. They place more emphasis on automation and cost control rather than all the tenets of HyperLeveraging communication that I discussed previously. Answering systems that shunt you from one menu to another only to be put on hold endlessly or end up in a call center in a foreign country, has become the bane of the consumer's experience.

The above process may help a company keep its expenses in check, but it has a negative effect when it comes to leveraging customer goodwill. It's not just telephone customer service that is the problem. The same goes for providing an easy-to-access and navigate two-way means of communication between a company and its users. The user experience of corporate communication is rarely leveraged to the benefit of the user. Statistics abound on how toxic this can become. A company will lose more customers and empower them to provide poor reviews or seek solutions elsewhere when they experience poor customer service. It may be a numbers game, but numbers end up becoming finite, and the cost of retention has almost always proven to be lower than the cost of acquiring new customers.

So why not flip the switch and HyperLeverage this fact and use it to your advantage. In this case, why not leverage more resources and a proactive effort into improving communication with existing customers.

There's a reason that Zappos has been at the top of America's top brands for most of its 19 years of existence. Because communication with the customer and listening to them has been its primary focus since day one. The company is maniacal about customer service. Starting with how easy it makes it for customers to talk to a real person, as a part of their CLT – Customer Loyalty Team 24/7. It empowers its CLT team to take ownership of an issue. After all, that is why someone would communicate with the team. It sounds like common sense, doesn't it? Why doesn't everyone do it?

To further this discussion of HyperLeveraging customer service as a core communication tool, we have all been a witness in recent years to companies overdoing their customer service ratings and survey requests. I doubt that many companies are taking note of the actual responses. The emphasis on collecting data—like who is responding, in what frequency and through which device—appears paramount. There is no actual communication going on here and certainly no HyperLeverage.

Getting relevant feedback from customers is very important to HyperLeverage people. It's crucial information that should be used to create proper strategies or improve existing systems. In my experience, the higher the quality of the interaction with customers will always trump getting mass quantities of questionable responses.

Many companies may think that this is a form of HyperLeverage – collecting data from customers to serve them better. However, the way most companies do this, it is hard to show that the means justify the end, at least in the eyes of the customers. Because everyone is doing it today – it has become a new form of spam.

Here's a better technique – one that comprises the big three of HyperLeverage – Proactive, Intentional, and Meaningful. Why not "wow" and "delight" your customers, vendors and anyone you wish to get actionable feedback from. To begin with, make it exceptionally easy for someone to contact customer service, instead of hiding the "contact us" emails or phone numbers in the small crevices of a company's website. That's just one of the things that Zappos does.

Another method is to completely retool how you create and present FAQs. Most customers are not interested in scrolling or sorting through them to find an answer to their question. Certainly not in the way they are presented on most websites. Make it more intuitive and more personal. Make it more immediate, accessible, and use the modern tools of communication I cited before, such as video, imagery, audio.

As in all things HyperLeverage, it begins with a strategic decision to put the company into the "shoes" of its customers. The User Experience and Buyer's Journey doesn't end with a purchase. That's just the start. It's what comes afterward that determines how much leverage you can apply.

Unfortunately, customer service has become a way to save money on expenses, instead of recognizing that it can be a significant and perhaps even the most powerful positive brand reinforcement. For most companies, especially online service providers, it is the only direct person-to-person contact that a company has with its clients. They are missing a golden opportunity to leverage this communication beyond putting out fires.

HyperLeveraging Internal Communications

Let's now divert our attention inward and look at internal communications. Because after all, how can a company HyperLeverage any of its business opportunities if it can't effectively communicate internally? People at all levels and positions in a company have got to be on the same page.

Take a moment and consider how information flows to everyone in your company. Is there a unified communications system or even guidelines? Are new employees trained in what methods are best? Does anybody get training on software systems, email, and phone etiquette (especially those that have direct contact with customers or vendors)? Are communication protocols in place in the event of emergencies? Most companies "pooh-pooh" the need for this, but things happen from natural disasters, utility shutdowns, and the like. Reviewing the major activities that make up HyperLeverage in an internal communication system might look something like Figure 10.

When I'm called to assist a company that wants to uncover HyperLeverage around its internal communications, I start with a deep understanding of what is currently used and what has been tried in the past. That is the essence of the deconstruction depicted

DECONSTRUCTING
INTERNAL COMMUNICATIONS

INTERNAL
COMMUNICATIONS

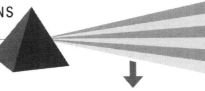

COMMUNICATIONS SOFTWARE

SOCIAL MEDIA

EMAIL

TELEPHONE

TEXT MESSAGING

DIRECT & ONLINE MEETINGS

REPORTS/MEMOS

HAPPY HOUR/SOCIAL EVENTS

COMPANY EVENTS (OFFSITES)

INTERNAL VIDEO MARKETING

FILE SHARING

FIGURE 10: DECONSTRUCTING INTERNAL COMMUNICATIONS

in Figure 10. I then drill down to understand what information needs to "flow" to whom and why.

I have seen companies that look at the tools of communication as a panacea and replacement for a comprehensive strategic communication plan. That is a big mistake. Ask any handyman, and he'll tell you that the tool must match the problem it's supposed to solve. To begin with, the real internal communication issues must be defined.

I find the story of how Virgin Trains in England dealt with its internal communication challenges enlightening. It illustrates how one "decentralized" company with a highly mobile workforce of over 3000 employees, many of whom work at the "front line" on trains and stations throughout Great Britain, employed HyperLeverage. As I studied the actions this company took, I came to realize that its activities represented a methodology similar to my DOIT Leverage Method, the system I described previously in Chapter Three that combines analysis, critical thinking, and planning to uncover and exploit all leverage opportunities and sources.

To begin with, it began by deconstructing its communication challenge and determined the requirements it would need to rapidly communicate with all its people about news and pertinent decisions that affected their jobs. The company's technology assessment showed that most of its mobile workforce lacked access to the Internet and other communication channels used by the company. Virgin Trains management recognized the flaws in its communication system and took action to connect colleagues directly with each other.

First, the company tackled the communication delivery engine by replacing its existing IT infrastructure with a cloud-based system that was easier to maintain. It transitioned from "word-heavy" communication content to more interactive, "bite size" content. Finally, it implemented a process of measurement, analytics and reporting to ensure that communication was flowing properly at all times to the entire workforce, thus closing the loop of continuous improvement of the system.

To make this happen, it HyperLeveraged the expertise of others and opted for a software as a service (SaaS) approach with significant flexibility and room for growth. Taking action by hiring an outside vendor rather than trying to do it entirely on its own, and by deploying a Microsoft Office 365 solution in conjunction with Yammer, an enterprise social networking service for private communication within organizations, the company hit a home run.

The story of Virgin Trains is illustrative of many other modern businesses that have a dispersed workforce and need to HyperLeverage communications in order to thrive. In the case of Virgin Trains and its remote workforce, the need for immediacy and reliability was critical. With software tools like Zoom, Slack and others that incorporate audio, video and file sharing, many more companies can HyperLeverage both internal and external communication with remote clients and build a virtual business environment.

As in every HyperLeverage internal communications system, you have to understand the objectives and craft a strategy before any tool or tools can be chosen. However, from a HyperLeverage perspective, these tools have one reason for existence—to make sure that all internal information and communication gets to the right people, in a manner that is easy to access and helps to produce results that are beyond the norm.

Entire businesses and technologies have been created to solve this complex issue and help organizations leverage internal communications. Take Slack, for example. By adopting what was the Internet's first community building communication tool—the Chat Room—the company created a powerful platform for teams to collaborate through chat and voice communication. Slack is one of hundreds, if not thousands, of companies that have sprung up to address the types of internal communication challenges that companies face every day.

Companies that develop communication protocols can be more productive, make quicker and better decisions, and adapt to change promptly. But HyperLeverage in communication requires a good understanding of all the "Ws": Why are we communicating? To whom do we need to communicate to get the job done? When should we communicate and how often? Where (or how) is the most effective channel to communicate? Let's look at what the prism shows us to deconstruct internal communications.

Takeaways

⚠ Companies that HyperLeverage communications do this by intentionally aligning their external and internal messaging and content creation. Their messages are consistent, cogent, relevant, intentional, and build awareness and trust—both inside and outside the company.

⚠ HyperLeveraging communication means connecting with others in a two-way manner, both conveying information and listening. This type of communication creates a relationship of trust and respect that increases your influence.

⚠ Finding HyperLeverage through communication begins with a strategic decision to put the company in the "shoes" of its customers. The User Experience and Buyer's Journey doesn't end with a purchase. That's just the start. It is what comes afterward that determines how much leverage you can apply.

⚠ Effective communication is accomplished through transparency, authenticity, and responsiveness. Raising the bar of communication in this manner leads to HyperLeverage.

CHAPTER 8

Clients, Vendors & Partners

I n today's online, social world, companies have become keenly aware that consumers, vendors, and partners are now empowered with the ability to provide immediate, real-time feedback and ratings on the products and services they buy. This process gives consumers important leverage and the ability to influence how large organizations conduct business.

In many circumstances, this shift has completely reversed the supplier-client relationship. This means businesses, both B2C and B2B, must learn to be proactive and leverage the relationships they have with their clients, vendors and partners.

One needs to look no further than two phenomena that businesses have leveraged to tell their story: influencers and social media. An example of this is Lush Cosmetics. Eschewing the traditional method of celebrity sponsorships or high-priced commercials, Lush Cosmetics opted to leverage its clear brand message of ethical cosmetics and support for social and environmental issues via a proactive social media and content generation campaign. Reinforcing the brand story and how it aligns with its customers' core values, coupled with a quality product and buying experience, generated an opportunity for HyperLeverage. Lush's followers are passionate about the brand and share this freely and frequently by word of mouth on Instagram, YouTube Blogs, and other social platforms.

This "ethical cosmetics" company has gone from having a small cult of ardent followers to a retail giant with sales figures of over $1.3 billion. All by HyperLeveraging what it already had, it is based on young women willing to share their stories with others. Lush Cosmetics is not alone in understanding that its customers represent the most authentic and powerful broadcasters of its products. It leveraged what has been understood by all of us for generations, that people prefer to do business with people they know, trust, and have an honest dialog with.

HyperLeveraging a network of people, whether it's customers, vendors, or partners, requires honesty and openness to form a bond of trust. Once the bond is broken, the leverage disappears—often quite quickly.

The story of Theranos, a health technology company made famous for its false claims to have devised breakthrough blood testing technologies, is indicative of a company that found HyperLeverage through its partnerships, network connections, and the reputation of its board of directors. It used this leverage to sell employees, potential clients, vendors, and investors on the promise of a purported groundbreaking technology and the potential for enormous returns on investment. Theranos founder Elizabeth Holmes stacked her board of directors with well-heeled, uber-connected non-businessmen with little or no relevant business experience to build the Theranos brand, despite its being an "empty suit." Caught in her net of deception were such internationally recognized dignitaries such as former Secretaries of State George Schultz and Henry Kissinger, former Secretary of Defense Bill Perry, former Senators Sam Nunn and Bill Frist, and former military men, Navy Admiral Gary Roughead and Marine Corps General James Mattis. Elizabeth Holmes was able to leverage this formidable list of famous individuals to gain access to investors and major corporate accounts such as CVS. This board, however, failed to leverage their collective strengths and instill the integrity, discipline, transparency, and accountability that were the hallmark of their personal brands and careers. The promise of imagination that Theranos represented became the ultimate failure brought down by hubris, dishonesty, and fraud. Within months, the company went from a valuation of over $9 billion to zero as a result of the activities of the CEO and the ineffectiveness of the board.

HyperLeveraging Clients

Despite the avalanche of money that companies spend on marketing and advertising, word-of-mouth recommendations and referrals still rule when it comes to consumer-purchase decisions. Online rating tools and social media have only magnified this trend. After all, who better to tell the story of a company than those who have had a positive, real-world experience with that company's products or services? The opportunity to leverage these relationships is abundant.

How can a company HyperLeverage its clients and its ability to provide powerful, organic, word-of-mouth marketing? Let's pull out our Leverage Prism and see what it reveals.

Unfortunately, few companies understand how to leverage the referral marketing power of their customers. Bombarding customers with pop-ups and follow-up emails that beg for immediate ratings and feedback are a new type of SPAM. Companies that work this way may glean a few insights or gather some worthwhile data, but they're not nurturing long-term relationships. In other words, they're missing out on the ability to turn leverage into HyperLeverage.

If it's the feedback you want to get from real people to inform you, then you've got to communicate with them in a personal manner.

DECONSTRUCTING CLIENT RELATIONSHIPS

CLIENTS & CUSTOMERS

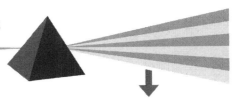

RATINGS/REVIEWS

TESTIMONIALS

REFERRALS/WORD OF MOUTH

LOYALTY PROGRAMS

DISCOUNTS/COUPONS/REBATES

INFLUENCERS/SOCIAL MEDIA

BRANDING/REPUTATION

LONG-TERM CONTRACTS

PERSONALIZED COMMUNICATION

SAMPLES/FREE TRIAL PERIODS

FIGURE 11: DECONSTRUCTING CLIENT RELATIONSHIPS

The quality of the data is so much more important than quantity. Graham Kenny, managing director of Strategic Factors, writing in the Harvard Business Review in January 2019, accurately states, "The obvious answer is to talk with customers directly." There's no way that traditional impersonal surveys could deliver the same kind of direct and honest responses and data that can be leveraged for deep strategic analysis. To leverage clients or even vendors, Kenny continues…"To get meaningful customer input, you need enough interviews to get to the point at which you hear nothing new, and material is being repeated – so-called "saturation." You can reach this point surprisingly quickly and with better results through the "magic" of personal communication and connection.

Perhaps nothing is more impactful in business than authenticity. The driver and basis for almost any interaction between companies and their customers and vendors is trust. With all the advances in technology, we still cherish and strive for the personal touch. Any method that a business can use to exhibit and reinforce its connection to actual people is one that needs to be leveraged.

There is no doubt that social proof, especially authentic testimonials, that people can trust, believe, and depend on has impact far beyond almost anything else a company can do to promote itself, its brand, and its product. And it's something that any company can use. The opportunities and playing field are quite even and the barriers to utilize it are low.

For example, the use of video is available to all. Video Marketing has become somewhat of a business language, especially the use of testimonials. Any company can create and use customer testimonials to develop a story about its brand and the customer journey, and highlight the needs that the customer had and how your service was the ideal solution. It's seldom about the production values—it's about the authenticity and honesty of the everyday people expressing their experience. Gate1Travel, an international travel company, does this so well as it merges simply handheld camera (mobile phone) testimonial videos with images of the various travel destinations and trips it markets.

The use of testimonials and the word of others to tell your company story is not limited to B2C - direct to customer experiences. Wiley Publishing and Hootsuite are an example of how two companies came to create a testimonial video that focused on the benefits of collaboration. Obviously, from the perspective of HyperLeverage, these examples indicate the power behind a strategic and intentional use of customer and vendor relationships.

HyperLeveraging Vendors

Suppliers, distributors, and other vendors have a symbiotic relationship with the companies with which they do business. On the one hand, they want to maximize immediate profits, and on the other, they want to establish lasting relationships that lead to long-term value and efficiencies. These providers have a vested interest in the ongoing success of their clients, and companies have a strong interest in supporting their suppliers, distributors, and other vendors. It's in the symbiosis of this relationship that HyperLeverage can be unlocked. This approach requires the relationship to be properly managed and nurtured.

Before diving into our Leverage Prism evaluation, it's important to understand why companies have vendors. This will help us fully assess the different ways to utilize the company-vendor relationship and maximize its benefits.

Let's look at how companies like BMW leverage vendors in a symbiotic manner to reach their long-term business objectives. When BMW first set up an automotive assembly shop in Spartanburg, SC in 1994, it was one of its first major forays into manufacturing and assembly of vehicles outside of Germany. Far removed from the nexus of automotive vendors concentrated in the Midwest, BMW was in a virtual wilderness in the upstate region of South Carolina.

Opened at a relatively modest cost of $600 million as a small assembly point for North American-market 3-series cars, the BMW Spartanburg assembly plant has expanded into the largest BMW assembly plant in the world. It did not happen in a vacuum. As the company grew, suppliers began to relocate or new ones sprang up nearby, creating a symbiotic client-vendor relationship that nurtured each side.

Not all companies pay heed to the advantages of building long-term vendor relationships, all too willing to jettison the goodwill that has been built up for years of working together for short-term cost savings. This phenomenon has gained more traction and acceleration in mass retail chains that often use vendors, new and even long-term ones, to establish recognition and demand for certain products only to "knock them off" with cheaper private-label brands—store brands—imported from overseas. It is a somewhat cynical approach to providing the consumer what it wants as they deprive them in the long run with the choice and often, better quality of the original vendors' products to increase profits. In the early 2000s, stores like the toy chain Imaginarium brought on an early demise by treating its vendors in this way. Other major retailers walk a fine line with vendors between having too many store brands that compete with them or displace established brands.

The notion that everything can be accomplished and produced in-house is a legacy leftover from before the Industrial Revolution. Being vertically integrated—meaning that most resources, materials, and services required to produce, market, distribute, and sell are done internally—demands a large investment in infrastructure. These days, companies large and small find that working with specialized vendors is often more productive, less expensive, and produces a higher quality product or service than going it alone. This approach allows companies to focus efforts and resources on the components of the product or service that they do best. Today, it is almost impossible to achieve HyperLeverage in a company that is vertically integrated. It's just no longer as efficient.

For a company to effectively engage the right vendors, the leadership team needs to fully understand what business components they do best and identify and onboard vendors that provide an optimal balance of cost, quality, and reliability. Let's use the Leverage Prism to deconstruct the Vendor-Client relationship and study components that can be leveraged effectively.

As you can see in Figure 12: "Deconstructing Vendor Relationships," vendor relationships can be quite complex. Without a system to maximize leverage with vendors, opportunities can be squandered.

For example, in my work as a consultant, I've watched marketing departments miss out on opportunities to present relevant case studies because they were not made aware of major vendors that would be more than happy to give testimonials. Vendor relationships, which are often years in the making, can provide outstanding marketing materials if properly utilized. Short testimonial videos from core vendors can become marketing gold. Savvy marketers can use these in working with the different parts of the business to gain concessions from new vendors by demonstrating the advantages of working with the company. The marketing department must know when new vendors are onboard. This process takes interdepartmental coordination and collaboration, which isn't always prioritized by companies.

I've seen manufacturing companies waste precious resources on quality control because they failed to leverage their vendor

DECONSTRUCTING VENDOR RELATIONSHIPS

VENDORS

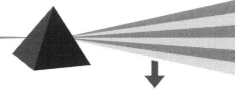

SUBCONTRACTING

LONG-TERM CONTRACTS

JUST IN TIME INVENTORY

FINANCING/PAYMENT TERMS

REFERRALS

DISCOUNTS/PROMOTIONS

INCOMING QUALITY CONTROL

WAREHOUSING/DROP SHIPPING

TEMPORARY/PART-TIME EMPLOYEES

TESTIMONIALS

FIGURE 12: DECONSTRUCTING VENDOR RELATIONSHIPS

relationship. They could have insisted that their vendors provide proof of quality control so that they didn't have to expend company resources taking on this role. These quality control checkpoints are especially important when a company buys entire components and not individual raw materials.

From its humble beginnings in 1905 in the small central Texas town of Kerrville, H-E-B, the dominant supermarket retailer in Texas, has grown (according to *Forbes* magazine) to the 12th largest private company in the country. It has over 340 stores and annual revenues estimated at close to $25 billion for fiscal year 2017. It did this in a manner that was not only congruent with its core values but by embracing those local and regional suppliers within whose community its supermarkets were located. Perhaps more than any other retailer, supermarkets—especially before the era of easy mass distribution—relied heavily on local vendors for their fresh produce, from vegetables and fruits to dairy and even meat and poultry. The symbiotic relationship that existed between customers and suppliers was critical to leverage properly.

Hugh Topper, group vice president, explained it succinctly back in 2011. "H-E-B recognized that years and years ago—that we want to have great relationships with growers and farmers."

Over the years, H-E-B not only "talked the talk," it took intentional, proactive measures to leverage its relationships with its suppliers. Its supplier diversity program is a model of how to partner with suppliers that understand the unique needs of H-E-B's customers and have creative ideas on how to serve them. HyperLeveraging these partnerships allows H-E-B to stay competitive in a grocery landscape that is undergoing significant competition from mass retailers such as Wal-Mart, Target, Costco, and Sam's Club as well as the growing disruptive marketplace for food and meals.

One of the keys to this multi-generational success has been the long-term strategic commitment to quality vendor relations. H-E-B uncovered HyperLeverage among its supplier network by creating a sense of community among its clients. Its efforts outshone many of its national, big-box competitors. The results are impressive, as H-E-B continues to be the most popular supermarket grocery chain in Texas after over 110 years in business.

HyperLeveraging Partnerships

The Red Bull-GoPro partnership is a perfect example of how to HyperLeverage partnerships. In October 2012, Felix Baumgartner jumped out of a plane and recorded the event live for everyone who was signed onto YouTube to see. It was nothing extraordinary at first glance; many others had videotaped such jumps before. Baumgartner, bedecked in a space-age uniform reminiscent of the ones used by space station astronauts, was about to break a world record from 128,000 feet—from the very edge of space. He was the main actor in a marketing event for Red Bull, the swashbuckling energy drink company that exploded out of Austria in 1987 and became a category builder in the sports drink arena. To take full advantage of this event, Red Bull leveraged social media, advanced PR, and the beginnings of a long-term business partnership with portable micro camera company GoPro, which has become synonymous with outdoor activities and extreme sports.

Strapping on a series of GoPro cameras to his suit, the world vicariously lived the experience of free-falling from more than twenty miles up. It was partnership marketing on steroids, and people went wild. The outcome of this "stunt"? GoPro drove global awareness to its brand and reinforced the capabilities of its product as it captured an extreme sports moment not previously captured on camera. Red

Bull crushed it by leveraging the event to a huge audience. In the short four minutes it took Baumgartner to return to earth safely, Red Bull had essentially left all energy drink competitors in the dust.

Two years later, Red Bull and GoPro formalized their partnership and joined forces on a multi-year, global partnership that included content production, distribution, cross-promotion, and product innovation. GoPro's product and brand accessed more than 1,800 Red Bull events across more than 100 countries. The company's share content rights on co-productions and related content were distributed across both Red Bull and GoPro's digital distribution networks, including The GoPro Channel, Red Bull TV, and Red Bull.com and in the Red Bull Content Pool, Red Bull's media service platform.

Why did this partnership work? Both brought something to the table that the other couldn't develop or achieve internally. Both companies share common business vision and goals but in completely different categories. They are both lifestyle brands that represent fearlessness, adventure, and extreme, action-packed activities. To date, it has been a perfect pairing. GoPro provides the tools to adventurers and athletes to capture their lifestyle feats on the 1,800 Red Bull-sponsored and produced events around the globe and Red Bull gets to promote them exclusively on its various online marketing channels.

Partnerships can be HyperLeveraged not just for co-branding purposes, as was the case for GoPro and Red Bull. Figure 13 lists the other impactful potential avenues where partnerships should be considered instead of "going it alone," delaying, or simply not pursuing business opportunities. Pooling disparate resources is perhaps the simplest approach that allows companies to develop products and services with less costs and less risk and get them to market quicker. Partnerships can also be useful in reducing customer acquisition costs and provide a mechanism for smaller companies to compete against and take market share away from industry leaders.

DECONSTRUCTING PARTNERSHIPS

PARTNERSHIPS

POOLED RESOURCES

REDUCED COSTS/INVESTMENT

INCREASED SPEED TO MARKET

DEFINED/LIMITED PROJECT SCOPE

NEW MARKET OPPORTUNITIES

CO-BRANDING

SHARED RISK

FIGURE 13: DECONSTRUCTING PARTNERSHIPS

The ultimate benefit of HyperLeveraging partnerships is to achieve better results with a limited pool of resources and assets.

Takeaways

⚠ Customers represent the most authentic and powerful broadcasters of a company's products and services, and this willingness to share their user experience can be leveraged in today's online social media environment.

⚠ HyperLeveraging a network of people, whether it's customers, vendors, or partners, requires honesty and openness to form a bond of trust. Once the bond is broken, the leverage disappears.

⚠ Partnerships allow companies to develop products and services with less cost and get them to market quicker. Partnerships can also be leveraged to reduce customer acquisition costs.

⚠ Companies should look to HyperLeverage vendors and partners who can perform tasks or deliver products and services that are not part of their core competency.

The DOIT Leverage Method: People
Case Study—UBER

From its beginning in 2009, Uber has hit the gas pedal full throttle to become the dominant player in the disruptive ride-sharing market. With a "take no prisoners" approach and aggressive "grow big quickly" expansion model, Uber became synonymous with ride-sharing. The toxic, misogynistic corporate culture that supported this breakneck growth was publicly exposed in 2017, leading to the ouster of key executives and founder and CEO, Travis Kalanick. His replacement, hired from outside the firm, was Dara Khosrowshahi, a seasoned corporate executive tasked with handling the growing backlash of a tarnished brand and establishing a more controllable growth trajectory.

In 2017, Uber was at a crossroads. It knew it had a serious people problem both in terms of its internal business culture and its tarnished reputation with customers and drivers. This DOIT analysis is a theoretical look back—with 20/20 vision—at how the new Uber leadership might have considered how to HyperLeverage what they had at their disposal to control their rapid growth and prepare for the eventual initial public offering (IPO), which took place in May 2019.

To begin with, Uber's new executive team had to deconstruct the foundations of their core business and evaluate how they handled the various issues they were facing. They had to organize resources and market opportunities to see what they were already HyperLeveraging and where more leverage opportunities existed. Next, they needed to assess what they could improve upon with the assets on hand. They had to take significant and immediate action to continue to leverage the core values they offered to consumers and drivers—values that were being overlooked because of the controversies in which the company was embroiled.

Deconstruct

- Leverage Technology—The ubiquity of mobile devices allowed for immediate and easy access to Uber's services.
- Leverage Limited Infrastructure—The company had little physical infrastructure or fixed assets. It only needed to invest limited resources in training, insurance, benefits, and other HR activities to trump those offered by legacy transportation companies.
- Leverage People—The company could pull from a huge pool of drivers from around the world who were looking for an extra source of income. Driving home the message that Uber provided them a way to leverage their spare time and their own assets (their cars) was a no brainer.
- Leverage Location—Uber is everywhere. GPS tracking technology allowed for drivers and customers to connect worldwide anywhere on the planet.
- Leverage Change—Massive lifestyle and transportation changes would likely increase Uber's usage for the next decade.

Organize

- Make it easy for consumers to access the company's services with continued support and improvements to the user-friendly app. Provide payment options that match the growing trend toward both credit card and other online methods of payment.
- Reinforce the company's core value proposition that consumers can control their transportation costs and conveniently schedule and plan their time.

- Continue to provide resources for people to sign up as drivers for all Uber transportation and delivery services.
- Continue to roll out delivery services to additional urban locations, specifically in Europe and South America.

Improve

- Invest in advanced driver tools to improve consistency and quality.
- Leverage existing driver pool to further expand the Uber Eats food delivery service.
- Continue expansion into other areas of urban transportation using scooter technology.
- Continue to invest in driverless car technology and forge partnerships with major automotive manufacturers.
- Contemplate expansion into LTL and full trailer delivery services to disrupt the long-haul freight market.
- Contemplate partnerships with existing automotive manufacturers to lease/purchase a fleet of Uber-owned vehicles to disrupt the rental car marketplace.

Take Action

- Name a new CEO from outside the company who could change corporate culture and bring in high-level executive management experience that can prepare for and lead the company toward a successful IPO.
- Apply a long-horizon strategic plan that focuses on ride-sharing market share, technology upgrades, and the core model of delivery as a service (DaaS)
- Deploy resources with more discipline on multiple fronts: ridesharing, food delivery, technology (driverless cars).

What were the results of the Uber team's assessment? They recognized that they had defined the space of ride-sharing services by providing choice, flexibility, and control of timing to the customer for their transportation needs. They established their brand worldwide (until "Uber" had become synonymous with ridesharing). They expanded into associated transportation services such as Jump.com to capture market share in the growing urban scooter market. They established themselves as a force to be reckoned with in the rapidly expanding food and home delivery services. By HyperLeveraging their key assets, specifically through the expansion into food delivery, Uber was able to report a 43 percent year-to-year increase in reported revenue to a total of $11.3 billion.

What are the key takeaways from the efforts of the Uber executive team? They proved that taking bold action as part of a long-term strategy can pay off. The Uber story reinforces the concept that taking action is the differentiator when it comes to creating a disrupted market. On the other hand, they recognized that being dismissive of key people issues such as conditions for their drivers, brand reputation, and corporate culture and ethics were major deterrents to accomplishing their strategic plans.

Uber's leadership showed that by HyperLeveraging key assets, they had the muscle to dominate new market arenas. They demonstrated that their strategic efforts in developing the technology of the future in driverless transportation indicate they have the patience, long-term vision, and strategy necessary to build the infrastructure for future growth.

HyperLeverage and Planning

"An organization's ability to learn and translate that learning into action rapidly is the ultimate competitive advantage"
~Jack Welch

DEFINITION: HYPERLEVERAGE AND PLANNING

1. Proactively maximizing all business resources, assets, potential, and opportunities to create a detailed and specific roadmap that accelerates growth and extends an organization's longevity.

2. Intentionally melding an organization's disparate business activities—including the use of data, intelligence and critical thinking—into an effective and actionable roadmap that drives an organization's exceptional levels of performance .

Chip and Joanna Gaines, stars of the HGTV cable show *Fixer Upper,* were not even teenagers when Bob Vila and his trusted sidekick carpenter Norm Abram made house remodeling "must-see" entertainment in the 1980s and 1990s with their shows *This Old House* and *The New Yankee Workshop.* Years later, the Gaines took the remodeling-show concept more than one step further, utilized modern media communications, and coupled distressed real estate with modern home improvement and interior design concepts. The result was a popular new remodeling-show genre that took the nation by storm, attracting more than five million viewers and becoming the flagship star of the HGTV cable channel. The couple then leveraged their newfound fame and created their brand of home decor and furnishings.

As an episode of *Fixer Upper* opens, we find Chip and Joanna walking through a rundown house that hasn't been maintained for years. They describe to the new owners what their vision is to make their new home not only functional but exceptional. Chip walks viewers through the various construction issues, and Joanna brings her keen sense of design to the finishes and small touches. The new owners are excited, and so are we as viewers.

Chip and Joanna make the steps that need to be taken seem so obvious. The *Fixer Upper* team then clip on their carpenters' belts, rev up their miter saws, and start cutting away. A few weeks later, Joanna comes in to put a dash of color on the wall, hang several decorative mirrors and art pieces, and *voila!* the house is fit for royalty. To the viewer, the exceptional results looked effortless. Of course, anyone who has ever worked in construction or interior design knows that's not the case.

What goes into making the latest *Fixer-Upper* project look so effortless? Planning. Lots of planning. Margins are tight in construction and variables can be high (unpredictable weather, surprise construction defects, etc.). The cost of making a mistake can mean the difference between a profitable project and a costly one. A miscalculation or surprise structural defect can lead to significant and costly project delays. The margin for error is small, and the stakes are high. That's why skilled construction contractors leverage planning, measurement, and forethought before acting.

Living by the simple credo, "measure twice, cut once," contractors and designers know that they must think strategically to cut costs, reduce production time, and build quality into the process. They leverage project management because they know that there are certain activities that must be done in a certain sequence. They leverage planning to know what tools, equipment, and supplies they will need. Before they begin, they have already determined how they are going to measure, construct, and finish the project. Even before they plan the production stage, they've done a different kind of planning: they've assessed the real estate marketplace to present the right homes to buyers in a specific price range. They've evaluated market intelligence and done product research on the home's potential finishes. Planning is *everything* in a successful construction and design process. Don't be fooled by their casual approach and relaxed style— Chip and Joanna Gaines are masterful planners.

The outcome of a *Fixer-Upper* segment is always the "reveal," that emotional moment when the new owners see their redesigned home for the first time. Chip, Joanna and the *Fixer-Upper* team know that this "wow" moment is their goal and they work backwards through the planning process to achieve it—it's the heart of their show. In my business engagements with clients, I use this same approach. I call it "thinking backwards"—clearly envisioning the end goal allows one to peel back the activities necessary to achieve it, one layer at a time. The process reveals the resources necessary to reach each milestone until the desired result is achieved.

Unfortunately, planning and strategy are often given "lip service" in pursuit of quick results. Striking when the iron is hot is enticing, but eventually, the fires go out, and you could be left with a big question mark on how to proceed. Many managers, professionals, and business leaders shoot from the hip and follow their gut instinct, rather than engaging in clear, rational, strategic thought and finding enough data to support their direction. This is what happened at Myspace, now a footnote in the history of social media sites. Before Facebook, Instagram, Twitter, YouTube, and Pinterest, Myspace ruled the online world of social interactions. Founded in August 2003, it reached a user base of 22 million before being acquired by News Corp for $580 Million in 2005. The company continued an upward trajectory for a while after the acquisition. When News Corp tried to monetize Myspace in order to pay for the acquisition too quickly and haphazardly, things began to unravel. People's personal home pages began to be inundated with ads of all kinds, and they were poorly targeted to the user's profile. End users were also allowed to significantly alter the design of their home page, which led to the platform taking on a sort of "Wild West" look of poorly designed pages capped off by very poor user experience. The oversaturation and intrusiveness of the ads, coupled with the hands-off approach to the site's aesthetics, opened the door for Facebook, which tweaked what Myspace had started and found the winning formula of controlling the user interface while slowly introducing revenue-producing ads. In June 2011, News Corp sold Myspace for a mere $35 million, a fraction of its previous value. Planning matters.

Of course, even with impressive planning, no business can completely control its fate. The world of commerce is too complex and unpredictable. No one can predict what nature might rain down upon us. We can try to be prepared for it, but we can't stop the rain. Business leaders can try their best to anticipate scenarios capable of knocking their business or projects off-kilter. When catastrophe strikes, leveraging an effective crisis plan can provide a welcome safety net that can save jobs and profits. A business's goal is to survive long enough to realize a healthy return on its investments and assets. It's rare for that to happen without adequate planning for both positive outcomes and managing unforeseen circumstances.

Now, making timely, impactful, and smart business decisions is the role of business management. It is an essential element of achieving HyperLeverage. The difference, often slim, between simply making decisions and HyperLeverage, though, lies in the proactive and take action emphasis of the latter. HyperLeverage is holistic in nature, taking a more wide-angle view of the entire business canvas. No doubt, to make smart decisions you should incorporate many of the same processes that make up the HyperLeverage system. But often, even the best decisions are made in a vacuum, devoid of context or data analysis.

In this section, I'll introduce key, underlying truths about the planning process and how understanding these truths can help companies achieve results well beyond the norm. I'll explain the importance of having data and intelligence to inform the decision-making and strategic-planning process. We'll explore how my "thinking backwards" process can help business leaders create a more effective, forward-facing strategy. Finally, we'll look at how time, location, and even size can play leading roles in achieving aggressive and higher-value business objectives. Taken together, these components are the underpinnings of successful planning. As you will find in the stories throughout this book, rarely do any of these sections or chapters exist in a vacuum. There are significant overlaps and interdependencies between the 4 Ps of HyperLeverage: People, Planning, Performance, and Progress. With this in mind, let's dive right in with the central lodestone of HyperLeverage planning: strategic planning.

CHAPTER 9

Strategy & Planning

The cornerstone of HyperLeverage is active and meaningful acquisition, refinement, and deployment of assets and resources to create added value and realization of stellar returns on investment. That investment can be both tangible (money and materials) or intangible (intellectual property, employee training). It all starts with intention—proactively creating a plan to make one plus one equal significantly more than two.

In today's highly competitive, fast-moving environment, a company's ability to create a HyperLeverage setting for optimal business results can mean the difference between success and failure, profit and loss, having a sufficient time horizon to realize a return on investment, or having to shut off the lights and close up shop. HyperLeverage doesn't happen by chance, and it doesn't happen overnight. But it *can* happen with strategic planning. Strategic planning is a company's ongoing exercise in evaluation, analysis, and prioritization of activities as they relate to the company's long-term objectives. It allows the company to match the right resources with the right goals to achieve the best results. The findings of strategic planning will guide strategic, tactical, and ultimately operational decision-making.

Most businesses already use the processes of analysis, planning, and strategy. More times than not, though, these processes are treated as separate and independent activities, rather than part of a cohesive, interconnected, and codependent system. For a more systematic approach to take hold in a company's culture, it must be inculcated throughout an organization. In other words, it can't just be isolated to a certain level of management or a specific department. It must become a core value that defines the company's decisions and actions. A cohesive, inclusive planning system can lead to maximum exploitation of a business's true potential. It is what separates mediocre and even good companies from top performers. It is also the essence of HyperLeverage Planning.

Everyone wants to leverage what they have. Business development and sales departments want to sell more of their current products and services to increase revenues. The marketing department wants to communicate its current value proposition to more customers. Operations teams want to extract efficiencies and productivity from existing teams of professionals. These are all a given. The secret is to figure out how to pull together all these disparate activities, so the activity gears start to interlock and work together as a whole. This not only improves efficiency, innovation, performance, and profitability; it ultimately starts to generate an additional level of efficiency, innovation, performance, and profitability—a sort of energy boost. And therein lies the HyperLeverage. It's not easy to do, and most companies fall short.

Strategic Planning is an Ongoing Process

The DOIT methodology is an ongoing activity and not just an isolated one-time exercise. The same holds true for strategic planning. The findings, recommendations, and action items of the strategic planning exercise must be shared, easily accessible, and open for collaboration.

The various strategies of a business, including those at the department level, must be congruent with the culture, business ethics, and mission of your organization. Thinking strategically is not an isolated exercise conducted only some of the time by a few top executives or managers. It's a mindset that should be nurtured throughout the company and should empower all corporate stakeholders to handle challenges that arise throughout the life cycle of a business. Strategic planning is a core tool for business growth. Let's find out how we can squeeze even more out of it to take advantage of business opportunities and to maximize growth.

HyperLeveraging the View from Above

Strategic planning requires a "big picture" perspective. Think of looking out of an airplane at 20,000 feet. What do you see? Geography made up of disparate parts—farmland, mountains, rivers, forests, lakes, and more. From this vantage point, you can see that the path from where you are to where you want to go looks different from up there. You can see the shortcuts, vantage points, opportunities, and threats. How does that translate into your daily life? Well, perhaps you'd discover your current business path does not consider a new market niche in which to sell your products or services. Remember how Play-Doh came to be? Perhaps you might discover a looming threat to your existing value proposition—a virtual mountain range that will require a jolt of innovation or product improvement to thwart. Anyone with a Blackberry can attest to how Apple's iPhone derailed Blackberry's strategic plans for dominance in the mobile phone arena. Former BlackBerry Co-Chief Executive Jim Balsillie conceded as much in an interview in 2015, stating that Apple's iPhone was the cause of the once-great Canadian company's fall from the pinnacle and represented a devastating blow to Blackberry's parent company, Research in Motion. Even though BlackBerry tried eventually to compete with the launch of its own touch-screen phone, it had been rushed through product development and was a massive failure. Balsillie admitted, "That was the time I knew we couldn't compete on high-end hardware."

Without the ability to deconstruct the marketplace landscape from a high vantage point, these crucial opportunities found amid the nooks and crannies of the geography can be overlooked. There can be no real HyperLeverage without the combination of the 20,000-foot vantage point and the process of assessing its parts and the space between them. If everything just gets lumped together, it's difficult to understand what part of a business is pulling the cart and which is being pulled.

Deconstructing the elements of the business landscape is just a first step. Getting the most out of planning requires reconstruction and emphasis of those elements that can achieve HyperLeverage. For example, it's not a leverage activity with a lot of promise to try to breathe new life into a product line that once held promise but whose market is diminishing. The resources should be diverted elsewhere. Large organizations shed divisions and departments often in a continuous molting process. Smaller companies are even more nimble and should be looking to do the same, while focusing on those business activities and market opportunities that provide the highest potential and ability to leverage resources.

The reconstruction of an existing strategic plan can be difficult. You can face leadership challenges, people challenges, business culture challenges, and more. There can be many off-limit questions, such as if your company's products and services truly have a value proposition that stands the test of time. Maybe you don't have the right people or even enough people to make the pieces of your strategy work. Maybe you need to shift resources around to achieve your strategic goals. The roadblocks can be formidable. It may take time, but you'll need to push through the problems of the past to focus on the future.

How can you do this? By organizing your evaluation of the business components and embracing a brutally honest "look in the mirror" mindset. Think of it as spring cleaning—discarding items you've collected over time but never really used. Reducing clutter and unnecessary activities—resource hogs that hold back progress—is essential if you wish to find HyperLeverage in your planning.

A Closed Look of Continuous Introspection

HyperLeveraging the power of strategic planning derives from the ability to identify underutilized resources and improve their incorporation into the revenue and growth activities that already exist in your strategy. For example, a marketing initiative that has not yielded the anticipated results might still represent a valid business opportunity but needs an improved marketing campaign, perhaps even including replacing staff or adding specific marketing expertise.

A strategic plan will always need a mechanism for being evaluated. Without it, how can you possibly determine whether it is on target or whether adjustments and refinements must be made? A strategic plan is only as useful as a roadmap if the road continues to lead to the right place. When you get in your car, you have a destination in mind and a good sense of how to get there. You are constantly adjusting to road conditions and traffic. You change lanes, you take shortcuts to avoid bottlenecks, you avoid driving at certain hours of the day. Your strategic plan of how to get from point A to point B is under continuous review, albeit often subconscious or semi-automatically. That's how you leverage your time behind the wheel. So, too, when you are driving a strategic plan. I'm sure that BlackBerry had a strategic plan. Did it have a continuous method to test it, or did it just dust it off once a year?

A strategic plan is not a one-off exercise done just to check it off your to-do list. All the hard work of analysis and forward-thinking that goes into planning is worthless if you don't put everything into action. You've built the roadmap and are ready to leverage the work and thought that went into building it. That's very important and often hard work. Now turn the key and get the leverage engines running. Whether it's a company-wide or departmental strategic review or simply a strategic plan to address specific marketing, operational or sales initiatives, driving down the path you've built, even if it seems scary and unfamiliar, is only meaningful if you follow through. Implementation of planning is how you unlock HyperLeverage.

HyperLeverage Planning is proactive, as are its three basic elements: full and active support from upper management, employee participation and input, and truly effective communication. The latter should include a clear understanding of the need for the strategic plan and its ramifications for all involved. Your strategic plan can't be just words on paper. Susan Heathfield in writing on thebalancecareers.com blog in May 2019 cites that organizations whose employees have a clear understanding of the strategic goals enjoy a 29 percent greater return than firms that keep it close to the chest.

They see what HyperLeverage of strategic planning can look like in a highly successful company. Look at the famous Amazon Flywheel in Figure 14, conceived originally in 2001 by the company's founder, Jeff Bezos.

Figure 14 reveals that the key to success in online retail is *a bias towards leveraging and investing in infrastructure*. It became the long horizon vision that has informed the strategic planning used by Amazon to

FIGURE 14: THE AMAZON FLYWHEEL: BEZOS VIRTUOUS CYCLE   SOURCE: JEFF BEZOS 2001

conquer the Internet through extraordinary growth. In 2018, Amazon recorded revenues of $233 billion, close to doubling its 2016 level of $136 billion. As a sign of how it was able to find HyperLeverage in its strategic investment in infrastructure, the company has amassed an astonishing 288 million square feet of warehouses, offices, retail stores, and data centers. In 2017, it added close to 80 million square feet.

How did Bezos conclude that was the way to dominate the emerging online e-commerce space? He deconstructed his industry and the prevailing approach to his business. He analyzed, reverse-engineered, gathered intelligence, and created a new roadmap for Amazon. As a result, Bezos was able to suspend the prevailing tendency of dot.com companies to think in the short term and instead play the long game by investing in infrastructure. This enabled him to grow very quickly and attain economies of scale that were previously unthinkable.

HyperLeverage at Hubspot

HubSpot also offers a great example of HyperLeverage Planning—in particular, the power of strategic planning. In 2004, two MIT graduate students, Brian Halligan and Dharmesh Shah, met for the first time. Little did they know that the copious amounts of coffee and beer they were to share over the next couple of years would result in launching HubSpot, a company that would disrupt business marketing and change the way that almost every other company in the world utilizes the Internet.

In 2006, Halligan was helping venture-backed startups with their go-to-market strategy. Shah was busy with his blog, "On Startups." What they both noticed was that the blog, with practically no marketing budget, was experiencing massive traffic growth. Meanwhile, companies with big budgets and professional communication teams using traditional marketing techniques were struggling to grow traffic to their websites. Halligan theorized that traditional marketing was being tuned out by the masses. People found it annoying. It was unsolicited and unwanted. Halligan also recognized changes in the way people were shopping online and learning about new products and services. They were spending more and more time on social networks. Using techniques that mimic what I call my "Leverage Prism," he peeked into the future and foresaw the social content revolution that was to be fueled by Facebook, Instagram, and Twitter, even before those companies had hit the scene. People don't want to be interrupted by marketers or harassed by salespeople. They want to be helped so they can make better decisions. Halligan believed he could merge these two realizations into one strategic vision and build a company around this vision.

Together, Halligan and Shah built HubSpot based on a strategic plan that would flip the world of marketing—from one with an outbound focus to an inbound marketing focus where helpful content would draw people toward a company's products and services. Their strategy was a simple series of interconnected activities. The more information a company gave away to a prospect, the more it empowered it. In turn, these empowered prospects would see HubSpot as an authority and a company they could trust. When a company was ready to subscribe to a marketing platform or service, it would naturally turn to HubSpot because of the strong connection that had already been made.

I love the simplicity of their vision. It shows that you don't have to create complex paradigms to be successful. They were not going to reinvent the wheel. Instead, they were going to leverage existing and independent marketing concepts and bundle them together in a platform that marketing teams could use to more productively communicate their company, product, and brand stories to customers. Their achievement is a true demonstration of HyperLeverage Planning. They proactively exploited existing leverage opportunities with intent and purpose.

HubSpot began with blogs, eBooks, and social media posts. Its platform leveled the playing field and allowed small companies with limited budgets to produce quality content that would draw people to the websites and landing pages where they could explore the products and services being offered there. Its strategic plan considered the historical and current methods of marketing and recognized the dramatic shift the Internet and social media would create in empowering the consumer from a passive to an active participant in the business equation. Again, the founders of HubSpot offer a great example of HyperLeverage Planning: they intentionally drew from the past and married this idea to future technology and communication patterns.

To prove its point, HubSpot ate its own dogfood. The company used the techniques it was espousing to demonstrate that the platform worked. They had deconstructed the opportunity, organized the necessary building blocks of a business model and plan, improved upon what already existed, and were ready to act. Halligan and Shah's plan worked stupendously. HubSpot found HyperLeverage in its strategic planning to achieve exceptional results. Its inverted the traditional marketing approach from outbound to inbound. The company went public in 2014 and now generates more than $500 million in sales and has a market cap of over $6 billion. It is still one of the largest and most dominant inbound marketing software platforms on the planet, despite the entry of a slew of competitors.

Think Backwards

Generally, strategic planning is thought of as a forward-thinking management discipline designed to set priorities and focus a company's time, money, and energy around a common set of goals, outcomes, and results. It's meant to bring the whole team on board and get everyone aligned around future results. Strategic planning, as it is commonly understood, begins with the next step to achieve those goals.

It is more effective to think backwards from a tangible and well-articulated goal. Why? Looking forward is an exercise in futility. It underestimates the challenge ahead. There is a tendency to think of pie-in-the-sky possibilities. It puts the focus in the wrong place and fails to align everyone around the critical assessment and decision-making process. This process is necessary to determine the time and challenges that must be overcome to achieve each of the smaller goals required to achieve the larger goal. Additionally, it does not focus on the discovery and assessment of current and potential assets that could be leveraged along the way.

HyperLeverage planning is like crafting the story that you want to have told. Before Disney learned the lessons from its work with Pixar, the company followed a traditional, forward-thinking path in its strategic planning of blockbuster animated movie releases. It was when it reverse-engineered its goals that it was able to unlock HyperLeverage. Reverse-engineering a goal means going deep. It means taking the time to systematically assess where you are, what you have, what you need to do, what you need to change, and what you must leverage to get to your end goal. There's a clear methodology behind this type of strategic planning, and it looks very different from most of what passes as strategic planning in companies these days.

There will always be hard and fast planning deadlines that a company can't ignore or circumvent. For example, the holiday and Christmas season comes only once a year. A manufacturer that wants to get its latest and best products into top retailers and online distributors for that lucrative season must be cognizant and plan around the specific time milestones imposed upon it by these entities. No matter how great a product is, if you don't close the deal and get your supply chain set up in a certain timeframe, you will not be able to distribute and sell your products during the upcoming holiday season.

There are situations where there is value in being quick to action. Fads and fashions change constantly and require a different approach to strategic planning. In these cases, those companies that have readymade supply chains, existing distribution outlets, and can repurpose marketing campaigns and assets can ride the waves like a professional surfer. Others who might be late to the "game" have little to leverage. Rarely does short-term business activity translate into HyperLeverage, as it is mostly reactive.

Why do you need this runway of time? Because rarely is success drawn in a straight line. I learned this lesson in my early 40s, when I decided to learn how to sail. The image of men of my age at the helm of a boat enthralled me. I could see myself standing confidently, staring straight ahead, rudder in hand, cool shades on my eyes, and the wind blowing in my hair (when I still had some). To me, this vision oozed success, confidence, control, and a sense of purpose. As an A-type personality, it is in my nature to seek control of my environment. Sound familiar to any of you? That describes so many business owners, entrepreneurs, and executives. I was used to charting my own course, bending the curve to my advantage.

At this same time, I was also building my first company, Colorations®, and I could see my goals. I had a strategy in place, a roadmap, and I knew what I was going to leverage to get to my destination. I was cocksure that I knew exactly where to go and how to get there. Time to hoist the sails and go down that straight line to the finish line, right?

Turns out that rarely can you sail straight to your destination. The winds, currents, and other influences and obstacles force you to adjust your path. All you can do is learn how to read the winds and the currents and let them inform you where you can and cannot sail. The same was true for building my company. I had to make constant adjustments along the way. I had been naive. Luckily, I had built my company like I had provisioned and captained my boat—with all the correct tools and knowledge to adjust my course. I had the processes, infrastructure, and assets I needed to capitalize and harness the winds of business on my road to success. I was able to create and benefit from HyperLeverage...if only I could shift my mindset from one of straight-line arrogance to one of humble, constant learning.

Learning to sail put an end to my naïveté and changed my approach to business planning. It taught me humility. A good sailor knows to work backwards, to plot a course toward the destination, and to assess the challenges along the way. A good sailor utilizes the skills, sails, and rudder to adjust as he or she constantly gauges the currents, winds, and weather ahead. Planning HyperLeverage comes from keeping an eye on the destination while intentionally adjusting to maintain profits and efficiency as market and business conditions change.

Even Amazon, which is now known as the "Everything Store," learned the ropes in one vertical, at first: selling books. As it made money selling books, it worked on its larger strategic plan to develop the infrastructure and software systems it would need to leverage for success in other business verticals. It is now reaping the rewards of that HyperLeverage Planning. It never fell into the swallow-the-entire-elephant-in-one-gulp trap into which many companies fall. Rather, with a very smart application of high-growth planning and long-term thinking, it rode the wave of technological disruption. It chose to start in an area it could disrupt and thus dominate. Then, it moved on to conquer the next market.

Planning for the future is an essential task of business management. A company that incorporates "think backwards" strategic planning, with an emphasis on supportive data and information, sets itself and its employees to achieve and reap the benefits of HyperLeverage planning. Whether its managing time and resources, working with others, or simply making an effort to think critically about the tasks at hand, a business succeeds when its components are intentional in what they do and in how those tasks relate to the overarching business strategy.

Takeaways

⚠ Planning is a proactive exercise that leverages the collection and analysis of information and intelligence to reach informed decisions.

⚠ To leverage strategic planning, it pays to have a "Think Backwards" approach to visualize the result and understand the milestones and obstacles to overcome.

⚠ A cohesive, inclusive planning system can lead to maximum exploitation of a business's true potential. It is what separates mediocre and even good companies from top performers. This is the essence of HyperLeverage Planning.

⚠ HyperLeverage through planning can be achieved by figuring out how to pull together all disparate business activities so that they mesh like interlocking gears. This generates an additional level of efficiency, innovation, performance, and profitability—a sort of energy boost. Therein lies the HyperLeverage.

CHAPTER 10

Decisions & Risk

A key trait of successful companies and leaders is their ability to make good and timely decisions. The quality of the decision-making process is directly related to the success of the outcome. Good decision-making requires good intelligence, critical thinking, and planning. Intelligence requires good information and data. Garbage in equals garbage out.

No path can be paved, no project management plan can be implemented, and no acquisition or deployment of assets or resources can be done without making meaningful decisions. Unfortunately, few businesses emphasize learning how to make decisions effectively and communicating this process to the entire organization so that there is a consistent, uniform, reproducible, and proactive approach to decision-making.

So why are haphazard, piecemeal systems that often lead poor decisions still tolerated? Bernard Schwartz, in his influential book, *The Paradox of Choice*, explains the conflict that allows these systems to flourish in today's business culture. The human desire to have options leads to a continuous search for something better. In today's terminology, it's called FOMO (Fear of Missing Out). It shackles decision-making and impedes progress. FOMO in the business world can have serious negative consequences that squander resources. It can lead to emotional, gut reactions that are counter to the fundamentals of rational and fact-based decisions and planning.

It is all the more reason to develop a decision-making process that overrides FOMO and works for your organization. Perhaps it is entirely data driven. Perhaps you need a system that can manage experience and is subjective. Are decisions made unilaterally without peer or team review in your organization? When does the spigot of intelligence and information get turned on or off? When is it wise to hold off on a decision until more information can be collected or analyzed? These are all worthwhile questions that should be answered as you craft a strategic-planning process that fits the culture of your business. In the answers, you'll find the building blocks of your decision-making process, which should be a useful blend of historical data, current operational and market information, intelligence about trends, technology, personal experience, and demographics, among others.

"Just the Facts..."

In one of the first famous TV cop series, "Dragnet," Sergeant Joe Friday did not like to beat around the bush. He didn't have time for small talk and preferred to get straight to the heart of the matter. One of his famous catchphrases when interrogating suspects was, "Just the facts." Friday's style comes close to how many decision-makers operate their businesses. They want to reduce the subjective "gut feeling" component of any decision to a minimum. For them, business decisions are based on cold hard data alone.

There are a lot of very sophisticated techniques about decision-making, which are outside the scope of this book. They all share a common thread that leads to HyperLeverage. They all rely on an intentional collection of data that can be vetted, measured, and evaluated against existing or pre-set norms. And herein lies a dilemma. When do too much data and analysis lead to poor decision-making? When does data become a barrier, a roadblock in the decision-making process? By insisting on data collection from a wide variety of sources—many that may serve to verify previous information—a company can create a data pool that gives them enough of the right information to make good decisions.

HyperLeveraging Risk

When is it prudent to employ risk? Is going out on a limb—either by taking on more debt or by deploying a disproportionate amount of resources to one facet of your business—ever the smart option? Is that sort of risk worth it? When does being conservative and risk-averse become the smarter leverage play? Holding back is more often the more difficult option because we are wired to favor brisk business growth over a slower build. Is the ongoing pressure from various stakeholders, like investors and upper management, shaping your risk strategy?

The story of GoDaddy is illustrative of how a small start-up can leverage risk as part of its strategic plan. Its plan worked, as GoDaddy is now the world's largest Internet domain registrar, is a publicly traded company with more than $2 billion in annual revenue, and has 6,000 employees worldwide. That's a pretty sweet return on its $1 million investment.

In 2005, founder Bob Parsons reportedly had a little more than a million dollars allocated for marketing his new venture. The prudent thing to do would have been to use that money in a variety of reliable marketing channels to grow the business. Parsons felt the safe strategy would take too long to yield the results he wanted. He calculated that he needed to make a splash and capture market share and awareness quickly in a business that had little inherent protections or a clear value proposition. He decided to leverage the largest viewing audience in the country, the Super Bowl. Instead of the typical Super Bowl TV ad spot, Parsons and his team devised a highly controversial ad that would shock and awe the audience...and get the company a ton of PR as a result.

It was a big risk. With no inherent intellectual property or unique technology to support the growth of GoDaddy, Parsons went for brand awareness and ubiquity. GoDaddy's ads appeared to work well enough with its target audience that the company continued with a similar strategy for the next couple of years.

Where is the HyperLeverage in this example? GoDaddy's risk strategy was intentional. It went all in and used risk to hit a home run, knowing that this would also be a storyline that would be commented upon. Parsons could have taken the safe route that other companies take when faced with limited budgets. They would have apportioned their marketing dollars in a more even and allocated manner. They would be hedging their bets that multiple channels would result in a more balanced marketing campaign and relied on the adage that increased frequency of ads is better than a single big splash campaign.

I recall that when I started my first company, Colorations®, my friends thought that I was a big risk-taker, just like GoDaddy's founder. The truth is, I was not. I had done my research and planning. The real risk-takers are those business managers that don't do their homework. Those that don't avail themselves of the tools and systems I've described in these pages. Collecting data and intel, making informed decisions, and using a DOIT process to think critically and develop a living and breathing strategic plan are not HyperLeveraging risk—they are taking a risk. Exploiting the leverageable resources reduces potential issues. It is how you leverage risk. Not taking calculated risks is the opposite of HyperLeverage. It's putting your head in the sand and hoping things will all work out on their own. The decision to purposefully avoid making changes to a strategic plan in the face of new information and market dynamics in the belief that these are temporary is an example of risk that can backfire.

The bigger problem in business is an aversion to risk. Eastman Kodak is perhaps the most glaring example of a company that became so risk-averse, it slid into extinction. In the period before digital cameras and certainly before smartphones, Kodak ruled the roost of photography-related products. It was the global market leader and one of the most recognized brands in the world. Kodak failed to develop and implement a strategic plan that deeply examined all areas of its market. When innovative new technologies entered the market and consumer buying habits started to change, Kodak failed to assess or act on the challenges in a manner that adequately addressed the changing market landscape. As a result, the company was forced to declare bankruptcy in 2012. What might have happened if the management team made a bolder choice and weighed the risks of not acting versus the potential rewards of acting boldly? Could things have turned out differently? You bet they could have. Companies reinvent themselves all the time. Remember the Play-Doh story?

The absence of risk-taking in an organization is a leading indicator of other more substantive issues, such as poor data analysis, business intelligence, and strategic planning. Companies that are completely risk-averse slowly lose their edge and fade away. HyperLeveraging risk as part of the planning process can't be undertaken without setting up systems to manage and learn from the certain failures that come with risk. This means there must be processes and checks and balances in place to monitor, measure, and refine along the way.

Robert Kaplan and Anette Mikes expounded on this in their June 2012 *Harvard Business Review* article, *Managing Risks - a New*

Framework. "Beyond introducing a systematic process for identifying and mitigating strategy risks, companies also need a risk oversight structure. Infosys, for example, uses a dual structure: a central risk team that identifies general strategy risks and establishes central policy, and specialized functional teams that design and monitor policies and controls in consultation with local business teams. The decentralized teams have the authority and expertise to help the business lines respond to threats and changes in their risk profiles, escalating only the exceptions to the central risk team for review." Using the DOIT Leverage Method can be very helpful in these situations to uncover underlying opportunities for HyperLeveraging risk effectively.

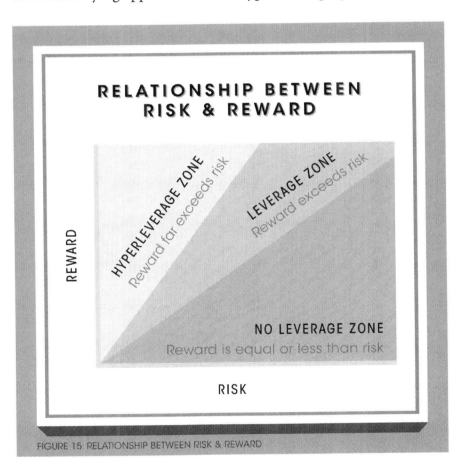

FIGURE 15: RELATIONSHIP BETWEEN RISK & REWARD

Figure 15: "Relationship between Risk and Reward" shows the relationship between risk, reward, and the degree of leverage that can be achieved.

Figure 15 demonstrates that when the reward is greater than the risk, then there is an opportunity for leverage. For most business activities, this would fall into the more moderate Leverage Zone because the ratio of reward to risk is greater than one. HyperLeverage occurs when the rewards of HyperLeveraging risk are far greater. Conversely, if the reward to risk ratio is one or below, then there is no point in pursuing this path as there is no leverage attributed from accepting any risk. This simple exercise can be used throughout any planning process as part of a "Go - No Go" decision tree. It requires various degrees of subjectivity based on the access to data and information to assign values to risk and potential or anticipated rewards.

Takeaways

⚠ To reach HyperLeverage, it may be necessary to leverage risk. Playing it too safe and under-utilizing assets can lead to loss of leverage and, consequently, loss of value.

⚠ The quality and leverage of a decision-making process are directly related to access to reliable intelligence and data analysis. Making reactive decisions based on gut feelings is the opposite of HyperLeverage, as it rarely exploits existing leverageable resources.

⚠ Decision-making is a fundamental activity for any leadership or management team. Organizations that HyperLeverage decision-making create a uniform process and inculcate it throughout their organization to create consistent, uniform, reproducible, and proactive decision-making

CHAPTER 11

Intelligence & Data

I n this chapter, I'll address how to HyperLeverage data and intelligence to gain business, market, and competitive advantages. I'll discuss the overlap of intelligence with other aspects of a business, such as measurement systems, business development, and communication techniques, to build strategies and implementation plans that go beyond simple leverage.

Big business is increasingly run on data analytics and business intelligence to make smart decisions that lead to the exploitation of existing assets and the development of new opportunities. Using a haphazard and cobbled together patchwork system of collecting, accessing, and analyzing information can be extremely dangerous to the viability and long-term health of a company. Since data is becoming an ever-increasing asset, albeit one that does not appear on a balance sheet, it needs to be handled similarly to other tangible and intangible assets, such as equipment or intellectual property. It should be assigned a value and shelf life. Because data—how it's collected, analyzed, filed and stored, accessed and ultimately used—is what determines if it can create HyperLeverage or ends up taking up space. Like everything I've written about in this book, the power of data and intelligence is unlocked through a proactive and intentional decision on the part of management. Companies that use intelligence in all its different iterations are the ones that stand out from the crowd. In short, playing it by the "gut" without reliance on good information is just not going to cut it anymore in a world of constant change, innovation, and open global markets.

To HyperLeverage data, analysis, and intelligence, companies need quality and trustworthy information. The wrong data can be disastrous. That is what happened on April 1986 in the worst nuclear reactor accident in history. In the first episode of the HBO miniseries, Chernobyl, the filmmakers depicted the critical decisions that were made by the managers and technicians of the nuclear power plant. It turns out these crucial decisions were based on faulty and incorrect data that the plant manager had received from the reactor mishap. He didn't recognize at the time the severity of the explosion of the nuclear core, as he was told the radioactivity measurement was only 3.6 Roentgen/hour (R/h)—serious, but nowhere near what turned out to be 15,000 R/h. Based on this incorrect data, key decisions were made in the first 24 hours that made the situation even worse. It was only when verifiable and accurate data was obtained that the true nature of the disaster became obvious and a comprehensive and correct strategy for containing the fire and radioactive fallout could be conceived and implemented. But by then, it was too late. Businesses need to trust the source of the data they use, whether it's collected through their means or purchased or derived from external sources. And for business operations that are "mission-critical," the ante is significantly higher. I'll address the importance and how to HyperLeverage Measurement in Chapter 14.

Business Intelligence

Many people confuse data analytics with business intelligence (BI). They are related, but intelligence is more predictive. BI comprises the strategies and technologies that are employed for the data analysis of information related to business operations. BI solutions are valuable data management tools that inform decision-makers about how to improve business operations. They are wide-ranging tools that can comprise data mining, reporting, benchmarking, analytics, predictive analytics, and other means to evaluate the ever-increasing mountain of information that can be leveraged.

BI software can handle huge amounts of data, such as external data from the market in which a company operates as well as internal sources such as financial and operations data. Data analytics, on the other hand, has a bias toward looking at historical data and pinpointing business trends. It's more of a leading-edge indicator, showing where to improve and make changes to prepare for the future. Combined, they provide a big-picture canvas that can't be derived from a singular data set or perspective. That is one of its big leverage points.

How do BI and data analytics fit together so that the big picture is greater than the sum of its parts? Through a non-stop process of collection, analysis, decision-making, measurement, and refinement. In this manner, a company can achieve HyperLeverage through an iterative process. It's the "rinse and repeat" that makes this possible—the fact that the process is repeated.

Companies that exploit BI and have a system to disseminate the findings throughout the organization, not just one specific business group, can have a significant competitive edge. These companies gain insight into new markets, assess current and future demand, and even gauge the impact of their marketing efforts. Meaningful intelligence can be used for better decision-making, development of strategic initiatives, deployment of personnel, and use of physical assets. That's a powerful tool! You don't want one area of your company "starving" for meaningful intelligence to conduct its activities while another has a rich vein of it to mine and exploit.

Many companies invest in fancy tools and platforms to handle these tasks, but they are only a piece of the puzzle. HyperLeverage can only happen when these tools are coupled with human decision-making processes and critical thinking skills. Additionally, not every asset has a "number" attached to it. How do you measure brand trust, for example? How do you use BI to inform your business about the effects of business regulations? There are simply too many important human interactions that require subjectivity. We don't live in the Matrix, run by super-smart artificial intelligence supercomputers. At least, not yet.

I'm sure that some of the items in Figure 16: "Deconstructing Intelligence," are already utilized in your organization. Perhaps others are cornerstones of how you develop your strategies and various operations, business development, sales, and marketing plans. But can you identify areas that you are lacking or have been overlooked? For example, could your organization benefit from team insights to achieve a more multi-dimensional perspective in your decision-making process? Are intelligence and data leveraged in other aspects of your business? For client acquisition and retention? Innovation? Even using it for opportunities to improve both internal and external communication? These are all questions worth asking.

DECONSTRUCTING INTELLIGENCE

INTELLIGENCE

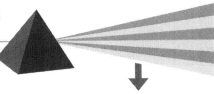

DATA COLLECTION FROM MULTIPLE SOURCES

BUSINESS INTELLIGENCE ANALYSIS

COMPETITIVE MARKET ANALYSIS

ARTIFICIAL INTELLIGENCE (AI)

MACHINE LEARNING

IMPROVED DECISION MAKING

IMPROVED STRATEGIC PLANNING

VENDOR & CUSTOMER FEEDBACK

REAL TIME DATA & INFORMATION

REDUCED RESPONSE TIME

FIGURE 16 : DECONSTRUCTING INTELLIGENCE

HyperLeveraging Intelligence
From Disparate Sources

Often the path to uncovering HyperLeverage through intelligence is to look elsewhere for data and information and use it to solve other challenges. To a large degree, that is what has been playing out in real-time in the world of driverless cars where a culmination of decades of incremental technological advances in measurement, data, and intelligence is changing our transportation systems.

There is no doubt that vehicle automation is a wave of the near future. The fuel that is making this happen is data and artificial intelligence. Companies that have jumped into this arena may be dreamers to many. To me, they are HyperLeverage machines!

Driverless cars will have a dramatic, disruptive effect on how we move our bodies and products from point A to point B. They may already be in your corner of the world. Companies like Apple, Waymo, Tesla, Ford, Honda, BMW, Nissan, Intel and Uber are all testing driverless cars. The common thread is this technology is highly dependent upon real-time data and its immediate analysis.

It's not just this kind of intelligence and data that is being leveraged in their development. Driverless car technology leverages many of the technologies developed for and used by auto-piloted planes and trains. They also incorporate the advances in data collection, technology, and intelligence systems that have become standard in most new automobiles for years.

Have you been to a new car showroom lately? Do you recognize how "smart" these cars are compared to ten years ago? Twenty years ago? What about your parents or grandparents' car from thirty or more years ago? The difference in the use of data and intelligence— not only in the design and manufacturing of modern cars but also in their utilization of real-time data—is night and day.

An examination of the systems that we take for granted as standard features shows how data and intelligence have been utilized to build the cars of today and of the future.

- Electronic Stability Control helps correct a skid if your car begins to slide.
- GPS Satellite Navigation collects real-time location data.
- Radar-based Cruise Control collects vehicular speed intelligence and adjusted vehicular speeds in a continuous manner.
- Continuous Tire Pressure Monitoring has probably saved the lives of thousands.

All these advances in technology were intentionally instituted to increase driver safety and vehicle reliability. They were also advantageous to car manufacturers and their bottom line. They were able to collect intelligence from these technologies and make better and more informed strategic and tactical decisions on a wide array of key business activities, from marketing, infrastructure, and dealer support. And it wasn't by accident. Some were mandated through regulation, but most were proactively implemented.

Competitive (Market) Analysis

Competitive intelligence (CI) or Market Analysis is like BI but with an emphasis on the external environment in which a company operates. It focuses on gathering, analyzing, and distributing information about a company's products, services, and customers as well as competitors and their products, services, and customers. Essentially, CI gives companies the big picture regarding their competitive landscape. CI is what I consider the "opportunities and threats" component of a SWOT (Strength, Weaknesses, Opportunities, and Threats) Analysis, only more detailed and systematic.

All these tools have become extremely impactful, important, and easier to integrate into business operations because the entire world is connected continuously to the Internet. Almost all commercial and personal activity can be monitored—including social media, online activity, and at-home activity—through the introduction of smart devices such as Alexa and the coming "infiltration" of smart home devices using IOT (Internet of Things) platforms. The challenge then becomes how to leverage it for profitable and sustainable business activities.

In 2015, Brett Hurt was ready for his next big idea. After successfully taking his previous startup, Bazaarvoice, public, he came to appreciate the power of data. He saw how it was changing the world in which his children were growing up. During his nine years at the helm of Bazaarvoice, he helped to guide the company to prominence as the world's largest network of active shoppers, connecting more than half a billion consumers to retailers and brands throughout the globe. Hurt recognized that the shortage of data was not a critical issue going forward. He saw that the world of business might drown in it unless systems could be put in place to effectively comb through the vast oceans of data and make sense of it. In other words, Hurt wanted to help businesses leverage data for maximum gain.

He founded his latest venture, Data.world, with a mission to help organizations nurture a data-driven culture. Recognizing that data collaboration would be the key that unlocked treasure chests of useful information, he created a platform for sharing data that could be as powerful as the Internet itself. It would provide unlimited opportunities for companies to leverage not only their data but the collective intelligence of this new data network, just as the Internet provides unlimited interconnected paths of communication. "Even today, data collaboration too often relies on 20th-century tools like email, FTP, and USB drives," Hurt said in an interview with VentureBeat. "Data.

world is changing that by giving everyone access to technologies that are currently only used within large, wealthy, advanced companies."

Data knows no boundaries, geographies, or politics. According to the underlying premise of Data.world's philosophy, business leaders who strive to incorporate a data-driven culture will recognize that it's more than just a technology solution. It's the convergence of people, data, and analysis. "Raw data is like crude oil. It needs to be refined to power the world," said Hurt. "Right now, up to 80 percent of data work is spent on cleaning, formatting, and otherwise preparing the data, which leaves only 20 percent for analysis. No one likes to spend so much time on data janitorial work to get to the sexy part. We're changing that in a big way."

The Promise of Artificial Intelligence

Software and technology go hand in hand with business as the world of commerce becomes driven by data collection, analysis, and artificial intelligence. The access to mounds of data that seems overwhelming today will in short order be replaced by entire mountain ranges of raw data sets waiting to be efficiently utilized for everything from marketing strategies, operational efficiencies, mass personalization, and communication initiatives to dynamic pricing. It's hard to overstate the changes that are coming and how data and intelligence can and will be exploited in the future.

Think of how social media changed our world. Did anyone accurately predict the consequences of Facebook in our daily business lives back in 2008 when Mark Zuckerberg and his cohorts started it? They certainly didn't. Did anyone recognize how social media would fundamentally change how we communicate as individuals or in business? In the year 2000, as we welcomed in the new millennium, no one was talking about this. In 2030, we will be looking back to today as "medieval times" as it relates to how all of us use data in our daily lives.

The advance of technology is relentless in the pursuit of better and cheaper ways to solve problems. According to Byron Reese, futurist, technologist, and author of *The Fourth Age, Smart Robots, Conscious Computers, and the Future of Humanity,* we are entering the next age of technological advancement. It will bring artificial intelligence into the very fabric of our business and personal lives. Artificial intelligence is at the intersection of technology and data. According to Reese, "Being technology-driven is a way of thinking where you are looking for opportunities to multiply your abilities by using knowledge." This quote sounds exactly like HyperLeverage to me.

The quantity of information now being collected makes it difficult to assimilate. We can only cherry-pick data using pre-determined filters. These filters introduce bias and can create distortions that lead to incorrect decisions. Artificial intelligence can help us assimilate the data quicker and more efficiently. However, as Reese explains, there can be deep systemic biases in how the data is collected that will skew results. And we might not understand the conclusions that artificial intelligence gives us.

Becoming A Data-Driven Company

The havoc that artificial intelligence and big data may exact on our existing way of doing things will be profound. It will place a premium on HyperLeveraging big data and BI in ways we are just now experiencing. One of the most important aspects of data is to get the information that provides an historical, current, and predictive view of a business and its operations.

Here's a dirty little secret: as hard as companies large and small try to treat data as an important asset, inculcate data analysis into their culture, and adjust their strategies to emphasize data and analytics, most are still failing to HyperLeverage it. Writing in the *Harvard Business Review* in February 2019, information experts Randy Bean and Thomas Davenport posit that companies are failing in their efforts to become data driven. They cite a survey conducted by Bean's company, NewVantage Partners, that 72 percent of survey participants report that they have yet to forge a data culture, 53 percent are not treating data as a business asset, and 52 percent of large enterprises are not competing on data and analytics despite their deep pockets, large technology infrastructure, and human capital. This only indicates how difficult the challenge is to HyperLeverage data and intelligence.

It's hard to understand the impact of one's efforts or the potential impact of business assets without being able to assign some measurement to it. Even if it's a subjective and relative scale. Without assigning real and financial value to the data and intelligence that a company possesses, it diminishes its acceptance as an asset and, indirectly, to the need to leverage it to the max, like other aspects of a business that we've talked about in this book.

Treat data, data analysis, and the subsequent intelligence that is derived from it something of value on par—often exceeding—how you might treat intellectual property. Give it a value. Communicate this value to your employees so that they understand the impact and role that data and data analysis plays in your company. You'll be surprised how quickly people will accept the ramifications of it from a big-picture perspective.

It's a challenge to forego the classic approach to business assets and accept that the tangible has been replaced by the intangible. Future generations, who will exert a profound influence on business, are more inclined toward the abstract. They grew up in a non-tangible world dominated by the Internet. We see the evidence even in the financial markets as data-driven technology companies—based on the accumulation of "non-tangible" assets such as data, innovation, and intellectual property—are supplanting "tangible" asset and non-data driven companies.

Takeaways

⚠ Finding HyperLeverage in data requires the use of proper filters and guidelines to avoid collection and analysis of unproductive data. All data will have a degree of bias as a result of the filters and measurement techniques used to collect it.

⚠ To create a data-driven culture, a business should approach data and intelligence as a company asset that has a monetary value, a resource to be shared throughout an organization, and a limited use shelf life.

⚠ Data will become commoditized as open or shared data sets become accessible to more businesses. The companies that learn to HyperLeverage data through assimilation of it into normal business operations, planning, and decision processes will be the market leaders.

⚠ Artificial intelligence is the next frontier for HyperLeverage through data and intelligence. It will play an increasingly disruptive role that can be leveraged to jeopardize the hegemony of many legacies and established businesses.

CHAPTER 12

Time, Location, & Size

There are three soft assets all companies possess that can be leveraged to gain competitive advantage. These are time, location, and size. They deserve special attention because they exist in every organization, no matter how big. Each can be readily leveraged if a company handles these soft assets proactively and with the intention to further its long-term objectives.

Business leaders and managers must be very cognizant of time as it can be both a limiting and a limited asset. Business decision-makers should understand how location can open superhighways of commerce or lead to dead ends. Finally, business leaders need to understand that size does matter, and they should take full advantage of it. I will explore these three concepts below and how successful business managers make it a point to proactively and intentionally leverage these soft assets for exceptional results.

Keep an Eye on the Horizon

Time is an interesting concept in business. It manifests itself in many ways: from the time it takes to get something produced and brought to market, to the time spent by employees to get things done, to the right time to introduce a product to the market. Time becomes like a thread that weaves itself like a vine around almost any and every business activity.

I once read that the ultimate key to business success was to last one day longer than your competitor. Think about that for a moment. If your competitors close shop, where will their existing customers go? If you are still around, chances are very likely they will find you. Bingo! Just by sticking it out a little longer than your competitors, you win through attrition. Most business growth does not happen through obstinacy. Rather, it happens because companies learn how to leverage time in a way that provides enough lead times for their assets to become fully formed and utilized. This is how companies stick around one day longer than the competition *and* outcompete them.

To leverage time, a company must allow a long enough time horizon that aligns with the buyer's journey and other external market dynamics. The CEO or sales director who instructs or even demands his sales and business development personnel to close three new deals within a month without accounting for these considerations, risks expending resources on a futile effort by imposing unrealistic time constraints. The time horizon was too restrictive, too short.

The pressure of reaching certain revenue or profit milestones takes precedence over the implementation of a well-constructed strategic plan that is based on correct intelligence about the opportunities that can be realized in a specific time frame. Finding HyperLeverage opportunities in time, therefore, means coordinating several activities:

- Gather inputs from the "front lines" on where and how many customers or clients are in the current company's marketing funnel and where they are in their buyer's journey. This information informs a company on developing realistic timelines and expectations. It can also inform as to any additional steps that might be taken, such as increasing and using a more focused communication campaign or even providing pricing incentives that could shorten the sales cycle.

- Create a corporate culture that understands the value of time and aligns it with accomplishing the objectives set out in the strategic plan. Being able to communicate the underlying connection between the time it takes to reach milestones and the revenue and profits that arise from it should be shared throughout an organization. Employees want and need to feel that their time and efforts have meaning.

- Inculcate a practice of continuous DOIT-type evaluations to organize all business assets and activities in a way that leverages maximum productivity and efficiency about time. Employing modern tools and processes such as project and time-management software, agile-management techniques, and information and file-sharing programs are just some of the ways that businesses create a web of coordination that harnesses the limitations of time.

It's not just startups that fall into the trap of not planning for a long enough time horizon. It happens to companies of all sizes. Being optimistic is great; however, being *realistic* about how long a project might take to accomplish and factoring in a buffer for unanticipated delays or setbacks allows for leverage to happen. How many good, even great, business ideas have fallen prey to an insufficient time horizon? How many businesses have invested significant resources only to pull the plug too early, paying too much attention to the inevitable setbacks, expecting quicker results, and losing sight of the future?

Many businesses and even well-funded and established startups deserve to fold it up and lick their wounds in failure. Many times, the reasons they don't survive are not a matter of their products. Rather, their failure emanates from the pressures of the marketplace to accelerate business performance in ever shorter windows of opportunity. It's not just startups that fall into the trap of not planning for a long enough time horizon. It happens to companies of all sizes.

Time Is Money

Having a deeper understanding of time is the first step in knowing how to leverage it. For example, good project managers certainly have a deep appreciation of time because it's the essence of their job. Time for them is not just a metric of performance; it's an asset that holds the key to efficiency and profit. Think of a bottling company and the incremental profits it realize from minimizing the time it takes to switch from one batch to another.

Southwest Airlines understood this. Early on in its history, it decided to employ the tenets of HyperLeverage and developed a system to turn around planes at an airport terminal in half the time as the larger legacy airlines. It understood that the longer its planes were on the ground, the fewer passenger hours it could fly and the fewer flights per day it could run. This meant it would need more investment and infrastructure, including more planes, to fly the same number of passengers. It was a recipe for slower growth, so it decided to address the problem head-on. If Southwest could find a way to leverage its systems to save time on the ground, it could save significant money and fly more people each day with the planes it currently had. Even shaving 15 minutes off a turnaround would save the company an hour or more a day of productivity, which could equate to an entire extra flight per route per day. That would translate into an additional 10 to 15 percent more passenger hours per day. Now that's real money! Moreover, the cost of doing this was very minimal and did not disrupt its customers.

How did Southwest find a way to cheat time? It leveraged what it already had—a flight crew that was already in place and could prepare the cabin immediately upon the last passenger deplaning. This not only saved precious minutes but also meant it didn't need to hire a separate ground-based crew to do this work. It streamlined the onboarding process by eliminating assigned seating, and encouraged passengers to check their bags, knowing that it would make boarding quicker as fewer people would be trying to squeeze their oversized carry-on suitcases to avoid the baggage fees that the other airlines charge. Southwest made up for this loss of revenue through the time saved and added efficiency of its turnaround process.

Not only did Southwest leverage assets it already had, it also added a value proposition to the flying public. No baggage fees. Like the bottling company manager, Southwest knew that the profit was in reducing downtime since the other part of the process, the actual flight time, was fixed and couldn't be changed.

Here's a way to get more out of the time constraints that exist in business. Think of your business day like a football or basketball game. There are set time rules. There are penalties for taking too much time. Force activities to become more efficient and/or reduce the scope of what can be done to get things accomplished. Even consider enacting a "two-minute" rule to create hyper-focus and get jobs completed rather than pushed out to another day.

It is the role and responsibility of good management to provide the resources to get the job done in what is determined to be enough time. A company that has an unspoken expectation from its employees to work beyond the nominal 8-hour workday leads to additional costs, reduction in quality, and employee issues of resentment, stress, and burnout. In short, overtime is symptomatic of a company's inability to HyperLeverage time. It's costly and rarely sustainable.

Timing Is Critical

Being a "first to market" company does not guarantee success. As Geoffrey Moore writes in his book, *Crossing the Chasm*, it is often the company that bides its time that comes out the big winner in a new and developing market. The companies that establish the initial beachhead for a product often are just the road and bridge builders, paving the way for others to cross in a manner that can take advantage of its superior assets, established infrastructure, and systems. These beachheads are more times than not just targeted at the vanguard of early adopters who are less discerning and willing to take a spin on the latest and shiniest new object or technology.

The barriers to entry based on geography, borders, and even protective tariffs are no longer walls that afford protection, as they did in the past. With unfettered access to information, getting a leg up on real or potential rivals using timing has different ramifications than it did years or decades ago. This only underscores the importance of timing in efforts to achieve HyperLeverage.

Let's look at this strategically. If you have a new product, service, or software that solves a major problem in the market, you want to get it out before others beat you to the punch. I've been there. It feels like there's a hole burning in your pocket.

Considering my experience, I now consider the question of timing to be key to attaining the right leverage. The difference between being patient and letting others do the spadework is accepting the short-term risk of missing out on the initial riches to prepare completely for your eventual move into the market, using HyperLeverage tools I've described previously,

Strategically, if you have created a strong foundation to go to market—meaning you have sufficient capital; have the resources and plans to scale quickly; have systems in place for customer acquisition, customer service, monitoring and measuring client satisfaction, and quality control...you get the drift...then chances are that being first to market is indeed the smarter move. That's a lot of work that needs to be done upfront for a product or service that has yet to be proven as viable or even wanted.

One of my business mentors, a high-level executive VP at Rohm & Haas, at the time a Fortune 500 company, once told me his approach to timing. A company has three choices: It can sell an existing product to a new market, It can develop and introduce a new product for an existing market, or It can develop and introduce a new product to a new market. The first two options he explained can be enhanced with good timing while the latter should not be taken by any startup or immature company, as it requires significantly more control of time, timing, and time horizons. Even well-established market leaders should have a healthy respect for the extra challenges this latter approach will face.

Let's explore how the record and music industry of today came about. It's the story of the upstart company, Napster, and how Steve Jobs, the legendary CEO of Apple, waited for it to self-explode before making his move.

Napster had the first-mover advantage. Its founder, Sean Parker, one of the original bad boys of market disruption, created a beachhead and avid fan base—especially amongst college students—for online sharing of music by bypassing copyright and existing music licensing deals. By demonstrating that the music-consuming public, composed of broke college and high school kids, wanted control over what they listened to, Napster had disrupted the music and record industry stranglehold on forcing consumers to purchase music albums with songs they didn't want.

The concept was strong. The executive and business model was not. Napster was not ready for prime time, and it didn't have enough resources nor time to iron out the obstacles it faced in a time frame it could control. It was not able to HyperLeverage its timing and first-mover advantage because it did not have the wherewithal and assets to make it happen.

Steve Jobs was quite appreciative. His business model at Apple seldom exploited the first-mover advantage. Apple, for all its reputation for innovation, rarely was the first to introduce new technology. From my estimation, Steve Jobs was a master of HyperLeverage. He was obsessed with detail and planning and controlling the ecosystem on which his products were used. Apple, under Job's tutelage, became the experts at exploiting timing and time horizons.

With more cash and financial reserves than over 80 percent of the world's countries, and the ability to let new products and services take hold in the market, Apple swooped in and leveraged what it learned from Napster. iTunes was born in conjunction with the iPod music player Apple created to play the songs people were buying. Apple had a built-in user base, and had the resources to pay licensing fees to musicians and record labels that Napster couldn't. Apple's tagline for the first iPod, "1000 songs in the palm of your hand," was introduced at just the right time, and it said it all. The rest is history.

Patience and choosing the right time to introduce innovation is part of Apple's DNA. It has used it as leverage time and again. Its systems, culture, and willingness to let others cross the chasm first set the stage for HyperLeverage in this area.

Today, one of the strategies of the "Lean Startup" movement that has been emulated by more and more established and profitable companies is the importance of Minimum Viable Products (MVPs).

The underlying premise is that even if you don't have all your ducks in a row, you've bought yourself enough time before others catch up. Many startups look at the MVP as the first important milestone for their companies because it provides them with a powerful story that can be used to soak up investment capital, knowing that the pool of investment money for any product or service is finite. Rarely will you find more than a handful of companies that can garner significant private equity investment in a field that has been "discovered." Often, it's only the top two or three companies that get green-lighted.

The story and the promise of a startup company are more significant than the actual product or service that may already exist. Rarely is the initial product anywhere close to a refined and well-oiled one. There will be countless improvements and innovations along the way. From the perspective of HyperLeveraging clients and the public at large, I'd be wary, though—both for startups as well as mature companies to take that path too quickly. There is only one chance to frame your initial story. Consumers have long memories.

Well-capitalized companies can also use the MVP approach. Putting on my "Dr. Leverage" hat, though, I view this as not the best HyperLeverage move for them. The risks far outweigh the benefits. Companies with established infrastructure, workforce, and systems are better served by using the DOIT Leverage Method and proactively planning to leverage every possible asset and advantage they have and acquiring those they don't. This is preferable to doing a "dip your toes in the water" approach with an MVP or other not fully formed products. The risk to your brand, your value proposition, and the trust you have nurtured for years is at stake. Your customer base expects a higher level of performance than what a startup can offer.

The real opportunity, then, in terms of timing is to capture the second or even the third wave. Being at the vanguard is not as important as a leveraged asset in this case for larger companies. Since most of the first-to-market companies are not properly capitalized, don't have the necessary distribution, or can't communicate effectively to the widest audience, their first-mover advantage is diminished. Companies with deeper pockets of financing, established business systems, and the ability to scale are better served by waiting and pouncing when the time is right. That's when smart business leadership with a good view of the wider business canvas can swoop in like a hawk and grab the prey or develop their own versions of the product or service with business and competitive intelligence on what the market really needs and wants. That means achieving HyperLeverage with regard to timing *and* size. It's what Apple did when it introduced iTunes.

HyperLeveraging Time for Your Customers

Today, we are witness to another great example of how companies are trying to leverage time and timing. It's happening in real-time in how we buy and consume food, still the largest retail sector of the entire economy. In the late 1990s, the Internet was beginning to take hold as a new method for shopping. It had not yet revolutionized the retail sector and certainly not the grocery and restaurant business. The former being the single largest retail sector, with tentacles in every corner of the country. The potential of capturing even a small part of this market was enticing. After all, the higher-spending consumers were already early adopters of the Internet. Why not introduce an on-line version of the grocery store? Almost every major grocery chain has either partnered with a grocery delivery service like Instacart, Peapod, or has created its own delivery service. Other stores have acquired a company with established delivery systems, like H-E-B did when it purchased Favor. Companies like Uber with its UberEats,

DoorDash, and others, are looking to capture even a small slice of this market opportunity.

The early movers in this space were technology companies, not supermarkets, and they had very limited or no understanding of the dynamics of why and how people shop. Companies like HomeGrocer.com and Webvan spent a tremendous amount of their initial investment dollars building warehouses and creating the infrastructure necessary to grow. They were in a race against time to establish a beachhead in major cities to prove their business concept.

What they failed to do was employ the basic tenets of HyperLeverage. Their models were unproven and based on unsubstantiated exuberance. Their strategic planning, as it existed, either ignored or discounted a basic fact of the grocery sector; margins are very low except for a select number of items and the profits only come from tremendous volume. Also, as much as consumers may dislike the inconvenience of driving to the supermarket to do their shopping when they did, they got what they wanted in real-time, without having to wait. They could control the time and timing they spent on this activity. From a business perspective, the consumers were the ones spending the time putting things in the cart and spending the money to take them home. The new businesses were banking on consumers willing to place a dollar value on their time. As the dot.com era came to a head, in 1999, online grocery shopping accounted for less than 0.1 percent of the total market. Nowhere close to "exit velocity" to create a sustainable market. The bottom line: the idea may have been logical, but the timing was way off.

Fast-forward to 2019, and we find that the pure-play technology model of the dot.com era is a thing of the far distant past. However, the idea is not dead, far from it. What has emerged is a hybrid model based on the merger or partnership of online retail technology and the expertise, buying power, and infrastructure of supermarkets.

With the wave of mergers and acquisitions in the grocery market, including the entry of dominant retailers like Wal-Mart, Target, and Amazon, the introduction of smartphones, the ubiquity of mobile devices and apps, and, most importantly, the changes in buyer habits through changing demographics, the time is ripe for disruption. It is not a solution trying to find a problem, more of a solution exploiting an opportunity.

This is where HyperLeverage is uncovered in time, as it has been done at Apple and Napster. Apple didn't have to convince its target audience of the value proposition. It just had to deliver a system that made sense. In the case of online grocery shopping, the tipping point has not yet been reached. The time may be right to prepare for HyperLeverage by utilizing existing grocery infrastructure and logistics, along with the massive economies of scale that allow these much larger businesses to possess and squeeze additional profits which can be used to absorb the cost of developing the online grocery shopping experience. Only then will late adopters begin to cross the chasm en mass.

The two stories in this section are quite instructive for any business, small or large. Even with the advantages of size, innovation, and even good planning, without a component of time and timing, business opportunities can go bust in a big way.

Timing An Exit

Finally, I would be remiss if I did not discuss the important aspect of timing regarding business exits. Most companies will miss out on an optimal exit by not investing the time to create a strategic and implementable exit plan, not allotting for sufficient time horizon for a company to be at the optimal point of growth to exit, and not allocating sufficient time to identify and negotiate with the right buyer.

Why do I bring this up? After all, an exit means an end of the road for business owners in its current configuration. It normally does. If you have set and met certain business growth objectives, perhaps it is the best strategy to follow both for management and the long-term health and viability of the company. Exits should not be viewed as negative events. With advanced and proper planning, they can be leveraged to consolidate profits and move on to the next big idea.

In my work as a certified business exit planner, my focus was always on the strategic aspects and not the mechanics, such as accounting or legal negotiations. Because from my perspective, the strategic component takes time to develop and implement and puts the company in control of the timing of its exit. It requires thinking backwards and looking forward.

Rarely will a company outlast its current ownership before it is either sold, merged with another company, or go out of business. The number of family businesses that survive even a first to second-generation transition is small. Second to third-generation handovers are even rarer. Third generation to the fourth succeeds at a rate of only 3 percent, at most. For the third and fourth generation, transition time and business history are not on their side. It's probably best to exit, reap the rewards, and move on.

It's no different from any other major business initiative, product, or service. They all have a certain lifespan before market forces impose a change. Perhaps the original objectives have been met. They all are exits, and therefore the same principles apply.

Let me illustrate with this hypothetical example: Company A was a private venture-backed food-service software company. Its board of directors and the executive team recognized that their industry was primed for a major disruption because of new technologies being developed and introduced. They were going to experience a period of consolidation, as bigger enterprises viewed the market as ripe for entry. They were growing and scaling quite well, far above average. They had done their homework over the years and had been able to gather reliable information on industry competitors, purchasing and pricing dynamics, and technology trends. They certainly were HyperLeveraging data and intelligence much better than others in their field.

While they were showing good revenue expansion and high profitability, reaching higher profit margins was still an elusive goal. The leadership decided to revisit their original long-term strategy, which identified an exit event through either a merger with a smaller or similar sized entity or an acquisition by a larger enterprise.

Upon review, it appeared that the original time horizon they had anticipated and worked toward was being shortened. The point in their business life cycle at which they had planned to entertain offers of the acquisition was upon them. They had a decision to make. Continue the same growth path and continue to strive for HyperLeverage in all areas of the company and thus become a truly exceptional company that could maintain a dominant position in the changing business landscape, or focus on the activities that would make them an attractive acquisition target. Company A took a hard look at the evolving business canvas and realized that the only thing it could control was its timing. It opted for the acquisition strategy.

It was going to do what millions of people do every day when they look to sell their biggest asset, their house. They clean it up, fix the cracks in the wall, and make sure all systems are running smoothly. They make improvements that add value.

Using a system of evaluation and decision-making that parallels the DOIT Leverage Method, Company A organized its efforts to ensure the most impact within the allotted time frame of 12 months. A lot had to happen in the ensuing period, and it forced the entire company, from management on down to entry-level employees, to work smarter than it had ever done before. It was as if it had a countdown clock staring it in the face.

The market indeed changed dramatically over the next year or two. The smaller competitors were being gobbled by others already in the space. Almost like an alarm clock went off, the big Fortune 500 companies took note and began to seek out strategic acquisition targets in earnest. Having controlled its destiny by proactively preparing for such a situation, Company A became the most sought-after company in the industry and sold for a valuation that was almost twice what it had originally planned for.

The key HyperLeverage lesson here is how a company can use time and timing in an even more impactful way, especially when it is combined with a more holistic approach to business. Company A had its eye on the ball and the entire business playing surface. It understood the "game clock" and used it to its advantage.

If we've learned anything from the increased velocity of business growth, it's that all businesses should be mindful of the compressed product life cycles and align assets accordingly to gain maximum advantage sooner rather than later. Being mindful of where your business is on the classic business life cycle spectrum, which informs you when to put an exit plan into play. A high-growth business should consider an exit during the "hockey stick" portion of its life cycle. A mature business should consider an exit before new technology or new market forces pose a threat. A business in decline should exit as soon as possible or invest in a reorganization. A startup may want to exit earlier than later, pocket the gains, learn from the experience, and take the core team and move on to the next big idea, with more resources in the pocket than the first time around.

HyperLeveraging Location

It was October 21, 1995, and the baseball world series between the Atlanta Braves and the Cleveland Indians had just begun. The Atlanta Braves had its ace, Greg Maddux, its Hall of Fame pitcher on the mound. Maddux was the closest thing to a "money pitcher" as you could get in the big leagues. Even though he had a two-run lead, he insisted that he was going to pitch the last inning and close out the game. He was pitching a masterpiece, having given up only one hit. When he gave up another hit and allowed another run to score, it seemed like his day on the mound was over. But not to him or his manager. Known as Mr. Cool by his colleagues, Maddux knew he possessed the one thing that the batter did not have. He possessed the ultimate leverage in baseball: he knew the exact location of his next pitch. He had the control to make it happen. If it was possible to "place" a baseball at a certain position as it crossed the tiny box of the batter's box, it was Maddux. He was the master of location.

Maddux was a pitcher, not a thrower. He did not possess a pepper-hot fastball. His opponents knew that he wasn't going to blow them away with a 100-mph pitch. Maddux rarely threw a ball above 90 mph. He didn't have to. Speed was not his secret weapon. In the context of HyperLeverage, Maddux was one of the most prepared pitchers of all time. He exploited his main leverage asset: his pinpoint accuracy in a manner that kept his opposition in a constant state of confusion.

Maddux did what I've been writing about throughout this book: he invested the time to understand what his assets were—accuracy and consistency. As a student of the game, he spent countless hours between starts, pouring over the hitting stats and proclivities of his opponents. He leveraged this advanced scouting (intelligence) to plan the right pitches, a sequence of pitches, and target locations. He communicated this detailed game plan to his catcher and other team members so that they would be prepared.

For Maddux, location was a leverageable resource. He controlled the location of his pitches. In business, possessing foreknowledge of location yields tremendous leverage. Predetermining a location based on business intelligence and being intentional in collecting that information is the way companies can leverage location and timing.

This is what large national retailers such CVS, Costco, Wal-Mart, and others do. The stakes are high where they locate their stores because these decisions involve the expenditure of large sums of money—often borrowed at variable interest rates. It can be a risky high-wire act trying to guess where urban growth is headed and purchasing the land years in advance when it's cheaper and at depressed valuations. This is the type of leverage needed to make these business bets viable. The HyperLeverage component comes from utilizing the same systems and procedures I've laid out before.

Take my new adopted hometown of Austin, Texas. The population of the greater Austin metropolitan area is growing like weeds after a spring rainstorm. Austin is also one of the hottest startup technology communities in the country. With this comes tremendous building expansion. Successful retailers and large technology companies such as Apple, Amazon, Facebook, and Google are not blind to this. They are way ahead of the curve, sometimes even by a decade.

For example, H-E-B got a whiff that certain roads were going to be expanded in Southwest Austin over a decade ago and quietly snatched up undeveloped land where it could place its anchor stores. Instead of waiting for the urban sprawl to happen and then try to buy land at inflated prices, it preempted the demographic boom, bought the land at bargain-basement prices, and just let it sit for years upon years, being willing to finance and pay the real estate taxes until it was time to build. After all, it figured it could always sell off the land and pocket a tidy profit. That's how it achieved HyperLeverage through both time and location.

It's not that difficult to identify areas where any business, large or small, can leverage location to the max. It's not unique to just real estate. Location is extremely impactful in how a product is merchandised, how a website is laid out, or even how a book cover or a label is designed. Here is a simple three-part methodology to uncover your HyperLeverage options to get the most out of your location options.

1) Deconstruct how location plays a role in the operations and future growth of your business. This can be anything from access to distribution and transportation, to "owning" the right corner lot, to "elbowing" out the competition, to where you present key information on your website. Everything has at least one location element to it. Dig deep to uncover them. Perhaps the location of your files needs to be updated and leveraged for easier access.

2) Organize your location in a way that allows for optimum use of assets. Merchandisers are pros at this, especially during peak holiday periods. Production facilities need equipment to be situated to minimize time and increase efficiencies. Just picture an Amazon distribution center, with rows and rows of pallets stacked up to the roof. It organizes its warehouse using data, automation, and other technologies to locate items in the most effective locations in the building.

3) Improve your location. For example, if your business relies on foot traffic, then either move to a place that your data and intelligence inform you where your customers are, or devise

a mechanism to make it easy for people to do business with you. If your workforce is increasingly far away from your office, consider setting up satellite offices or virtual locations. If you merchandise products, identify the best locations to have them displayed—in a store, on a store shelf, or on a website.

Large chain stores spend a fair amount of time studying buying habits and in-store traffic patterns to gain the intelligence they need to understand and create a buying experience that will lead to greater sales. They situate merchandising racks, lighting, aisles, etc., in a meaningful way to capture the potential buyer and hold on to them, if possible.

According to Paco Underhill in his influential book, *Why We Buy*, an increase of just a few minutes spent in a store has a direct correlation to an increase in sales revenue. Sounds perfectly logical. The correlation to websites and landing pages is straightforward. The more time someone stays on your website, the greater the opportunity to connect with him or her and lead the person down the marketing funnel and to the desired buyer experience. Bounce rates are leading business indicators of this. Heck, we've all been enticed to purchase something from the impulse display situated near a cash register. It's a deliberate use of location to entice the consumer. That cold bottle of soda looks so refreshing on a hot summer day. Why not have a Snickers bar as well. After all, it's just a couple of bucks at most. Sound familiar? Those impulse purchases are all about location.

A major factor in the success of online retail sales is also location-related. It is not at a physical location, but where your business shows up on the Internet and where the information you wish to communicate to your customers is located and laid out. One does not physically walk into an online store. Nevertheless, understanding how people interact with your website and using data collection and analytic tools such as Google Analytics, informs us on the user's path through the labyrinth of pages and content. It's not by accident that some sites have no "back" button forcing the user to stay longer at a specific location.

Previously, I wrote about HubSpot and how it flipped the conversation from outbound to inbound. It championed the use of landing pages, target locations that a company uses to channel its target audience. It's all about forethought and intention that supports a strategic plan.

The design of a modern website is all about leveraging location to provide the best user experience and to showcase a company in the best light. There are places on a webpage that are known as power areas. These areas, when used properly, are leveraged to drive a long time on a page or a website and reduce bounce rates.

I've explained the increasing importance of intangible assets such as data. Where is that data coming from? Increasingly, it comes from how we access the information that is presented to us online. Where do we go when we use the Internet? What portions of a page do we go to first? Do we scroll down a page or look at the content above the fold?

All of these are location-based decisions that must be determined as much as possible by data and intelligence. Design must be a continuous and progressive activity to reach the heights of HyperLeverage. It is the essence of good modern industrial design. Simply placing items on a page without intention will not give it maximum impact. Just because a website might be strikingly attractive in terms of color, images, and layout does not mean that it converts. Making it easy for users to get immediate context while leading them in the direction you wish for them to go and take the action you desire from them, is the ultimate objective.

Size Matters

Don't be led astray by people claiming that size does not matter. It most certainly does in almost all aspects of life. We are inclined, based on our upbringing and social norms and our biology, to react to size in all its manifestations. As humans, we have an innate ability to "size things up quickly." Our ability to collate discordant information quickly is part of what makes us successful as a species—survival of the fittest. The business has often been described in these same Darwinian terms. With the underlying assumption by many business leaders that this means being the biggest. Size matters in the world of business, and the opportunities to leverage size are numerous.

The larger the company, the more there's a smooth overlap of critical business functions. It can negotiate, often dictate, favorable deals. Few businesses can survive long term without creating a greater ratio of assets employed to revenue earned. This concept is called economy of scale, and it's often the determining factor between success and failure. We all have heard the joke, "I'll make it up in volume," to describe the sale of a product at cost or even below. The theory is that as you increase volume, you lower unit costs and thereby increase gross margins.

So being able to increase the scale of one's operations is an exercise in leverage. A business leverages the fact that it can produce larger quantities to negotiate deeper discounts from suppliers. In most cases, a company that purchases increasingly larger quantities can negotiate a better deal, thereby leveraging its purchasing power to get a lower unit cost.

There is a limit to how much size is too much before the risks outweigh the benefits. In the previous example, if we had increased production size to 1000 gallons per batch, we would have produced enough for two years in one shot. However, since the paint had a shelf life of two years, it might have gone bad before we could sell it. We would have lost all the advantages of leverage. The point is that there are limits to how much size can or should be leveraged.

Many follow a curve that flattens out and tends toward a limit. At some point, there are no more increases in economic benefit. Risk, costs, and administrative and operational inefficiencies arise that offset the reduction in expenses. Important sources of leverage such as company culture, openness to change, and a fertile environment for innovation and creativity suffer. A deleveraging effect can happen where resources are expended with nominal added value. Not every business can be like Amazon, with a massive vault of resources and the time horizon available to create monumental levels of size and scale. However, forward-thinking companies that develop and implement comprehensive strategic plans can unlock HyperLeverage in their size. They can absorb years of financial losses as they gobble up market share, expand operations to meet changing market dynamics, and acquire technologies that will serve them into the future.

Takeaways

⚠ Companies must plan for and allow a long enough time horizon to leverage their business activities to bear fruit. This time horizon must align with market dynamics and increasingly with the changes in the buyer's journey.

⚠ Time is not just a metric of performance; it is also an asset and a limited resource that always needs to be considered and leveraged.

⚠ Timing is an intentional activity that any organization needs to leverage proactively to gain advantages in the marketplace.

⚠ Organizations, both large and small, can HyperLeverage Location to the maximum. Whether it's the location of an office, store, or warehouse, where a product is merchandised, how a website is laid out, or even how a book cover or a label is designed.

⚠ The objective to maximize economies of scale should be front and center but tempered by the recognition that there are limits to how much size can be leveraged before it can have negative consequences.

CHAPTER 13

Mergers and Acquisitions

For many companies, the easiest path to realizing a greater return on investments and greater shareholder value lies in leveraging their ability to finance an acquisition or create a situation that leads to an advantageous merger or acquisition. Mergers and acquisitions are generally completed to expand a company's reach, gain market share, or acquire resources and talent to create shareholder value.

As companies grow bigger and experience the classic business life cycle, it's harder for them to maintain the same pace of organic growth. They become more bogged down by size and bureaucracy, and get further removed from the entrepreneurial mindset that propelled the company forward in the beginning. They need to access external growth levers. Acquiring another company or companies is the classic mechanism for this.

Let's examine some mergers and acquisitions that have been considered successful and what leverage was generated by it. In 2005, consumer goods giant Proctor and Gamble (P&G) used something akin to a Leverage Prism to recognize that the world of retail commerce would eventually change and that it needed to be proactive to prepare both strategically and operationally to meet future challenges. One of those was a realization that it lacked the top talent and processes to drive innovation across the entire spectrum of its business. After considerable research and planning, it bought Gillette for the princely sum of $57 billion, at the time one of the largest corporate acquisitions ever made. Both companies were considered "best in class" in their respective areas of consumer products. It was something that many business analysts had been expecting for years.

The leadership of both companies recognized that the way to leverage the combination of their two companies was not to look at this as one company acquiring the other, rather as a merger of equals in most areas. The leadership of both companies knew that the fight for premium shelf space was only going to accelerate in the years to come as the threat of e-commerce became a larger reality. The combination of the two companies would create a behemoth—essentially, the largest consumer products company in the country. It just made sense on so many levels—compatible corporate cultures, complementary distribution channels, and financial considerations. Together they could negotiate better shelf space and reduce distribution costs.

What were the real leverage opportunities and how were they going to be implemented to reach what we now can recognize as HyperLeverage? In hindsight, we can recognize they realized leverage in three areas: people, planning, and performance. In my estimation, they conducted what I have called a DOIT Leverage Method evaluation.

It all began with planning. P&G approached the integration of Gillette into its corporate umbrella with an extensive strategic plan. This plan was based on detailed research into the best methods to merge the best processes and talent of both companies into a single and larger profit-generation machine.

To begin with, P&G recognized the complexity of the task at hand and leveraged the collective wisdom, experience, and creativity of employees from both companies by forming close to 100 global integration teams, with each team having two executives, one from each company. Second, it took its time and did not rush into anything, thereby controlling the changes that were inherent in the implementation phase.

Perhaps the most critical factor in the long-term success was communicating through words and actions a message of inclusion. By using the word "merger" versus "acquisition" and by holding town-hall-style meetings throughout the integration process, it made the transition easier for all employees, especially those from Gillette.

P&G understood that the key to HyperLeveraging the acquisition was to act inclusively, not just talk about it. It made a point of choosing from the best practices and procedures from both companies. It established cross-company connections and mentorships by matching seasoned P&G employees with the newly integrated Gillette talent.

Bringing two different companies together under one roof is a daunting task, fraught with missteps, insensitivity, and clashes of culture. It is a time where many employees, especially top managers, feel most vulnerable and seek employment elsewhere. P&G met its revenue goals within a year and retained over 90 percent of Gillette's top managers as well.

More recently, we marveled at the foresight that Facebook had in 2012 when it purchased the upstart photo-sharing network, Instagram, for $1 billion. At the time, Instagram had 30 million users and was growing quickly but had no revenue and no apparent path to profitability. What Facebook leveraged was the manifold. It could leverage the almost one billion users it already had and introduce them to the Instagram platform. It could take its time to build it up while determining the most advantageous method to drive ad revenue through it.

The acquisition also created a much-needed confirmation, just ahead of the company's IPO, that it had the vision to develop and build multiple products and platforms at the same time. It reinforced in the highly competitive battleground for tech talent in Silicon Valley, that Facebook was the place where hypergrowth was going to occur for the next decade.

The acquisition was genius. It removed a potential competitor and category killer from the game. This undertaking was no small feat, considering that Instagram was just launching on the Android platform and would have provided archrival Google, owner of Android, with an opportunity to elbow in on Facebook's social media hegemony.

The history of Facebook's dominance is known to all. But this first big acquisition was instructive to the company's leadership of its ability to HyperLeverage its market opportunities and resources.

Making timely, impactful, and smart decisions is the role of business management. It is an essential element for achieving HyperLeverage. The difference between simply making decisions and HyperLeverage lies in the proactive and intentional approach of the latter. HyperLeverage is holistic in nature, taking a more wide-angle view of the entire business canvas—both present day and future. All business leaders must make decisions and capitalize on the leverage they see around them. But companies that understand the power of HyperLeverage dominate their categories by setting up processes to systematically analyze, identify, and unlock leverage for maximum future growth and return. It's what separates good companies from great companies. All companies benefit from leverage some of the time, but all too often, decisions are made in a vacuum, devoid of context or data analysis.

Is the acquisition or merger approach the best way to leverage a company's resources, position, and financial capital? Is it good for the company and not only shareholder value in the long run? Unfortunately, the answer is no. According to the *Harvard Business Review,* more than 70 percent of company acquisitions are deemed unsuccessful. Most mergers and acquisitions are therefore not properly leveraged, unlike the examples of P&G and Facebook, let alone be HyperLeveraged.

You would think that large, highly successful, and well-run organizations would have both the workforce and resources to make this happen. The history of business shows otherwise. Even large companies such as Amazon, Microsoft, Apple, and others have bet both big and small on HyperLeveraging the acquisition of other companies to gain market share, technology, or a bridge to new growth opportunities only to find that they were unable to leverage the upside they perceived.

Take the case of the AOL-Time Warner merger in 2000. It was a blockbuster of a deal. A $162 billion deal that destroyed so much value and goodwill and squandered so much potential, resulting in a loss of stock value of over $100 billion when the two companies split apart ten years later. What went wrong? What was not leveraged? It's a story of trying to mix oil and water; diverse corporate cultures didn't work together.

The merger occurred at the height of the Internet craze, when AOL was the up and coming Internet media darling, gunning to dominate the world of media. Time Warner, established in 1990, was the old-school media giant created by the merger of Warner Communications (parent of Warner Brothers movie studio) and Time Magazine, established in 1990. Merging AOL and Time-Warner was a revolutionary move to fuse the old with the new to leverage the new age of the Internet with the rich content of the legacy media company. It was considered the combining of the best of both worlds: print and electronic.

Unlike the P&G story, there was no long-term or strategic plan to get the two company's management teams on the same page. AOL was in the dominant position, and it drove the bus. There was no synergy between processes, systems, or strategic vision. AOL was in a hurry. It didn't have the foresight of the older company.

When the dot-com bubble burst at the end of 2001, it accelerated the demise of the merger even before it could gain traction. Coupled with AOL's inability to quickly embrace wi-fi technology at the expense of dial-up Internet access, the marriage failed to exploit and leverage their combined resources and opportunities.

The Leverage Prism is a great way to view these decisions from the buyer's perspective. The more alignment the prism reveals, the easier it becomes to find agreement between the parties on a realistic price that ultimately provides leverage to both sides. Figure 17, "Deconstructing Mergers & Acquisitions (Buyers)" and Figure 18, "Deconstructing Mergers & Acquisitions (Sellers)," portray this from the perspective of the buyer and seller.

Say you are on the opposite side of the equation and your company has reached a point where it may have come close to achieving maximum growth and profits from the existing workforce, product lines, and investments. You're considering whether it's time to cash out and move on to other ventures. To do a proper assessment and maximize your profit in an acquisition, it's important to develop a strategic exit plan. I encourage you to work backwards from the end goal. This type of assessment isn't something you can leave until the last minute. If you want a profitable exit, strategic planning is required. You'll need to take into consideration possible market changes that could arise and impact your company's value. You'll also need to be able to assess timing. Is it better to sell your company now before increasing your investment in new products, new markets, expanded distribution, or a workforce that is required for

DECONSTRUCTING MERGERS & ACQUISITIONS (BUYERS)

MERGERS &
ACQUISITIONS

INCREASED DISTRIBUTION

NEW PRODUCTS/INNOVATION

ECONOMIES OF SCALE/BUYING POWER

INCREASED MARKET SHARE

MARKET/PRODUCT DIVERSIFICATION

PHYSICAL ASSETS/PLANT & EQUIPMENT

REDUCE COMPETITION

PROFESSIONAL TALENT

INTELLECTUAL PROPERTY

COST REDUCTIONS

FIGURE 17: DECONSTRUCTING MERGERS & ACQUISITIONS (BUYERS)

DECONSTRUCTING MERGERS & ACQUISITIONS (SELLERS)

MERGERS &
ACQUISITIONS

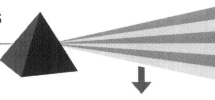

LEVERAGE UPSIDE GROWTH POTENTIAL

LEVERAGE EXISTING MARKET SHARE

LEVERAGE PHYSICAL ASSETS/INVENTORY

LEVERAGE BRAND/REPUTATION

LEVERAGE INTELLECTUAL PROPERTY

LEVERAGE REAL ESTATE/LOCATION

LEVERAGE EXISTING/TRAINED WORKFORCE

LEVERAGE ECONOMY OF SCALE

LEVERAGE OPERATIONS

LEVERAGE MARKET CONSOLIDATION

FIGURE 18 : DECONSTRUCTING MERGERS & ACQUISITIONS (SELLERS)

continued growth? If your answer is yes, you'll want to create a few exit scenarios, research potential buyers, and outline the reasons they might want to acquire your company.

Takeaways

⚠ Successful mergers or acquisitions must be carefully planned and managed with enough time horizon to allow for maximum leverage of financial assets, infrastructure, market dominance, and talent.

⚠ Acquisitions are a powerful leverage approach that reduces the time aspect of business growth by acquiring business activities that might not be a core competency rather than developing them organically.

⚠ To find HyperLeverage in mergers or acquisitions and gain the benefits of economies of scale in both operations, marketing and distribution also require attention to how the changes are received by both workforces.

⚠ To successfully leverage mergers or acquisitions, there needs to be a mesh of business cultures, good communication, and strategic long-term vision.

The DOIT Leverage Method: Planning
CASE STUDY—PRICELINE

Priceline is arguably the most famous online travel company in the world. Many consider it to be the best-run Internet company after Amazon. When it first came online in 1998, at the beginning of the dot.com era, it was an immediate success. For the first time, the Priceline website allowed users to purchase airline tickets, book hotel rooms, and rent cars at discounted rates. Nothing of the kind existed, so customers flocked to Priceline's one-stop solution for all their travel needs.

In 2001, when the dot.com bubble burst, Priceline was faced with an uncertain future. The business landscape had changed dramatically and suddenly. A strategic plan was needed to adapt to these new realities. This DOIT analysis is a theoretical look back—with 20/20 vision—at how the leadership team at Priceline might have faced this new challenge. It will help us understand what it had at its disposal to weather the dot.com storm and how it turned things around and became the largest online travel company in the world. Within this case study, you'll see the type of proactive and intentional planning that are the hallmarks of HyperLeverage.

First, the executive team at Priceline had to deconstruct its core business as it was in 2002. Next, it had to organize resources and market opportunities and review the existing strategic plan to see what it should maintain, what should be discarded, and what it could continue to leverage. After that, the next step was to assess what it could improve and leverage to increase existing assets. Finally, it had to take action based on the resources and opportunities it could leverage.

Deconstruct

- Leverage Inventory—Leverages the excess inventory of hotels
- Leverage Internet—Provides hotels a single platform for customers to book online
- Leverage Customers—Give them a bargain and a way to control their travel costs
- Leverage Authority—Use a widely recognized actor who played an authority figure, William Shatner, to actively promote the company's unique selling proposition—Name Your Own Price
- Leverage Change—Recognized that people, for both personal and business, are not using travel agencies and want to be in control of their travel

Organize

- Make it easy for consumers to research multiple hotels and lodgings based on geography and ratings.
- Create multiple revenue streams selling the same things:
    1) Name Your Own Price
    2) Purchase of hotel rooms on Priceline website
    3) Affiliate links when people purchase directly on the hotel website
- Make the company's value proposition simple. The consumer can control his or costs and value shop.

Improve

- Utilize and expand on the concepts of gamification by getting people vested in the outcome using the "Name Your Own Price" tool.

- Expand the "Name Your Own Price" system to car rental, airfare, and other add-on services.
- License the "Name Your Own Price" system to eBay.

Take Action

- Become ubiquitous with ad spots featuring William Shatner and the "Name Your Own Price" campaign.
- Make the "Name Your Own Price" tool part of their "DNA" so that customers associate price savings with the Priceline brand.
- Survive the dot.com bubble by focusing on improvements in performance and supporting its core services—travel.
- Apply a long horizon strategic plan that focuses on performance and capturing loyal repeat customers.

What were the results of the Priceline team's assessment? It defined the space of online travel services by providing access, control, and choice to the customer. It purchased other associated and competitive travel sites, such as Booking.com and Kayak.com, to expand its reach across various travel sectors. By maximizing its leverage of key assets (aka HyperLeverage), Priceline was able to average compounded 42 percent earnings growth from 2007 through 2017, despite the formidable challenges it faced in a changing marketplace.

What are the key takeaways from the efforts of the Priceline executive team? It proved how important it is that accepting and proactively planning for rapid change in both the business environment and consumer expectations arena had to be part of the strategic plan going forward. Priceline understands what motivates customers and gives them simple, actionable solutions. It showed that a focus on quality and consistency of service is key. Finally, its efforts made it clear that a long horizon strategy wins and that adhering to that strategy based on a core value-added proposition leads to success.

HyperLeverage And Performance

"All good performance starts with clear goals."
~Ken Blanchard

DEFINITION: HYPERLEVERAGE AND PERFORMANCE

1. Taking concentrated, focused, and planned actions to implement plans and develop procedures that attain or maintain the highest levels of quality, consistency, and adherence to performance standards for extended periods through a continuous monitoring and refinement of processes and business activities.

2. Achieving exceptional results through effective and efficient implementation of pre-planned procedures and processes.

On any given Sunday during football season, any NFL football team is capable of winning. The individual talents of the athletes are at such high levels that often the biggest differentiator is the combination of individual and team performance. Which teams and which individuals actually "show up" on game day has more significance than the hours of practice and the wealth of skills and experience accumulated over the years by individual athletes and coaches. This is the story of HyperLeverage that we've been exploring throughout the book. It's about dedicated exploitation of the assets that one possesses to reach new heights and attain phenomenal results.

The best teams, not just sports teams, are the ones that leverage the ability to perform at the right time and the highest level. Performance on the field is not a matter of luck. It's a matter of putting all individuals on your team in a position to "get lucky." It's the result of preparation, planning, using the best and latest technologies, and having the right people in the right place at the right time. It sounds like the Four Ps of leverage doesn't it? No surprise.

The NFL is a multi-billion-dollar business built around the concepts of HyperLeverage: intentional, proactive exploitation of the talent, resources, and assets it possesses, culminating in reliable peak performance week after week.

All businesses should strive for the type of peak performance exhibited during a football season. Like the NFL, companies must build solid infrastructures that enable continuous exploitation of company assets and resources. It means developing measurement and metrics that accurately provide insight and inform as to what modifications, adjustments, or improvements might need to be made. It means embracing and systematizing a culture of quality throughout an organization's activities

The benefits of HyperLeverage are not achieved through a single event or change. Rather, they become embedded in the DNA of an organization or business through ongoing, progressive "learning" experiences that lead to continuous improvement. In this chapter, I will address some of the main areas where companies can leverage performance to achieve HyperLeverage. These include investments in measurement, quality, and infrastructure. Of course, like all sections in this book, performance HyperLeverage can't be achieved in isolation. It is dependent on the leverage of people and planning that were discussed in earlier chapters. Without this foundation, it is nearly impossible to attain performance levels that are exceptional.

Incorporating the type of change that will lead to improved performance is not simple. Buying a new piece of equipment or incorporating the latest software platform won't cut it. Those are tactical solutions. They can provide opportunities for leverage, but not HyperLeverage. All too often, however, such assets are underutilized or not fully or properly integrated into a company's workplace processes or infrastructure.

The story of how Japan turned itself around in the 1950s and 1960s following the devastation of its industrial and manufacturing base after World War II is instructive. It shows how a community can come together and make the difficult and necessary actions to change direction and embrace a path to better performance.

In the late 1950s, the leadership of Japan's industry recognized that it had a problem—actually, many problems, some within their control and some the result of World War II. Japan did not have a wealth of natural resources, such as coal, oil, or minerals. Additionally, the country was geographically distant from any of its big potential trading partners—Europe and the United States. Japan's society was also going through significant internal upheaval as a result of its defeat in the Great War. The country was in shambles. Infrastructure was decimated, and the people of Japan were demoralized.

Domestic Japanese consumerism was not enough, especially after the ruination of the industry base at the end of World War II. Wartime industries were not the ones that could be easily converted to produce peace-time products and services. The country's business leaders recognized that they needed to become export-oriented to survive. They were faced with a dilemma. What could they leverage amid the devastation?

The United States had emerged from World War II as the biggest and fastest-growing free-market economy in the world. Consumerism was on the rise in America as the middle class expanded by leaps and bounds. There was an aura of positivity across the country. The government was investing in big infrastructure projects. It was time to think big.

How did the Japanese take advantage of its export opportunities to America, overcome its significant raw material and distribution disadvantages, and in 1980—after a decade of hypergrowth—overtake the United States to become the world's number one automobile manufacturer? Japan focused on world-class performance and quality. Japanese corporations embarked on a decades-long strategy to embrace the concept of continuous improvement. They invested in improved quality control and refined measurement techniques, and embraced the power of consistency. Japanese companies and Japan as a whole developed sophisticated and interconnected infrastructures and a culture of heightened performance that captured the imagination of the world.

The result was Japan's industrial dominance long before China usurped this mantel at the beginning of the 21st Century. As a country, Japan became a model for performance HyperLeverage. This didn't happen overnight. A key lesson of the Japanese turnaround is the importance of a long-time horizon and the patience to stay the course.

As Japan modernized and rebuilt its industrial base after the destruction of World War II, a quick solution was to produce inexpensive, cheaply produced products that could be exported and compete on price. This created the stigma of "Made in Japan," a moniker of low quality and cheaply produced goods. It took an entire generation 20 years or more of investing in and embracing industrial and societal changes to turn around the way that consumers viewed Japanese goods.

One of the big hurdles Japan had to overcome in the U.S. was trust. Back in the 1950s and 1960s, there was a gigantic chasm— literally and figuratively—in the trust between the two countries. Japan, with the assistance of Douglas MacArthur and others, began to modernize after the war. American consumers did not forget Pearl Harbor and the sacrifices they had made fighting Japan throughout the Pacific. The consumer generation of people in their 30s and 40s had lived through this period, and it was still fresh in their memory. Capitalism be damned, Americans were not interested in Japanese goods, no matter how affordable.

To help address these issues, the Japanese brought in two American consultants, Joseph Juran, a quality control expert, and William Edward Deming, a mathematician and statistician who introduced what he called "Statistical Product Quality Administration" concepts to Japanese industry. As Japan rose from the ashes between 1950 and 1960 to become the second-largest economy in the world, Deming became an almost godlike figure among Japanese industry leaders. Many in Japan credit Deming with what became known as the Japanese post-war economic miracle.

Deming taught the Japanese quality control and high productivity measured through statistical analysis. In America, Deming had butted heads with corporate management teams that rejected his contention that poor quality products were not the result of worker ineptness, but rather the outcome of their management failures and improper performance systems. In Japan, Deming found fertile ground to put his theories into practice.

Over the course of the next two decades, Deming advised the Japanese industry to reject the American-style system of post-production inspection and instead incorporate quality control principles directly into the design and production process. Basking in their postwar economic success as the greatest industrial powerhouse the world had ever known, American executives had gotten lazy and rested on their laurels when it came to performance and quality control. They rejected Deming's notion that companies should pay attention to the needs of their consumers. American industry scoffed at the notion that any other country, especially a Southeast Asian country, could compete with them.

Deming recognized the opportunity for Japan to revolutionize its industrial sector and compete directly with the inattentive United States. He went to work. To begin with, he instructed Japanese companies to find and secure the right raw materials for their products. Next, he helped them establish an organized workforce with a good management system and understanding of statistics. That workforce, Deming said, would need to highly value company loyalty. Finally, Japanese business leaders would have to develop a culture of discipline and steadfastness of purpose unsurpassed by any company in the United States. Though Deming didn't know the term at the time, he knew that with all these things in place, Japanese industry would have all the underpinnings necessary for performance HyperLeverage. And he knew that meant that Japan would become a fierce industrial competitor on the global scene.

At a more granular level, Deming leveraged the Japanese culture's strong sense of commitment. He encouraged companies to develop long-term training programs for all their employees. He recognized that elevating the skills and professionalism of *all* employees—not just managers, but assembly line workers as well—as the golden key to unlocking massive untapped potential.

Deming's background in statistics gave him the insight to deconstruct the issues at their core, using an approach like the Leverage Prism. He saw that the Japanese workers were industrious and dedicated workers. However, working harder could only be leveraged so far. He understood that the answer to increased consistency, quality, and efficiency lay in working smarter by building a new infrastructure based on new machinery, new technology, and new management techniques.

Using statistical analysis and measurement, Deming taught the Japanese how to create a virtuous cycle of high performance and continuous improvement. He helped the Japanese learn to maximize people, planning, and performance. He recognized that an emphasis on higher quality forces innovation down through the organization and that a strong training regimen and a focus on engagement encourages everyone to have input. The result is a system that reliably delivers outstanding performance where the high quality of the product remains the same (or improves) today, tomorrow, and after that. In turn, quality raises consistency, which eliminates waste and improves the ability to measure progress that leads to product improvement and innovation. This is what HyperLeverage looks like in action.

It has been decades since the moniker "Made in Japan" was associated with inexpensive and poorly made products. Under Deming and Juran's watch, Japan became globally recognized for the quality of its exports. Meanwhile, in the 1990s, China began its timid steps into worldwide capitalism and took over the mantel of cheap. "Made in China" became synonymous with inexpensive, poorly made products when it began to export products en masse to the world in the

1990s. Japan was only too happy to let China and India fight over the low margin and low-quality portion of the economic bell curve. Japanese industry continued to leverage its cumulative brainpower, innovation, and industrial infrastructure to create high-margin, high-quality products. However, the dominance that was the result of this decades-long transition to quality and consistency could not be sustained forever with the emergence of South Korea and continuous improvements in Chinese manufacturing systems. As these countries have become the world's powerhouses of manufactured goods, many previously underdeveloped Asian countries have taken over the production of labor-intensive manufacturing.

A case in point and an example of how other third world countries can leverage performance is the story of Vietnam as a manufacturing powerhouse, which in manner mirrors the economic miracle of Japan, both countries devastated by war. Emerging from the Vietnam war era, it became a cheap source of labor and goods to the rapidly expanding Chinese industrial market. However, that was just the beginning.

Vietnam enthusiastically embraced the concept of free trade, enacting deregulation reforms, and effectively lowering the cost of doing business. With a stable political environment, it was able to invest heavily in both human and physical capital, thereby creating the infrastructure for foreign companies seeking the establishment of overseas production facilities. In 2017 and 2018, a period of global trade stagnation, exports were 170 percent of GDP and exports to the U.S. and China grew by 3.6 percent, when most other countries experienced declines up to 5 percent.

The stories of Japan, China, Korea, and Vietnam are chock full of lessons on the power of HyperLeveraging business performance. They also show that to gain HyperLeverage in the area of performance, it is necessary to follow the path of deconstruction and improvement of existing assets and resources and to make concrete strategic investments with an eye to the long-term horizon.

In this section, I'll introduce four underlying truths about performance and how they pertain to and are necessary to gain HyperLeverage.

- Knowing what to measure, how to measure it, and how to evaluate results is a prerequisite for improvement.
- Building quality into a process or product reduces costs, increases profits, and builds strong brands.
- Performance and adherence to the long term with continuous monitoring and incremental improvements lead to consistent growth.
- Investment in and improvements to infrastructure are a necessary and constant activity for any business.

As you have seen throughout this book, rarely do any of these concepts exist in a vacuum. There are significant overlaps and interdependencies. You'll see that in the performance section as well. We'll start by examining a prerequisite for HyperLeveraging any business activity: measurement and improvement.

CHAPTER 14

Measurement & Improvement

Performance is not a singular event in business. It's those companies that exhibit consistent and reliable performance time and
time again and over an extended period that stand out. What do I
mean by performance, you might ask? How does one determine if it
is enough, too much, or too little? The answer is simple. We measure.
Using measurement is akin to using a trained K-9 dog. You want to
"sniff out" the business practices that are working and those that
aren't.

Performance is not only an internal business activity whereby
you measure how business systems are performing, how processes
are meeting standards, or how employees or vendors are contrib-
uting. These are indeed tremendously important items to measure
so that refinements, replacements, and improvements can be made.
Performance HyperLeverage requires measurement with a holistic
view that incorporates all aspects of a business, from how products
and services meet the expectations and needs of users and customers
to how a company interacts effectively with the marketplace in which
it exists. They all need to be monitored and compared to acceptable
or unacceptable values. In short, every business needs to master the
science and art of measurement to experience HyperLeverage.

If You Can Measure It, You Can Improve It

Without change, there can be no improvement or added value. It's the same for measurement. Without it, HyperLeveraging performance can't exist. Without improved performance, products go stale or obsolete, and companies begin to wilt and eventually die.

Measurement can be a tricky little subject because it begs the questions: What do we measure? How precise should our measurements be? When do we measure? Do we measure everything all the time or just random samplings?

Herein lies the truth about measurement: the tighter the measurement tolerance, the more exact the analysis must be. Thus, the more exact the measurement process, the more costly and time consuming it becomes. Therefore, to leverage measurement, we must deconstruct the problem and assess the resources at hand. It starts with understanding the how, why, what, when, and even sometimes the where of measurement.

Back in the early to mid-2000s, before the real estate crash of 2009, I investigated securing a business. I was looking for something with consistent and reliable cash flow. My broker suggested that I look at a local laundromat that came on the market. The owners were retiring and seemed to have done okay. I was hesitant, as I didn't know how to measure whether it was a successful and sustainable business. I had no experience with that kind of low-tech business nor any direct knowledge of the target customer base. I was schooled in the traditional metrics of business: profit and loss reports, balance sheets, cash flow projections, and more. My broker laughed when I asked him to get these from the sellers.

"Joel," he said, "This is a cash business. The profits are in the amount of cash you can pocket *without* reporting it. You can't push the envelope too much on what you *don't* report, or you'll be audited. No more than 20 or 25 percent can go under the table. Understand?"

How was I supposed to know what that number was? I wondered. How was I going to measure the viability of my investment? Could I make this work be being completely above board?

I analyzed the problem and decided I would have to think differently about a very simple metric that would tell the financial story of the laundromat. It couldn't be the gross revenue or the gross or net profit—all those numbers could be fudged. I decided to measure the laundromat's monthly water bill. By knowing how much water the facility used each month, I could determine how many loads of laundry were done each day or each month. From that data, I could extrapolate how many dryer cycles were used and estimate how much soap was sold. This gave me a simple, yet quite accurate, picture of the business. It showed me how much of the laundromat's capacity was being used and what was the upside potential. It allowed me to measure what kind of profits could be realized. This was all based on water consumption—nothing else. My story illustrates the importance of looking at measurements from different viewpoints. Most buyers would pass on the laundromat opportunity because of the lack of classic business metrics. I'm sure the "cash under the table" aspect was a major deterrent as well. I was still mired in the old school of thought of using classic financial metrics. At the time, I could not understand nor accept the valuation the owners believed their business to have. I opted to pass. Years later, I noted how the eventual new owners had the foresight and vision to add a coffee shop and small grocery area to the site. Business was booming. They recognized they had a captive audience and leveraged the laundry with additional services that addressed other needs of their customers.

The lesson here is that if you're creative and resourceful, you can almost always measure something useful to answer the questions you have about your business. You must think through what to measure to answer your question. We measure many things in business. Most of what we measure is the traditional metrics that I asked for in my initial assessment of the laundromat. In this case, the traditional metrics, even if they existed, might not have told the real story of this business. I needed a more meaningful metric to decide whether the laundromat was a worthy investment to meet my goals. So, those are the questions I pose to you: Do you measure the most meaningful things in your business? Is there an overlooked metric or group of metrics that can be monitored to provide a more direct correlation as to your product, system, or service's true performance? Are there metrics that you should measure to gain a more accurate picture of your company's performance? You want to measure something that has meaning, but also something that will show you how to modify or make improvements, if necessary.

For me, the water usage not only indicated what the laundromat's current state was, it also revealed its untapped capacity, which was something I could exploit to make the business generate additional revenue. What would I have to improve in the laundromat's operations and marketing to grow the business? That would require a closer look at other, different metrics. The only way to grow your business and achieve HyperLeverage, is by measuring the right things, assessing your findings, improving where you can, and measuring again to confirm your progress toward your goal of continual improvement. Look at Figure 19: "Deconstructing Measurements & Improvements," to get a clearer picture.

We use the Leverage Prism in Figure 19 to examine various activities and resources that could be led to HyperLeverage in the area of measurement. The exercise reveals several components that, individually or combined, are the basis for a comprehensive system to leverage measurements and improvements.

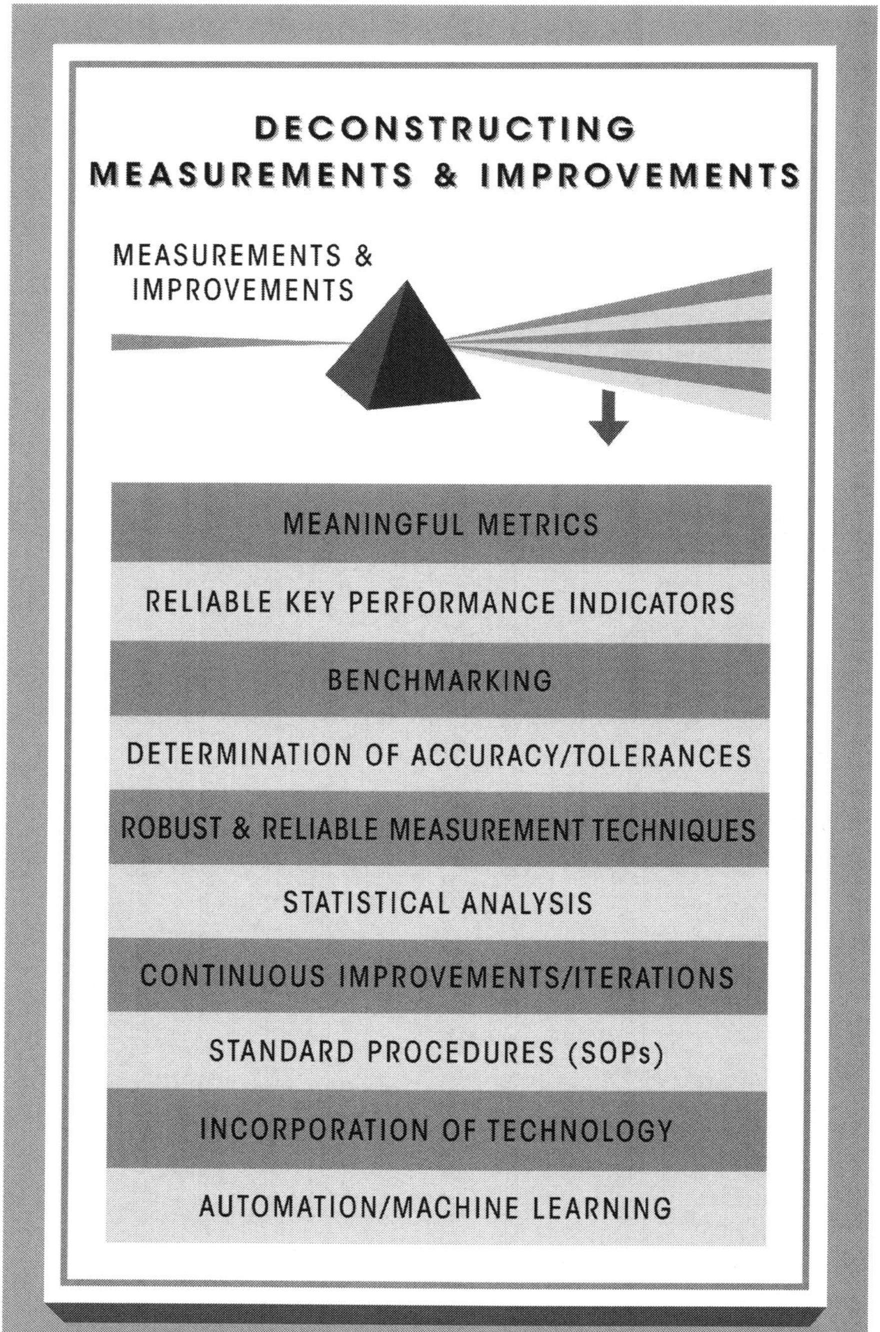

FIGURE 19 : DECONSTRUCTING MEASUREMENTS & IMPROVEMENTS

How To Hyperleverage Measurement

Today, it seems possible to measure almost anything we can think of. Whether it's the classic metrics of finance, the number of visitors to a website, or even the length of time someone watches a video. All these measurements spew out numbers. But the question you need to ask (and the answer) is whether this information leads to actionable intelligence. Can you make things better, cheaper, faster—whatever the desired objective is based on the measurements you collect? That is when and how you can leverage measurement.

We are wired to love large numbers. The bigger the number, the more significant it must be. A million hits on YouTube, hundreds of thousands of followers on Instagram, tens of thousands of retweets. You get the picture. The larger the number, the more we attach meaning—often false meaning to that measurement.

I recall when video marketing started to become an accepted marketing, communications, and branding tool. People were all excited about the number of views they got when they posted on YouTube or Instagram, thinking that this metric had real meaning. The problem is, it rarely tells anything close to the full story.

Measurements That Matter

Marketers rely heavily on metrics to measure the effectiveness of their campaigns. With the rise of video marketing, the number of video hits has become a popular metric to measure success. But the number of times a video is viewed is not necessarily a meaningful measure as to whether that video is resonating with an audience. Why? Because it's a metric that has little actionable significance. Someone can click on a video for one second and immediately turn it off. The number of views is the same no matter how long the viewer stays engaged with the video. In other words, the number of video "hits" does not provide any clue to whether someone actually saw the content of the video.

The more meaningful metric in this situation is how long someone watched the video and at what point did he or she stop watching it. This is like Google Analytics' measurements that show how long someone has stayed on a specific page of a website or how much of a blog he or she has read. The length of the engagement is the more important measurement for a video marketing campaign; not the number of views.

To leverage measurement that leads to enhanced performance, you must match the metric to the objective. In the case of video, the objective is to get people to watch enough of the video to take further action. We can extrapolate that the longer a video is watched, the more likely someone will see the call to action. We could also measure conversions if there were a direct link from the video to a landing page or retail page. All those measurements can inform the marketing team as to whether the video is working as planned. The number of hits does not provide information that can lead to change or campaign optimization; it's the measurement that is meaningless.

When I started podcasting back in 2010, I wondered if anyone was truly listening. At the time, podcast analytics were in its infancy. But even as podcasting has become extremely popular, creators still have limited visibility into metrics that matter. They can measure how many times their podcast was downloaded, but not how long someone listened or when they tuned out. The latter are the metrics that really matter. But very few podcasters can measure this information. As in the case of videos, conclusions about the effectiveness of their content may be completely wrong.

There are thousands of examples in hundreds of industries to demonstrate the ineffectiveness of measuring the meaningless. You must measure what matters. Without data that provides actionable insights, why measure at all? If the data doesn't answer the questions you have about how to improve and grow your business, where's the value in measurement? The only measurement that matters is the type that can provide actionable information that leads to continuous improvement. That's where the leverage is found—in companies that build meaningful measurement systems and integrate them into their culture, their communications, and their technology infrastructure.

Building A Company Around Measurement

Consumer Reports took the idea of HyperLeveraging measurement and ran with it like no other company had done before. By conducting independent testing of an entire array of consumer products, from the big-ticket items such as household appliances to the mundane, such as carpet stain removers, *Consumer Reports* became the go-to address for ratings and product reviews long before the development of the Internet. It did not collect information from others and turn it into lists and ranks, rather, it created its own set of performance metrics. Through a strategic decision to leverage measurement and establish a reputation for honesty and trustworthiness around that measurement, *Consumer Reports* showed what HyperLeverage looks like in action.

Before James David Powell III founded the marketing and information services company that bears his name, J.D. Power and Associates, he worked doing customer research for Ford Motor company. He quickly came to recognize that customer satisfaction was given little attention and generally overlooked. Working from his kitchen table and employing his associates, his wife, and his children, he collected and organized existing measurement data and created surveys and other studies that measured an entire array of automotive performance issues. Whether it's an Initial Quality measurement, Auto Dependability studies, or Ford's Automotive Power Execution and Layout metrics, vehicle manufacturers around the globe have come to use them to leverage and position themselves versus the competition.

Benchmarking Measurement Techniques

A smart company also learns to leverage the work of others when it comes to HyperLeveraging measurement. Perhaps after doing a DOIT Leverage Method evaluation as I described in Chapter 3, you determined that it is quicker and more cost-effective to emulate others, rather than create measurement techniques and determine appropriate metrics. Benchmarking is a way of evaluating performance metrics in each organization by comparing them to similar performances in one or more (usually external) sources—these may be competing organizations, an industry-standard, or a compilation of industry bests. It leverages the practices of others to establish baselines, define best practices, and identify opportunities for improvement. It is a technique that incorporates the basic tenets of HyperLeverage through measurement: proactiveness, intention, and impact. It's a simple method that shortcuts a learning curve by emulating the success of others who have had to grapple with similar issues.

The benchmarking process can be incorporated into a DOIT Leverage Method during either the Organize or Improvement stage to identify processes and metrics, gain an independent perspective, and enable and reinforce a mindset of continuous improvement.

Making Business Metrics Count

Every business grows because it has developed a product or service that solves a problem at a price that yields a profit and returns on investment for its customers. Using metrics that show a direct correlation between the use of resources and assets and the attainment of these objectives provides the raw material of information necessary to rinse, repeat, and refine. This is the progressive nature of HyperLeverage in the area of measurement. A continuum of meaningful measurements that move the ball forward.

For example, marketers are always interested in getting the customer acquisition cost (CAC), an invaluable measurement of how effective a company's marketing dollars are being spent. However, since a business has a broad time horizon, it is perhaps more important to assess and measure the lifetime value (LTV) of a customer, rather than the initial cost to capture new ones. After all, it may cost a lot to land the big fish only to find out that it's a one-off event that doesn't lead to repeat business. The lifetime customer value puts the measurement in the context of time, rather than a singular event.

With regard to HyperLeverage, the more meaningful measurement is the ratio between CAC and LTV. If the LTV is $100 and you're spending $120 in customer acquisition costs, you are in a negative leverage situation. The math simply does not make sense. On the other hand, if that same $100 investment in securing a customer results in $2400 of revenue, now we're talking turkey. The measurements of CAC and LTV by themselves have limited meaning in isolation. It's only when used to paint a holistic picture that combines time, investment, and reward that they can be leveraged meaningfully.

Without attaching an intentional meaning to the measurements, there can be no HyperLeverage. For example, measuring retention is an essential holy grail metric of SaaS companies and other online and app-related subscription service solutions. In theory, retention rates are indicators that the solution is working. Being able to track how long customers "stick" around provides important information that leads to better product development, customer service, marketing, and financial performance. It's hard to plan for growth if your customers are dropping off like leaves from a late autumn tree. The point is that measurements must have meanings. They are not just raw data.

Takeaways

⚠ If your measurements are to lead to any significant impact or meaningful change, you'll need to understand why, when, and where you will collect information and how you will use it.

⚠ The only measurements that matter are the types that provide actionable information that lead to continuous improvement, otherwise there is no path to HyperLeverage.

⚠ Benchmarking leverages the practices of others to establish baselines, define best practices, and identify opportunities for improvement. It is a technique that incorporates the basic tenets of uncovering HyperLeverage through measurement: proactiveness, intention, and impact.

CHAPTER 15

Quality & Consistency

Quality is one of those visceral concepts that we feel in our gut. We have an emotional reaction to it. We recognize quality products and services. We understand they have superior benefits. We want them, even if we can't always afford them. We value and strive to have quality in our lives.

Even though it compels a somewhat subjective reaction, quality can be measured. Businesses can define specific parameters to define quality in their organization. And because quality can be measured, it can be monitored and, more importantly, it can be improved and leveraged. The problem is that quality is rarely absolute. A quality product in the eyes of one person may seem defective to another. And therein lies an opportunity for HyperLeverage. If a company can determine how its stakeholders define quality, it can proactively pursue that definition of quality and communicate it effectively. If the market has already determined an objective quality level, a company will need to exceed this to maintain its quality moniker.

Quality, however, is not the same as perfection. There is no such thing as perfection. Inevitably, there are failures and defects. But when a product or service doesn't meet a customer's expectations, that person doesn't care that 99.99 percent of all your customers receive quality products or services. He or she only cares that quality expectations were not met. That's why quality must be defined. It's the only way it can be properly leveraged. A standard must be set.

Quality control is the old way of identifying and filtering out defects. Items or services that don't meet established standards are discarded or reworked. This is still the most common method to ensure quality, but it's costly and inefficient—perhaps because the costs are not as apparent and can often be hidden. We'll discuss why shortly.

A quality approach to business systems is, by definition, a performance issue. Maintaining and sustaining acceptable levels of quality mandates adherence to performance guidelines. The higher the quality standards, the more other factors in the business ecosystem come into play and must work in conjunction.

To me, it seems logical and basic that every business on the planet would embrace quality. Alas, quality is a concept that is paid a lot of lip service without much to back it up. Over time, the lack of quality or lack of commitment to continual quality improvement leads to the demise of a brand, and ultimately the end of many companies. Often, it takes a crisis to awaken companies to the importance of quality. Such was the case back in the 1990s when the titans of the American car industry—General Motors, American Motors, Chrysler, and Ford—were lagging far behind Japanese and German car companies both in the perceived and actual quality of their automobiles. They had a lot of catching up to do. They were experiencing a significant drop in competitiveness in global markets. They were in trouble.

This was the objective of the Malcolm Baldrige National Quality Award established by Congress in 1987 to promote improved quality of goods and services in U.S. companies and organizations. The program was established to identify and provide role model businesses (think of the Benchmarking component of the Leverage Prism diagram), establish criteria for evaluation of quality and improvement, and disseminating and sharing best practices.

The establishment of this award is a leverage story in its own right. Industrial leaders, major trade associations, think tanks, and ultimately Congress recognized that U.S. manufacturers were falling behind their Asian and European counterparts.

Motorola was the winner of the first Malcolm Baldrige award in 1988. In the years leading up to the award, Motorola had set the bar of acceptable quality at a level of 6 defects per 1,000,000, or three standard deviations on either side of the norm. It called this methodology Six Sigma. This was quite revolutionary because it seemed impossible to attain. Rarely had a large manufacturer of mass-produced items, especially in the area of electronic circuitry, set quality standards so high. Rarer still, was the onus for achieving this goal that it placed directly on its suppliers. Motorola leveraged its massive purchasing power to impose its will and require its vendors to dramatically improve their quality- control systems.

Motorola used the requirements needed to win the Baldrige award and applied Deming's teachings about how to unlock HyperLeverage through quality. It baked quality into everything and "leapfrogged" the competitive landscape by bending the quality curve to its advantage. It was both proactive and intentional. The prerequisites of HyperLeverage. The result of the massive investment in quality paid off handsomely for Motorola. It documented over $16 billion in savings as a result of adopting a Six Sigma methodology. In the years that followed Motorola's award, its Six Sigma quality approach was benchmarked and adopted by tens of thousands of companies around the world. If that's not Quality HyperLeverage at work, I'm not sure what is.

However, not all businesses have melded quality into their business DNA. American car companies for years simply applied window dressing rather than embrace real quality management. Marketing materials exhorting quality popped up everywhere. Ford tried to leverage its slogan, "Quality is Job One" as a reason to buy its cars.

Maybe Ford thought that if it repeated its heir slogan repeatedly, that would be enough to overcome its lack of quality performance systems, its absence of robust measurement techniques, and its very visible performance problems. Ford did have it right with the slogan, though. To leverage quality, it indeed had to become "Job One."

To HyperLeverage quality, you need time; it can't be achieved overnight. It must be built into a company's processes, systems, infrastructure, and culture. You've got to plan for quality, you've got to think about what quality means to your organization and your customers, you've got to determine how or if you can measure quality. If you want to leverage quality to the point of HyperLeverage you have to think and act holistically. Quality affects everything on the business canvas.

A slogan or banner is nice in that it communicates the vision and mission of the company. However, if it's not backed up by actions, it's little more than a marketing gimmick. In the case of Ford, consumers didn't buy it, as evidenced by the decline in market share.

Obviously, back in the late 1980s and early 1990s, Ford didn't get the memo about building quality assessments into the entire process. The adherence to a quality culture had changed everything for its Japanese and German competitors and they began to capture significant market share at the expense of the American brands. So, how can a company make quality job one and leverage it to attain higher levels of performance?

Let's start by deconstructing the quality problem that plagues many businesses. We'll use the Leverage Prism shown in Figure 20: "Deconstructing Quality & Consistency," to examine some of the components and systems that can lead to a clear definition of quality products and services and a pathway to creating the goals, processes, systems, infrastructure, etc., necessary to truly make quality job one.

DECONSTRUCTING QUALITY & CONSISTENCY

QUALITY &
CONSISTENCY

QUALITY CONTROL PROCEDURES

ACCURACY/TOLERANCE LEVELS

PERFORMANCE PARAMETERS

INCORPORATING TECHNOLOGY

TESTING METHODOLOGIES

INCOMING QC TESTING

IN PROCESS/CONTINUOUS TESTING

IMPROVEMENT PROCESSES

REDUCTION IN REWORK & REPAIR

INCREASE IN RELIABILITY

INCREASE IN BRAND EQUITY/TRUST

FIGURE 20: DECONSTRUCTING QUALITY & CONSISTENCY

As we have discussed, quality must begin with a definition of the term—both for internal purposes and external communications to the client. These two are not always the same. If quality is poorly defined, if the term remains a nebulous concept in your organization, you won't be able to leverage the concept. Without clarity, there will be no way to gauge consistency, improvement, or degradation of quality. Quality cannot exist in a vacuum.

Once the quality has been defined, the definition must be adequately codified and communicated internally to all stakeholders. Creating a culture obsessed with quality is the first step in creating a Quality HyperLeverage environment. Determining quality standards is indeed the first step, but without appropriate testing or measurement techniques, it can't be leveraged. Are your techniques sufficiently robust, accurate, and reproducible? Do you need to incorporate new methods, new technologies? Have people been trained? If one were to use a DOIT Leverage Method to evaluate how a company leverages quality, these issues and questions would be addressed as part of the Organize and Improve phases.

Without proper and robust procedures and guidelines, there can be no leverage, since there is no consistency of measurement or performance. Without this, there is no way to give direction on how to address deficiencies or adjust fix defects, or instructions on what the next step might be. Building quality into a system, a process, or a product is not a straightforward exercise in project or product management. HyperLeveraging quality requires a holistic approach.

Now let's assume that quality standards, measurement, and improvement techniques have been set. What now? Do you simply send a press release to the Internet and hope that people read it? No, quality is so directly related to perception and brand awareness that it requires a full and closed-loop system of progressive monitoring. People are programmed to have a gut feeling about the difference in cost and performance between a good and an excellent product. They inherently know that a quality product will cost more. It's not enough to yell, "Quality," and think that someone will believe you. It must be earned. And it doesn't happen overnight, no matter how much you might want to bend the curve. It takes time, it takes good communication, it takes consistency. The experience of quality by a consumer can rarely be manufactured just because someone says it exists.

Higher quality also is leveraged by differentiation. Not every product can be the best in the market. Not every brand can be considered the standard bearer in its market niche. If your brand is regarded as such already, then you have successfully elbowed out your competition. To maintain a HyperLeverage level of quality, you must be vigilant and defend your position aggressively. Always be constantly improving and monitoring. No slacking off. No complacency. Ever. That is a significant component that is revealed by the Leverage Prism.

Don't fool yourself that this all comes cheaply. That would be short-term thinking that can turn around and bite you. HyperLeveraging quality is a long-term investment. Yes, it often comes with additional and sometimes quite high costs and necessary changes to existing infrastructure. But that's what HyperLeverage is about. Making difficult decisions that magnify the significance of your actions. The highest levels of quality do not happen without it. If you want to telegraph that the expectations of your company should be higher, then your delivery and performance must keep pace at a minimum and exceed it to reach HyperLeverage. You can keep pace for a while but know that the competition will eventually understand what they need to do to change the narrative and cut through your temporary leverage position.

The salient point is that quality is a powerful concept that can be leveraged repeatedly in business. It's often the only "story" left over from generation to generation that cements a positive brand impression. Putting quality front and center as a business message and marketing campaign is powerful and brings with it a multitude of stories that can be woven from that cloth, but only if performance matches the hype.

Your business story must have "meat on the bone." It must be backed up by actual performance. In the case of Ford, it learned the hard way during the crisis that followed the great recession of 2008 - 2009 that the proof of quality was not in its slogans but in the actual performance of its product. Only when the two were in sync did the public recognize that the company's quality had improved. Companies need to be aware of the standards that must be maintained and weary of any chink in the armor of perception. Being vigilant in maintaining the level of quality that a customer has become accustomed to is necessary to keep HyperLeveraging quality. However, the slope can be quite steep on the way down. Companies that take their foot off the gas pedal can see how a deterioration in quality or even the perception of deterioration can be a deleveraging event.

Quality Requires Consistency

Once a new level of quality had been established, there is no going back. HyperLeveraging quality begets the need for consistency and continual improvement. What does it mean to leverage consistency? How can this attribute be purposefully exploited to reach a level of HyperLeverage?

It really starts with a decision backed by coordinated action to reduce variability and maintain a set level of quality and performance. Performance and quality levels may change over time as a result of market dynamics. The key to HyperLeverage in this situation is to limit the variation to a minimum by being vigilant and using improved monitoring systems. Advances in technology should be part of the solution.

Trust is the byproduct of consistency, consistency is the byproduct of quality, and quality is the byproduct of the right systems, processes, and infrastructure aligned with clear goals. Those, in turn, are byproducts of effective planning, strategy, people, and environment, and so on.

To reach HyperLeverage, you've got to be clicking on more than just one cylinder. When I get into my car, I expect that it will start up every time. I used to have to insert a key in the ignition, but now I can just push the ignition button. That required a significant leap of faith on the part of the consumer that the manufacturer had gotten the technology right. Consumers trusted the key to work without fail. Doing away with a physical manifestation, the key, was not intuitive to most car owners at the time the ignition button was introduced.

As you can see, there are many activities that work together. In the case of the automotive industry, technology and innovation had to be leveraged to build a reliable circuit board and chip for the car keys. Quality controls had to put in place with a determination of key metrics to make sure that faulty units were not installed. Testing methods had to be developed. It was a virtuous and holistic cycle of incremental leverage that ultimately led to HyperLeverage.

It is hard to overstate the power of consistency. A report done by McKinsey & Company, one of the most respected management consulting companies in the world, concluded that, "consistency is the secret ingredient to making customers happy. However, it's difficult to get it right and requires top-leadership attention. Brands rely on it for their inherent value. Consumers rely on it for decision making. Vendors and Employees rely on it to do their jobs."

Coca Cola, arguably the world's most recognized brand, puts a premium on consistency. Wherever you might find yourself on the planet, you will find a place to purchase a Coke, and it will look the same everywhere. The company has strict guidelines on how and where the logo can be used and the specific color of red to be used. This is how Coke leverages consistency. Disney and other worldwide brands act in the same fashion. They build the expectation of performance amongst their users through consistency of appearance that leads to trust and loyalty.

This is the central lesson of this chapter. Quality, consistency, and trust are interrelated. To achieve HyperLeverage in this area requires adequate planning and coordination. Together, these traits create a performance bar that should never be lowered.

Takeaways

⚠ Quality can't be achieved overnight. You've got to plan for quality, and you've got to think about what quality means to your organization and your customers.

⚠ Finding HyperLeverage through quality means building it into a company's processes, systems, infrastructure, and culture.

⚠ Quality must be defined both for internal and external communication purposes. These two are not always the same. Without clarity about what quality means in your organization, there is no way to gauge consistency, improvement, or degradation. HyperLeveraging quality requires specifics, not nebulous generalities.

⚠ The key to HyperLeveraging consistency and limiting variations is vigilance and improved monitoring systems. Advances in technology should be part of this solution.

CHAPTER 16

Infrastructure

n this chapter, I'll discuss a component that's critical to achieving performance leverage: infrastructure. It's another one of those "big" concept words like "culture" and "quality" that we have tackled before in this book. It means different things depending upon the context and situation. I think of infrastructure as the scaffolding upon which the operations of a business are built. It provides the framework that holds everything together so that it won't fold like a house of cards. The stronger and more comprehensive the structure, the longer the time horizon a company must realize its potential. Why? Because products and services can be developed and brought to market with more support. The company's workforce will have more resources to leverage their skills. Quality and consistency can be maintained with less effort. The systems, processes, and physical assets are in place to help the business achieve the objectives set forth as part of its strategic plan. The company can achieve more because it has built a strong infrastructure—a solid foundation for growth and innovation.

Of course, every business has different infrastructure requirements. Items that are essential for one business may not be as critical for other businesses. For example, the infrastructure of a digital marketing company that provides SEO services would require specific IT configurations, access to servers to store data, and specific software that could collect data and provide analysis. It would need an office to house the workforce. The emphasis of the infrastructure would be highly technology-driven.

A manufacturing company, on the other hand, would require a completely different kind of infrastructure. The type and amount of equipment, the capacity of the production lines, access to distribution centers, ports, highways, and airports all become a major factor in developing the right infrastructure needed. Controlling inventory and achieving viable economies of scale factor into its leverage equation.

The first thing to consider is that all infrastructure requires investment and certainly an outlay of time, money, and effort. These are sunk costs that in many cases take years to recoup. This harkens back to a basic premise of this book: you need a long enough time horizon to achieve HyperLeverage. Infrastructure is a long-term leverage activity. In fact, in many instances it could take years, even decades, to see actual returns. I recognize the difficulties of making decisions that could take a decade, if not longer, to come to fruition. However, that is ultimately the responsibility of business leadership—to set in motion those investments and activities that will bear fruit in the future.

Investment in infrastructure can be a major expense; it can also be a major advantage that can be leveraged significantly by those that have the foresight and means. Those companies that have the financial wherewithal to invest in long-term infrastructure projects can make it very tough for their smaller or less capitalized competition to compete. These huge infrastructure gambles can decimate markets when they come online. We need to look no further than Amazon to see how HyperLeverage works in the area of infrastructure.

Jeff Bezos had the foresight when he began building Amazon that to achieve his goal to grow as large as possible, he had to build

DECONSTRUCTING INFRASTRUCTURE

INFRASTRUCTURE

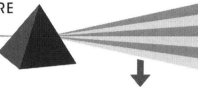

ECONOMIES OF SCALE

AUTOMATION/ROBOTICS

STANDARD PROCESSES

PRODUCTION CAPACITY

PROXIMITY TO VENDORS

PROXIMITY TO DISTRIBUTION

PROXIMITY TO CUSTOMERS

INVENTORY LEVELS

ACCESS TO WORKFORCE/TALENT POOL

PLANT, EQUIPMENT AND REAL ESTATE

FIGURE 21: DECONSTRUCTING INFRASTRUCTURE

fulfillment centers that could handle that growth. This infrastructure would separate him from his nearest competitors. The only way he surmised Amazon could become the "Everything Store" was to develop the technology and infrastructure that would create a moat around his business and protect it from the likes of eBay, Wal-Mart, and others. It was an integral component that made his virtuous cycle become a reality. The economies of scale would lead to improvements in infrastructure, which would lead to a reduction in costs, which would lead to lower prices, which would lead to increased volume.

It's almost as if we need to build our business frameworks out of elastic rubber, being strong enough to take the stress, but resilient enough to bend and be moldable. Rigidity in times of rapid change is not leverageable, and infrastructure as a leveraged investment is not a slam-dunk. There is significant risk involved. And not all infrastructure can be leveraged as planned, since market dynamics and technologies change quickly or the technology simply just doesn't work that well. Such was the case in the telecommunications industry. Unlike earlier generations of mobile networks, mobile operators did not see the big returns with the 4G system launched in 2009 as they had earlier technology iterations. Their investment in the 4G infrastructure showed flat or tepid growth. This infrastructure investment did not result in HyperLeverage. The reason? The technology outpaced the hardware. IOT, Streaming Video, and AI have advanced at blistering speeds, far outstripping the capabilities of the 4G infrastructure, which was not built to handle them. That's why building a 5G network has become a priority for top companies in this space.

Timing and Risk in Infrastructure

In 1995, Denver opened its new airport to great fanfare. It was hailed as the most modern and technologically advanced airport in the world. It had recognized that a key chokehold at older airports was the baggage handling system. The design and leadership teams for the Denver airport tackled this head-on by developing a more efficient automated baggage handling system. The new system would streamline the boarding and onboarding process and allow for more daily flights, and therefore more profits for the airport.

In the early 1990s, when the computerized baggage handling system was first conceived, enormous, expensive, and high-maintenance mainframe computers were used as a centralized command and control post to run the system. It was an old approach that would soon be outdated with the more affordable and scalable Cloud-based solutions that were being ushered in the 1990s. Today, decentralization, mobile computing technology, and Cloud applications have taken over almost every one of the tasks the centralized mainframe system was going to tackle. Airlines, warehouse operators, distributors, and shipping companies like FedEx and UPS can track an item in motion with a few clicks. The Denver Airport's huge computerized infrastructure was no longer needed. Alas, close to $600 million ($2 billion in today's dollars) of infrastructure investment was just flushed down the drain. The baggage system was never fully implemented, and left a relic of an infrastructure that became obsolete because it did not have the time horizon necessary to recoup its investment.

A company can be proactive and intentionally utilize existing solutions and assets, but disruptive technologies and unforeseen circumstances lurk just below the surface all the time. All you can do is shake your fist at the sky and shout, "Why can't progress just stand still for a decade or more so that I can make some money from my latest infrastructure investment?" It's true, infrastructure needs time to be fully utilized to see a return. Otherwise, it is just a big sunk cost with lost business potential. But most of the time, you have no choice but to continually build new infrastructure to keep up with changing times. It's just a reality of business. What's the key to achieving HyperLeverage of Infrastructure? You need great information to make the best possible decisions, a system to spot opportunities and trends and stay ahead of the curve, a willingness to accept a higher degree of risk and, in truth, a little luck.

HyperLeveraging inventory presents a similar situation. Huge up-front investments are made, but the inventory is susceptible to a variety of changes before it can be used to generate cash and profit. In my first venture, Colorations®, I thought I could leverage inventory to gain market share. I always had products on hand to ship out immediately. Back then, this was not the norm. Today, it is expected. But back then, most of my competitors took weeks to ship out orders to their distributors. They even had backorders on occasion. I recognized that if I could ship within 48 hours of receiving an order, I could capture many of the customers that were tired of having to wait and adjust their business practices to accommodate their suppliers. I went about producing much higher levels of inventory than my sales volume warranted at the time. The number of times I had to restock my inventory throughout the year was considered heresy at the time. I was taking a calculated risk, but I knew my clients didn't want to wait for their products. If I could help my customers maintain lower inventory levels by being their "just in time" supplier, I could have a strong impact on their bottom line. As a result, I saw an opportunity to leverage my inventory to gain market share. My investment in the infrastructure necessary to produce and warehouse a much larger inventory than my competitors was key to the success of my company. Sales skyrocketed, and Colorations® gained market share, capturing close to 5 percent at the expense of entrenched and larger competitors such as Crayola and Rose Art. As a silver lining, the increased demand allowed me to attain economies of scale that reduced my production costs by almost 25 percent. This more than offset the additional cost of carrying and storing the extra inventory.

These actions allowed me to HyperLeverage inventory and magnify my results far beyond what I could have achieved otherwise. Inventory became the leading edge; the value adds that Colorations® brought to the market created differentiation and established the brand. It solved a real and specific problem for my customers. It did not come about by accident. It was planned. It was intended to get specific results, and it was proactive and not reactive to market demands.

For me, the success lay in building a system where I minimized any work in progress. I converted incoming raw materials into finished goods as quickly as possible. This is yet another trick to HyperLeveraging inventory. The quicker the transition from raw material to finished goods gets done, the quicker a company has something to sell and see a return on its investment. This holds true for most industries. The pressure to get products to market before they become obsolete is paramount. Reducing the time where inventory is "in limbo" is critical to the success of the business.

So how can you reduce your work-in-progress phase and thus keep the time to market to a minimum? Where can you find leverage in this process? Let's go back again to the first tenet of developing a HyperLeverage Mindset. You must be willing to deconstruct every situation to find the nuggets of unpolished opportunity. Take apart your current system. Do you have a robust system to collect market data or BI to determine the appropriate level of inventory? Remember how Disney was so unprepared in terms of manufacturing infrastructure to handle the avalanche of demand for Toy Story licensed products? It didn't have the data at its fingertips to support proper inventory levels.

By anticipating demand or even creating demand, companies can decide on the amount of capital needed for inventory. Figure out if your sales and marketing strategies are aligned with the inventory you currently have and the competitive landscape. And develop a just-in-time inventory mentality with your suppliers and vendors. Instead of stockpiling raw materials, find a way to have the specific amount needed for production supplied just when production would commence. Put the onus of inventory on your suppliers so that you focus the resources on production, sales, and distribution of the finished items. Purchasing, manufacturing, distribution, marketing, and sales all must work together to make the investment in inventory truly impactful. There's a lot of homework to be done in order not to make inventory mistakes.

Even software development companies that rely on outside subcontractors for the completion of many of their projects can HyperLeverage "work in progress" inventory. The same concepts apply. Using agile management techniques has become crucial to HyperLeveraging time and infrastructure resources by making sure that team members can work in parallel while demanding that subcontractors deliver their products (software code) to coincide with when you need them. Getting them too early means that you have expended capital for an "inventory'" asset that is not ready to be used. Getting them too late means that you have created "work in progress" inventory that has been expensed but is not able to generate income.

Location

One area that companies can proactively and intentionally leverage is the location. Whether it's where a business decides to be geographically located, where it chooses to merchandise its products, or even how those items appear on its retail shelves or online e-commerce sites—all of these are decisions about location, and they have an impact on the bottom line.

The concept of an anchor store is not new. Shopping center developers scour the landscape for properties that have the best potential, demographics, and traffic and try to land a large brand name store that can attract other tenants that want to benefit from their proximity to it. Large manufacturing and technology companies are similar in that they can leverage the proximity to resources they can't develop or control on their own, such as an existing talent pool; access to suppliers, vendors, and subcontractors; and proximity to points of distribution and transportation such as ports, highways, rail systems, and airports.

In 2009, Boeing made a momentous decision to establish a second infrastructure complex in Charleston, South Carolina, on the opposite side of the country from Seattle, Washington, where the company is headquartered. The new facility was not only physically distant, it was culturally different. It was a gamble to duplicate the existing infrastructure it already had in Seattle and establish similar infrastructure in a new city on the opposite coast.

Though there were several important reasons for the move, the driving force was the production requirements of Boeing's 787 Dreamliner, a plane that constitutes a generational and fundamental change in technology and which will be Boeing's cash cow for the next 20 years. This story demonstrates how uncovering HyperLeverage opportunities in the area of infrastructure can become a key strategic differentiator and competitive advantage. The Dreamliner represents the first mass-produced jetliner that incorporates carbon fiber technology in the fuselage. Boeing needed to plan for an investment it felt would take at least 10 years and maybe longer to yield a profit.

The example of Boeing is instructive. Why Charleston? The city did not have decades of manufacturing history or a strong aerospace technology sector. It didn't even have a fully formed labor pool. There must have been something else—other than the

$1 billion or so in tax incentives. After all, the estimates to build this infrastructure at its new facility in Charleston ran as high as $28 billion, so $1 billion was not enough to tip the scales. Boeing's leadership clearly felt there were several major resources, as detailed below, that it could exploit in Charleston—resources that could result in HyperLeverage. Of course, there is never a single reason for this type of massive, strategic decision. The decision-making process is complex and multidimensional. In the case of Boeing, it was the intangibles that interested the company's leadership. Let's see this through Boeing's Leverage Prism:

⚠ There is a significantly lower cost of living in South Carolina. Boeing would be able to save tons of money over the life of its investment on lower wages and could provide a more affordable and healthier lifestyle to its employees. This would also make it easier to attract new talent to the area.

⚠ The regulatory restrictions in South Carolina are less burdensome than in Washington state. This would make it easier for Boeing to progress with fewer government roadblocks.

⚠ South Carolina is a "right to work" state and not heavily unionized. This would make it easier for Boeing to count on a workforce that would not go on strike, like what happened multiple times in the company's Seattle manufacturing facilities.

⚠ The future model of production for a project the size of the Dreamliner requires a global supply chain that makes the single location model obsolete and even risky. The Charleston location would provide Boeing the room for expansion needed to produce at least 50 percent or more of the total projected demand of 5,000 planes. As a major port city, Charleston planned to deepen its port to meet the demands of the Panamax cargo ships that would reduce Boeing's supply chain costs.

⚠ The state of South Carolina and the City of Charleston were enthusiastic supporters of a Boeing plant. Not only did they provide incentives directly to Boeing, they also aided the suppliers and affiliated businesses that would spring up around the Boeing core. Boeing had data on how BMW had been successful in establishing its manufacturing hub in the upstate region of South Carolina and could use the same playbook in Charleston.

In addition to the geographic considerations, Boeing is also an example of the necessity to consider appropriate time horizons when determining how to leverage current and future infrastructure, what business expenditures and assets will be needed, where they will be needed, when they will be needed, and how long they will be needed. This takes a "think backwards" approach like what was discussed in the section on Strategic planning. By first determining how many planes it needed to produce to break even, it could determine the infrastructure necessary to accomplish this, knowing full well that the real profits will be realized in years, sometimes decades, into the future after the initial investment has been paid off.

The story of Boeing is obviously one that few companies can or need to contemplate when HyperLeveraging location. Notwithstanding the size of a business, HyperLeveraging location, especially when it relates to infrastructure, will influence the performance of a company. It is an important consideration that most businesses are taking advantage of shorter-term and smaller-scale leverageable opportunities than the huge paradigm-shifting example of Boeing.

Size and Infrastructure

To take advantage of economies of scale, many companies expand their infrastructure beyond their current needs by factoring in the room for growth. They carry the cost of this additional infrastructure, either through direct cash investment or financial instruments of debt. In the short run, until the additional capacity is needed, they have underutilized assets, which would be the opposite of leverage. This applies to a multitude of businesses, not just manufacturers, but distributors, retail, and even technology companies. However, this excess capacity or underutilized workforce or even real estate, when done with the appropriate planning, is based on reliable information and analysis that constitutes the necessary pathway to HyperLeverage and not an underleveraged asset.

How does a company HyperLeverage economies of scale? Like so many of the lessons in this book, it comes down to the utilization of different components, many of which are not always as obvious. As a company grows, it can obviously leverage its growing demand for supplies and services into better-negotiated deals. It can muscle better distribution deals and added marketing and promotional discounts. Whether it's lower prices, free freight, or just-in-time inventory, there is a multitude of methods to strongly influence your vendors to "play nice" with you or risk losing your business. They know that size matters. Smart suppliers are never oblivious to the growth of their main customers. If they are on top of their client relationships, they are proactive and don't wait for their company to come looking for accommodations.

Often the key to HyperLeveraging economies of scale comes from taking a hard look at how operations are currently conducted and recognizing that there are other paths to accomplish the same objective. Using the DOIT Leverage Method is very helpful in uncovering these opportunities. When I took over the paint manufacturing operations at Excelligence, Inc. after my company Colorations® was acquired, I used this method effectively to HyperLeverage infrastructure through economies of scale. As a result, I was able to lower unit costs and drive demand up by more than 200 percent. I noted that the largest batch size of paint that was being produced was only around 50 gallons. That translated into 400 pint-sized bottles. That was the amount we sold each month. The problem was that we had six product lines with ten colors per line—this meant that we were making 70 different batches of paint. And I wanted to add another 100 new SKUs. Demand was growing exponentially as the company expanded in the preschool and elementary grades. We were selling close to 1000 gallons per color per year. And we had more than 100 colors.

Using the 50-gallon production equipment was not going to cut it. The paint department was working overtime just to keep from creating backorders. We had to improve our infrastructure quickly and dramatically. I decided to increase the batch size rather than hire a second and third shift of employees. We shifted from 250-gallon batches to 500 gallons at a time using the same amount of energy and labor as the original 50-gallon sizes. Not only did costs go down, but efficiency and quality went up.

That is a straightforward example of HyperLeverage. I was able to leapfrog capacity by a factor of 10 in one leap. For many larger companies, a much quicker method that leverages their size is to consider scaling their infrastructure through acquisition or partnerships. Why wait for organic growth to fuel the savings that can be realized from a quicker path to larger scale? Just shortcut the process and buy market share or increased production capacity. By combining forces, you can lower your per-unit costs and take advantage of the time by having the infrastructure to support more growth immediately.

There is a limit to how much infrastructure is too much before the upfront investment outweighs the short to mid-term benefits. In the previous example, if we had increased production size to 1000 gallons per batch, we would have overshot our infrastructure needs. We would also have been producing in one batch enough product for two years. However, since the paint had a shelf life of two years, it might have gone bad before we could sell it. We would have lost all the advantages of leverage. Companies that have excess infrastructure capacity are faced with a choice of absorbing the additional expenses until the company "grows into" the need for it, or downsizing, or doing something that few consider or put into action.

- Lease out excess space that is currently not being used. This could be warehouse space, office space, even entire buildings.
- Provide contract work for smaller companies that don't have the wherewithal or desire to build their own infrastructure. The Boston Beer company, known for its Sam Adams brand of beer, took advantage of this arrangement when it first started. It initially rented excess capacity at the Pittsburgh Brewing Company and later developed contract arrangements at various long-established brewing facilities with excess capacity, such as Stroh's and Hudepohl.
- Produce white label or private label versions of your own products. Even though this may seem like cannibalizing the market opportunity, often companies are not able to capture and service this additional market share by themselves. This allows a company to utilize its capacity and still gain a slice

of the market. It also provides leverage over its private label clients.

As the Boston Beer example shows, HyperLeveraging size is not just for those that are bigger than others. It had a proactive and intentional plan to exploit the infrastructure of others and place its efforts on marketing and distribution, rather than manufacturing. It's a great example of HyperLeverage.

Takeaways

⚠ Unlocking HyperLeverage in infrastructure is a long-term activity. Some projects can take years or even decades to produce tangible returns. It is the ultimate responsibility of business leaders to set in motion those investments and activities that will bear fruit in the future.

⚠ Developing a robust infrastructure can be leveraged as a defensive moat against competition because of the time and cost involved to attain economies of scale.

⚠ Almost every company can proactively and intentionally leverage location. Whether it's the physical location of its offices, stores, or warehouse or a company's use of space on the Internet...or even utilization of the location in a retail environment.

⚠ To HyperLeverage inventory, you need a highly correlated system that collects and analyses sales data, determines correct lead times, and considers cash flow.

The DOIT Leverage Method: Performance
Case Study—United Parcel Service (UPS)

Established in 1907 as a private messenger and delivery service, United Parcel Service (UPS) has grown to become the world's largest package delivery company and a premier provider of global supply chain management solutions. The company's performance is impressive. In 2018, UPS delivered an average of 20.7 million packages per day, which translated into 5.2 billion packages and total revenues of more than $71 billion for the year.

But in the late 1990s and early 2000s, UPS faced some major challenges. The Internet had ushered in the first major seeds of e-commerce and the company's leadership knew that a transformation would be necessary to stay competitive and continue growing. UPS knew it had to be proactive in preparing to address the new technologies, competitors and customer expectations that were emerging.

The leadership team began its preparation with a strategic vision to leverage the company's core strengths: performance and infrastructure. It also decided to position UPS as both the go-to address for reliable shipment of parcels and a logistic partner for e-commerce companies, which had begun competing directly with traditional brick-and-mortar establishments.

Let's imagine we were part of those initial strategic-planning meetings and bullet out the items that UPS's leadership team discovered as it sat down at the dawn of the e-commerce revolution and charted the company's course. This will be our DOIT Leverage Exercise, which is, of course, based solely on an external examination of the company from available public information. As we examine UPS's systematic search for acquisition of new resources and refinement, deployment, and exploitation of current assets, we will see how a well-established company turned leverage into HyperLeverage and became a world-class power in its industry.

Deconstruct (What are the key areas for leverage that UPS has?)

- Infrastructure. Utilize and expand existing package-processing centers, fleets of delivery vehicles and planes, and package tracking system.
- Consistency. Build on reputation for reliability, package tracking, and communication.
- Locations. Use its current package drop-off locations to allow for expansion of services throughout the United States.
- Scale. Continue to establish and grow delivery services in major cities around the globe, including in Asia and Europe.
- Demographics. Provide accessible package delivery services to the growing second and third rings of suburban sprawl.
- Capital. Expand business services through acquisitions.
- Change. Provide solutions for a growing population of self-employed and remotely employed professionals as well as growing e-commerce companies. Provide logistics solutions for companies to focus their resources on core activities rather than investing in their own logistics and supply chain infrastructure.

Organize (What current resources and market opportunities could UPS leverage?)

- Expand its dominance in local ground package delivery.
- Reinforce its commitment to real-time tracking and communication.

- Double-down on small package delivery as the core revenue generator.
- Disseminate its brand story: "What can "brown" do for you?"
- Continue to expand UPS's on-time money-back delivery promise.

Improve (What additional resources could UPS add, and which assets could be improved to achieve greater market share and profitability?)

- Improve infrastructure, from package handling to delivery and tracking using the latest advances in technology.
- Purchase and expand a retail consumer-facing company that can provide an easy gateway to existing and expanded UPS delivery services.
- Create partnerships with high-growth e-commerce retailers and startups such as Amazon, eBay, and others.
- Create partnerships and in-store kiosks with existing brick and mortar retailers.
- Create a new logistics division focused on providing supply chain solutions.

Take Action (What actions could UPS take based on the resources and opportunities it had identified as leverage opportunities?)

- Go public, which UPS did in 1999, in order to access capital for expansion and improvements for the next decade of growth.
- Purchase key assets, which it did with the acquisition of Mail Boxes, Etc. This enabled UPS to rebrand its stores to The UPS Store and create a strong interface with retail consumers.

- Expand The UPS Store to thousands of locations, including in-store kiosks at mass retailers such as Office Depot.
- Form a new unit to leverage the company's logistics expertise and economies of scale for medium and enterprise-level companies. The unit that was developed was called UPS Supply Chain Solutions.
- Develop major air hubs to enhance international service.
- Acquire package delivery operations and develop partnerships in Asia, China, and South America.
- Continue to invest in technology and tracking, with an emphasis on increasing efficiency and consistency.

What were the results that UPS experienced? First, it recognized that the Internet would change the expectations of the market dramatically and UPS would need to evolve in order to respond effectively to these new marketplace realities. Performance, it knew, was going to have a higher premium in a world that was undergoing significant disruption. UPS's leadership team realized that it had to leverage its strengths—superior infrastructure and execution—and expand both domestically and globally as the world's economies were becoming intertwined. The results of this early planner were impressive—from total revenues of $27 billion in 1999, it weathered the dot. com bubble and almost doubled total sales to $50 billion by 2010.

UPS's success, as a result of its executive team's long-term strategy and planning, proves that this approach pays off in a market that is rapidly expanding and results in exceptional results. The UPS team showed that existing infrastructure could be leveraged in a scalable fashion to "muscle out" smaller competitors and consolidate market share. UPS's decision to leverage its financial assets also gave the company the muscle it needed to enter into and begin to dominate new service areas and markets. And, finally, the leadership team knew it could leverage the company's reputation for consistency, quality performance, and attention to detail. The company's brand reputation could thus be leveraged in a competitive retail environment. The company's "What Can Brown do for You?" campaign was a brilliant client-facing communication approach.

There is no question that UPS had successfully attained HyperLeverage. It wasn't by chance that UPS is even more dominant today than it was back in the early 2000s. Rather, it was due to its management team's proactive and intentional search for opportunities to leverage current resources and opportunities that it reached new heights. The story of UPS demonstrates how taking concrete and bold action, which would take years to implement, led to exceptional improvement in its performance capabilities. It's these characteristics of HyperLeverage that have led to its dominance as the largest domestic ground parcel delivery company well into the dawn of the e-commerce era.

HyperLeverage And Progress

"Progress is not inevitable. It's up to us to create it."
~Anonymous

DEFINITION: HYPERLEVERAGE AND PROGRESS

1. Embracing a holistic approach to continuous improvement and refinement by the comprehensive and collective utilization of human assets, strategic planning, effective implementation, and judicious timing to advance an organization's objectives.

2. The intentional encouragement and application of innovation, technology, and intellectual curiosity to effect impactful changes, resulting in exceptional outcomes.

A business must continually progress to thrive. Gone are the days when barriers to competition and disruption can be held at bay. In fact, the velocity of change in our global economy continues to increase. The importance of having a hand on the levers of progress is paramount to long-term survival. But to achieve a meaningful degree of progress, your work and planning must be calculated with forethought. In previous sections, I have discussed how to HyperLeverage progressive changes in areas that relate to People, Planning, and Performance issues in an organization. In this section, I will address perhaps the most critical areas of HyperLeverage: progress, from innovation and technology to intellectual property and change. And why are they so critical? Because a business and its market environment are continuously going through transformations. Nothing stands still for long. The business world we live in demands constant improvement, i.e., progress.

Many companies don't have a clear understanding of the true meaning of innovation. They use the term as a broad brush to describe almost any new idea or tweak to an existing product or service. It's confusing. The word "innovation" has been overused, and often misused, to the point that it is now devoid of any concrete meaning. As Scott Berkun, a recognized author and speaker in the area of creativity and leadership states, "Innovation is a junk word."

How can a company harness innovation, if it can't even define it? Leadership teams that want to leverage innovation need to start by defining and communicating what these terms mean in their business culture.

What most companies miss when they try to innovate is the "deliberate application" and the strategic planning necessary to derive "greater or different value from resources." The result? Innovation becomes nothing more than a feel-good exercise with limited impactful results. New ideas might be generated, but they are not systematically converted into useful products that lead to a company's growth. A truly innovative company bakes it into the fabric of its organizational DNA. 3M is a shining example of such a company.

William McKnight, the legendary Chairman of 3M for decades during the past century, developed a profoundly progressive business philosophy that was light years ahead of his time. McKnight saw business and the workplace differently. He understood the interdependence of business activities and the importance of freedom to pursue innovative ideas as lynchpins of entrepreneurship and long-term progress. He also understood that innovation meant risk. It was a necessary ingredient to achieve success. Warning against micromanagement and the chilling effect that accompanies intolerance of failure, he averred that "Management that is destructively critical when mistakes are made kills the initiative. We must have many people with initiative if we are to continue to grow."

These core truths have been a source of leverage for 3M, long before the discovery of the computer, the Internet, or cloud computing. At 3M, innovation is not an activity that is done only in times of need. It is 3M's mantra of success. 3M has passed these core business traits from one generation of employees to another. And what are those traits? The importance of innovation, intellectual property, technology, and the need for perseverance to maintain progress.

The real winners are those companies, both large and small, that can align new and solution-driven ideas with customers and their problems before anyone else can. Sounds obvious today but being customer-centric is a relatively new phenomenon in American business. At 3M, they call this "spending time in the smokestack." It takes a combination of forward-thinking management willing to be flexible, willing to take risks, and willing to invest in and nurture creativity and innovation, and embrace technological progress. But at 3M, it's more than just the strategic alignment of objectives that is the fulcrum of progress. They systematize innovation and make the resources available to the workforce.

Businesses that want to experience HyperLeverage in this area must embrace many of the basic tenets that helped 3M survive and grow for the past century. However, it is becoming increasingly difficult to attain that level without a bear-hug of technology. Technology is another of our often-misunderstood concepts. We use the word with a very broad brush, defining almost any innovation or method of doing something, not just a scientific, engineering, or software product.

HyperLeveraging technology can manifest itself in many avenues. And there is a huge overlap with innovation, even though not all innovation is in the realm of technology and not all technology requires innovation—at least not in the context that I have defined it for HyperLeverage purposes.

One of the results of innovation and technology can be the development of intellectual property (IP), which can become an asset that can be leveraged in a multitude of ways. We are all aware of the application of IP as it pertains to Patents, Trademarks, Copyrights, and Trade Secrets. Entire business wars have been fought over these to gain leverage over competitors and corner a market.

But that's old news. Today, even though these classic mechanisms to leverage IP are still of great importance, in many circumstances, they are trumped by an entirely new set of IP assets. As the Internet became the canvas of business interactions, the ability—often the necessity—to take advantage of website IP addresses, URLs, and social media handles for communication, marketing, and branding has become paramount.

This leads us to the closing chapter on how to uncover HyperLeverage around change. Change is the mechanism that ties everything together. Because the premise of HyperLeverage is to take action, it follows logically that the only path to HyperLeverage involves change, often a significant degree of change. This can create stress and friction in a business because it is antithetical to our desire to have predictability, consistency, and continuity. Without change, it would be impossible to grow, let alone maintain, a business. Granted, not everything has to change all the time or at once. But it's impossible to hold it back for an indefinite amount of time. Especially in a business environment that has seen unprecedented disruption and globalization. Wave after wave of external forces bombard us and undermine the concept of business continuity. They are here to stay, and as business leaders we must get used to it and harness it to our advantage.

Those waves have been around throughout the history of business. Think back to the example of Kutol in Chapter One and how it pivoted and modified the entire focus of the company based on the changes in how people were heating their houses. Its product was no longer going to be needed, so it found a way to change and reinvent its product as Play-Doh. Kutol embraced change and leveraged it to survive and prosper in a new market direction.

In fact, few companies and even well-established products and brands are the same as they were 10 years ago, 20 years ago, and certainly longer. IBM, which started in 1911 as a computing tabulating company, has reinvented itself numerous times over the past decade, like a snake molting its skin as it grows. In the 1980s, IBM was the king of the hill when it came to the nascent personal computer revolution. Over time though, it realized that the commoditization of PCs was eroding profit margins. IBM was the big elephant in the room, slow to innovate and change. It made the smart decision to abandon what had become a core business and charted a new course on providing IT expertise and computing services to other businesses. By 2013, IBM was the number one seller of enterprise server solutions in the world. Today, IBM remains one of the world's largest computer companies and systems integrators.

But that was not the end of the story. IBM had come through its near-death experience from the PC era with a renewed commitment to innovation and change and was one of the first big companies to embrace the nascent technology of artificial intelligence. Its investment in intelligence-related research started with developing a winning computer program to defeat the world champion chess master and the all-time TV game show, Jeopardy Champion. It has paid handsome dividends in new business opportunities that would not have existed if it had not embraced change as part of its DNA.

In this section, I'll close the loop on the 4Ps of the HyperLeverage universe: People, Planning, Performance, and Progress and focus on the main areas that are the dynamos of progress—Innovation and Technology. And finally, I will conclude with a discussion of change—an area ripe for HyperLeverage in almost every organization. Ready to take the last plunge? Let's jump on in.

CHAPTER 17

Innovation

I n 2003, LEGO® was literally coming apart one small plastic brick at a time and appeared to be heading toward bankruptcy. The Danish toy manufacturer of the ubiquitous interlocking plastic bricks was having difficulties providing products that its customers wanted and controlling production costs at the same time. The company had retired many of the designers that had created the original LEGO® sets that were responsible for the company's growth in the 1980s and 1990s and replaced them with a new cadre of young innovators—graduates from the top design universities in Europe. Without a background in toy design and with no direct knowledge of the LEGO® culture, these young designers caused a logistics nightmare and cost crisis as the new products they introduced rapidly increased the total number of manufactured parts from 6,000 to more than 12,000. It was a shock to the company's system. The infrastructure needed to maintain this new production demand with no significant gain in sales, which was devastating to the company's bottom line. Something had to give. While it was great for these innovators to come up with new designs and ideas, they had to be reined in and have their creative energy channeled more strategically.

Jorgen Vig Knudstorp, who was hired as CEO in 2004 to balance the LEGO® ship, had his hands full. First, he had to instill fiscal controls. More importantly, he had to realign the company's products and product development with its core and target audience. He needed more focused innovation, not innovation at any cost.

Vig Knudstorp did something that even today might seem risky. He essentially handed over the creative direction of LEGO®'s products to his most avid customers, the core fans of the LEGO® brand. Embracing this concept, which has since become known as Open Innovation, LEGO® realized that it had a resource it could leverage for ideas: its adult customers who had grown up with LEGO® products and wanted their kids to enjoy using LEGO® to inspire their own creativity. To leverage their involvement, Knudstorp introduced an Ambassador program that provided a direct path for the company to access new product ideas from this community.

By being humble, recognizing that the best product ideas don't always come from within, and tapping into the creativity of tens of thousands of its customers, LEGO® was able to HyperLeverage this approach to innovation. The decision to nurture creativity and innovation completely changed the company and paved the way for a decade of phenomenal growth. In fact, it was pure genius! By 2016, LEGO®'s revenues surpassed €5.1 billion euros—up from €0.9 billion euros in 2005. That same year, LEGO® surpassed Mattel to take the mantle as the world's largest toy company.

As we can learn from the LEGO® story, a company's ability to channel, encourage, and harness the creativity of its fans and develop an ongoing culture of innovation proved to be a path to HyperLeverage.

Innovation and creative thought are indeed activities that can truly set a company apart from the crowd. It's something that every company should embrace. However, as the LEGO® story demonstrates,

HyperLeverage is achieved only when that creativity and innovation is shaped by a more inclusive approach to strategic planning that considers all the resources of the entire company. With no process to effectively channel its innovation, LEGO® struggled. Once it learned to expand and harness its innovation, LEGO® started to take off.

The Four Corners of Innovation

There are some absolutes when it comes to HyperLeveraging creativity and innovation that transcend any organizational structure or culture. These are the building blocks, as seen in Figure 22: "4 Corners of Innovation," that build the framework—the corner and flat-edged pieces of the proverbial jigsaw puzzle.

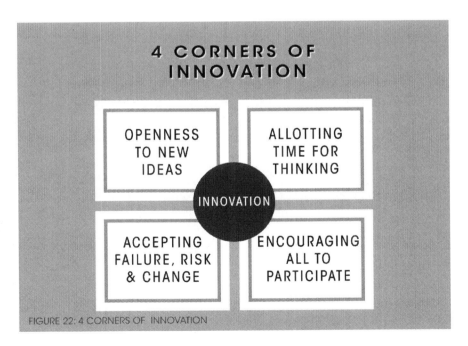

FIGURE 22: 4 CORNERS OF INNOVATION

Even small improvements in business activity can unlock innovation and creative thought. To begin with, there must be unencumbered openness to new ideas and a willingness to accept the changes and risks that implementation of these ideas might require. Without this openness to failure, who would want to go out on a limb or stick his neck out with a new idea? Nobody would be willing to risk antagonizing or even posing ideas that might be perceived as threatening to others. Innovation goes hand in hand with a change mentality. Having an acceptance and culture of change must be communicated company wide as well as on a personal level.

There is often a "not invented here" attitude that is pervasive in many organizations. It is especially prevalent when new employees join an organization. They start their new assignments with fresh ideas, different experiences and perspectives, skill sets, and a real desire to contribute as soon as possible. This is the perfect opportunity to get them on the HyperLeverage train.

My recommendation is to always actively seek out these new team members and encourage them to understand what has been done previously and how they might be able to leverage their experience for improvement. Without this initial push of inclusiveness, a company can send a clear message that innovation is not really valued, which can put the creative genie in the box for good.

Most companies are not as innovative as they think they are, and most don't leverage innovation well. Why is this? Because the underlying current of innovation is change and risk, which are kryptonite to most risk-averse management teams. Change and innovation go hand in hand. Without an agile culture that embraces change, there can be no innovation.

The most dynamic, change-driven and innovative companies reach a limit to the amount and degree of innovation that can be assimilated effectively at one time before the risks of disruption percolate throughout and instigate a state of disarray and paralysis. It is incumbent upon any organization and its leaders to find the balance between the agility required to handle change and disruption and the need to maintain control and consistency of operations. A steady hand on the tiller of strategic planning with a clear vision of the path forward is crucial to becoming a truly innovative company. Just think back to some of the issues of LEGO®, when it innovated too quickly.

As VP of Innovation at Excelligence, a leading school supply distributor and manufacturer, I made it a point to have an innovation strategy. And I recommend this for any company that desires long-term sustainable growth. An innovation strategy creates a deliberate alignment of current resources, collection of specific information, and empowerment of its human assets to challenge all existing processes. Within a short, three-year period, the number of new products expanded by a factor of three, resulting in an overall expansion of my department's revenue by over 300 percent.

Most organizations thrive on incrementalism by making slight variations or improvements to existing products, services, and systems. That's not truly innovation in the sense of creating something new. It's more about improvements, which are obviously a necessity in any business. However, it certainly does not rise to the level of HyperLeverage.

Crayola®, a company owned by Hallmark Corporation, produces and markets children's art materials. It is the worldwide recognized brand and the company is thought to be creative and innovative. This perception comes mostly because it sells art materials that children use to be creative: paints, markers, crayons, pencils, and modeling doughs. Selling items that others use for creativity does not necessarily make the producer of those goods creative or innovative. Notwithstanding, Crayola® makes a big deal about introducing new products. However, if you examine its new "innovations" more closely, you'll find that they are essentially line extensions of existing products. Crayola® often takes the same crayon or marker, changes the color, gives it a different name, and puts it in a redesigned package and touts it as new and innovative. Crayola®, however, is not alone in this practice. Many companies consider line extension like this to be innovation. Making slight modifications to existing products or services and developing new branding or packaging is not the intentional application of imagination to derive greater value. It may be smart marketing and good business, but it is not HyperLeveraging innovation, nor is it creative potential.

The question is whether a business can leverage creativity. And, if so, how does it raise it to the extreme? How does it make it deliberate so that it can be harnessed for true innovation? The answers lie in unleashing the performance activity of a company's workforce—a gold mine of talents, skills, and unlocked potential. What are the keys to unlocking the creativity that we all possess? How do businesses turn good ideas into great ideas and ultimately take action to convert them into real innovations? Let's find out.

Deconstructing Innovation

When deconstructing the major resources and activities that comprise innovation, we see that the keys to unlocking innovation come from many of the same business components discussed earlier in the book. A culture that inspires trust is necessary for innovation to thrive. Creating a corporate identity that is transparent and clearly articulates a philosophy of empowering employees, nurturing a culture of ownership and encouraging a "think first, act later" approach rather than the reactive "shoot from the hip" approach sets up the business canvas for innovation. Allotting time and encouraging active thinking while accepting failure and risk lets employees know they can venture outside the lines.

DECONSTRUCTING INNOVATION

INNOVATION

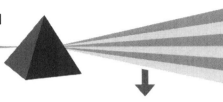

CREATE INNOVATION STRATEGY

ENCOURAGE CREATIVITY/CRITICAL THINKING

REMOVE BUREAUCRATIC ROADBLOCKS

BE WILLING TO ACCEPT FAILURES

PROVIDE INCENTIVES

SUPPORT OPENNESS & TRUST

SOLICIT CUSTOMER & VENDOR INPUT

ALLOT TIME FOR THINKING

UTILIZE BRAINSTORMING

LEARN TO SAY "YES" NOT "NO"

FIGURE 23: DECONSTRUCTING INNOVATION

Do you recognize any of the practices depicted in Figure 23 in your company? Which ones are missing? And most importantly, are any of the ones that make up your picture of innovation truly being leveraged deliberately? Does innovation just happen by chance, or is there a system in place to exploit it?

The Leverage Prism technique can reveal how innovation, research, and product development work within the framework of your organization. However, it takes a more strategic review to reveal if the result of these activities truly provides a long-term return on the investment of time and resources. In recent years, the concept of developing MVPs (Minimum Viable Products) as a mechanism to test certain innovative products or services has taken hold, especially in fast-changing high-tech environments. Borrowing from the concept of open innovation, the concept of MVP relies on feedback from the marketplace to direct innovation in a more focused, solutions-based manner.

Whereas innovation for almost any company is a must over the long haul, it does not have to be done internally. Rather, if management recognizes that it doesn't have the talent nor the resources available to leverage innovation, then a sound approach is to acquire them through hiring, licensing, acquisitions, mergers, or partnerships. This can be a very effective approach, allowing companies to leverage their financial resources differently and focus on those areas where they have a distinct performance advantage. This is more effective than attempting to force innovation internally in an organization that is not set up for it. This approach is quite common, especially with companies in fast-changing technologies, allowing them to essentially leapfrog a protracted development process and expand their product base or their market reach.

For example, Google has been especially active in acquiring innovation and incorporating under its brand umbrella. Google Docs, the online word processor app, was originally an app called Writely, created by Upstartle and purchased in 2006. Android, the most widely used operating system for smartphones, was a standalone company by the same name that was purchased by Google in 2005. More recently, in 2014, Facebook acquired Oculus VR, catapulting it into the world of technology hardware and software, a much different business market than the core social media base of the company.

Even though these companies are actively developing new products and applications internally, they recognized that it was advantageous to acquire these innovations in areas where they had little or no expertise rather than create them internally from scratch.

Developing a Culture of Innovation

Another core component to fertilize the landscape of innovation is purposefully budgeting time for people to think. This may sound like a somewhat odd, unproductive, and certainly immeasurable use of time, but the truth is that creative thought does not happen by turning on a switch. Innovative thinking requires stepping outside of the norm of everyday activity. And having permission to think is something that a business should provide. Steve Jobs was famous for taking walks when he needed to clear his head. Warren Buffet, by his own estimation, spends 80 percent of his time reading and thinking.

Years ago, I managed the R&D and product development for a group of highly skilled, highly educated materials engineers. Our building and lab were located no more than a ten-minute walk from the science library of Case Western in Cleveland, Ohio, one of the premier science and engineering universities in the country. At least one hour each week, I would make it a point to take a notebook and sit in the university's library, sometimes perusing the latest scientific journals, other times simply contemplating my department's activities. By separating myself from my normal business environment and daily routines, I gave my brain a break. It inspired me to think, digest, process, and explore ideas outside the norm.

I encouraged my team to do the same. I even let my team know that I considered these mini-retreats important enough to factor into their annual evaluation and review. To my dismay, few took me up on the suggestion. It was hard to blame them, as the concept of such a mini retreat was completely foreign to the company's upper management, who believed that only "real" work could be done in a lab.

In fact, one day, upon returning from my weekly library session, my direct boss, the VP of Operations, scolded me for wasting company time thinking in a library. "Joel," he said with a completely straight face, "We don't pay you to think, we pay you to develop new products." I saw the writing on the wall that day and very soon afterward found an opportunity to leave the company.

Innovative and creative thought are a combination of people, planning, and performance activities that require different mental frameworks to reach their full potential. Allowing people to carve out time to hang out in a different physical location—often as simple as moving to the coffee shop around the corner—can spur different thinking. It's a small investment relative to the long-term benefits.

All of these are activities that lead to an *improvement* in the amount and quality of creative thought and allow for leverage to happen.

Aligning Innovation to a Purpose

If business innovation is to succeed and improve a company's performance, be it internal operations, increased sales and revenue, improved systems, or new products or services, then the innovation cannot take place in a vacuum. The basis of HyperLeverage dictates that it must have a direct purpose with a relationship to the objectives and betterment of the company. To begin with, there must be a point of reference that would warrant the investment in the innovation and its implementation. Is there a void in the marketplace, a threat of new or disruptive technologies, increased competition, or other external changes? Is there a mechanism to measure the effectiveness of the innovation?

HyperLeveraging the potential of innovation means that leaders must have access to reliable information and data. But what kind of information and from where? Let's say that you have recognized the need for constructive feedback from your customers, vendors, fellow employees, and team members. You believe they could provide valuable insights to help your team determine whether to pursue an incremental upgrade or invest in a major product redesign. What are the different ways you could receive and assess this information?

This was the approach LEGO® used with its Open Innovation program: incentivizing and inviting loyal and passionate customers to feel ownership in the future innovation of its company. There are many other ways to accomplish this same objective. It may take some innovative thinking outside of your comfort zone.

For example, hosting a mini conference centered on sharing best practices and brainstorm ideas that could be the genesis for new product offerings or improvements to their existing platform serves many of these and other purposes. That is what Vidyard, a leading video marketing analytics company, began doing in 2014. According to Tyler Lessard, VP of Marketing, "we recognized the world of both B2B and B2C video marketing was changing so rapidly, that the only way we could anticipate and develop the next generation of services was to intimately interact with our current and potential customers." Over the ensuing years, the annual get-together became so successful that Vidyard created another innovation wrinkle to it. In 2017, the annual conference became a virtual event coupled with smaller in-market meetups. According to Lessard, "We are now able to interact with many more companies and individuals more efficiently while still maintaining the personal one-to-one connections that are necessary for idea-sharing. The objectives are the same and results are better than ever".

Today, many companies revert to social media, online surveys, email surveys, and similar impersonal and mass communication methods. I contend that this may be efficient in terms of getting mass amounts of data. But when it comes to innovation, quality will always trump quantity. Leveraging the power of personalization, either through direct, one-on-one conversations with customers or through the power of personalized videos with a direct request for feedback and ideas for improvement, will yield far better intelligence to inform your innovation strategy.

The toughest challenge of HyperLeveraging innovation comes with the follow-through. More than any other part of the HyperLeverage paradigm, innovation is a continuous activity. It's not something that you generally can turn on or off at will.

Even if a financial motivation is not at the top of the totem pole of items that drive employee performance, it's still important even if it's simply for recognition and employee morale. Having developed multiple new products for companies during my career, I can attest to being less than thrilled by the $50 patent bonus that was dangled in front of me. That was hardly going to buy a celebratory dinner— except perhaps at McDonald's. What was more important was that the attitude of the company towards the innovation and efforts on my part couldn't be clearer. It didn't truly appreciate my efforts or place high value on new ideas.

This happens at companies all the time and it can lead to a de-leveraged situation where employees opt to "shut down" and refuse to give their best ideas to a company since there is little incentive for them to do their best. To leverage innovation, a company should take actions that drive personal motivation. And as I discussed in Chapter Six, there are both tangible (financial, work conditions) and intangible (recognition, career advancement) methods that can be employed to create drive. Remember that your goal as a manager is to align innovation to meet the needs of the company in any and every way possible.

For me, the paltry incentive package I received was one of the reasons I opted to go out on my own as an entrepreneur. It's most likely a similar situation for thousands of people who leave their companies to go out on their own. The rewards offered to them to keep their ingenuity and creativity in-house are so much less than the risk they were willing to take to make it happen by themselves. In this regard, companies are continually shortchanging themselves and failing to leverage innovation effectively.

Think differently. Find out what can work for your specific situation and your specific team of employees. Perhaps think of giving your employees a share of the profits from a specific product idea that they helped bring to fruition. Another very simple and really cost-effective way is through recognition. Why not create a big PR campaign about the contributions of your internal team and its innovation? Get it out there on your social media. Pay for a good PR campaign.

It's really a win-win. A business earns new revenues and profits that wouldn't otherwise be realized. The individuals or teams of innovators get a direct sense of ownership and share in the financial rewards. It's a way to combine the 4 Ps: People, Planning, Performance, and Progress of HyperLeverage toward a singular goal.

There are myriad ways to motivate and incentivize. But the true renewal source of creativity and innovation would come as Daniel Pink has written in his seminal work on the subject, *Drive*, by nurturing Type I behavior. A way of thinking and an approach built around intrinsic rather than extrinsic motivators. Powered by our innate need to direct our own lives, to learn and create new things, to do better for us, and often to do better for our own slice of the world.

Innovation to Extend the Business Life Cycle

The need for HyperLeveraging creativity and innovation is vital to any organization because it provides new fuel to the business engine. Especially in an open market and global environment where ideas are easily shared, emulated, and even outright copied.

Rarely do a company's products or services last the test of time without modifications. The life cycles are being compressed into shorter and shorter periods. This is especially true with technology companies, especially those that are software-related. The constant need for incremental tweaks has overwhelmed many companies' abilities to break out of the "upgrade" cycle and truly innovate. That means that very little HyperLeverage is going on—just maintenance and staying current.

An innovative culture not only allows a company to stay ahead of the market, it also sends a powerful message to its customers, if done properly, that their interests are the driving force of the business, rather than a profit driver. This is just one example of how the connective tissue of HyperLeverage works. It strengthens the core of any organization. It reinforces brand equity. And, it connects customers, communication, and innovation in a thread that yields better products and, ultimately, better results.

There are various thoughts as to the level of innovation that is needed. I have followed a rule of thumb, like the 3M model, that new products should represent at least 10 percent and closer to 20 percent of a company's annual revenue. This calculation is tethered in the fact that existing products become old, stale, and out of favor because of competitive innovation. Without a continuous flow of new and innovative alternatives, a company can easily go from being at the top to the bottom in a few short years, just because there was not an emphasis on new and innovative products and services.

Now, a company does not have to be disruptive to be innovative. In fact, as I explained earlier, disruption is a result of change and innovation and requires a lot of moving parts to take hold. It requires a very dedicated culture of continuous and even radical change. It requires a risk-taking approach that many are not comfortable with, and it requires perseverance as it is harder to take giant leaps than to take incremental steps. Finally, disruption through innovation requires many intangibles beyond the control of a business, such as a receptive marketplace, a clear understanding of the benefits to the consumer, and a void in the market, free from established competitive forces.

The history of business is rife with innovative companies that created great products and services and crossed the chasm first with new and innovative products and services, only to find that the market wasn't ready, or they did not have the staying power. Many innovative companies experience HyperLeverage this way. They allow smaller companies to take the initial steps and allow them to establish a market bridgehead. They lay in wait, monitoring new advancements and technologies developed by others. When the timing is advantageous, they either copy or improve on the ideas with their more established and larger infrastructure, or they simply acquire the innovation outright.

Brainstorming - Proactive Innovation

Most companies do not start with an innovation strategy. That already indicates that not all resources have been leveraged. An innovation strategy provides the power of purpose. Rarely, as we learned from Edison's Menlo Park facility, is it done single-handedly. Furthermore, from a business perspective, there are distinct advantages to leveraging a team approach to innovation as it exploits the full complement of resources available.

One area that many companies have employed is the concept of brainstorming. It's used to squeeze the best ideas out of a group of individuals in a team environment. To squeeze the "nectar" from brainstorming, you need a safe, supportive, and systematic process. But many companies only give lip service to this concept. Brainstorming is done occasionally and is not part of an established process.

Veronique Lafargue, the global head of content strategy at Google Apps, explained in an article in Fast Company in 2016 how Google excels at brainstorming by using a simple, linear three-step process to come up with innovative ideas and turn them into actual products.

> 1. Know the user
> As Lafargue writes, "To solve a big question, you first have to focus on the user you're solving it for—then everything else will follow."

> 2. Think 10X
> Swing for the fences and think big, bold and even outrageous ideas. Incrementalism is the enemy of brainstorming.

3. Prototype

This is the part that I like best because it embodies HyperLeverage; taking action. As Lafargue explains, "You want to strike when the iron is hot–you *don't* want to walk away or agree to follow talk with more talk."

Google has learned to HyperLeverage innovation in this way by following through on ideas and building simple prototypes that don't have to be perfect. Rather, they represent a quick embodiment of the brainstorm that will test the basic assumptions of the idea.

I highly recommend that my clients develop a systematic, cross-departmental brainstorming process that incorporates perspectives from different angles. This ensures that brainstorming sessions don't become an "amen" choir of like-minded individuals with similar experiences and backgrounds saying "yes" to their own ideas.

Leveraging brainstorming meetings requires that the session ideas be collected, organized, and disseminated for further review and consideration. So, always find a mechanism to record it. Consider both audio as well as visual recordings. And consider using a transcription service to facilitate a first edit of what was said. In the end, to leverage brainstorming, you need to make the participants feel confident and trusting that their voices will be heard without judgment. The goal is to get free flow of information and ideas.

Takeaways

⚠ HyperLeveraging innovation requires an environment that incorporates four key elements: openness to new ideas, acceptance of risk and change, encouragement to participate, and time to actively think.

⚠ For companies that want to experience HyperLeverage around innovation, there should be a process and framework. Haphazard ideation is neither efficient nor scalable.

⚠ Effective innovation can be fueled from reliable information, data, and feedback derived from multiple sources, including vendors and customers.

⚠ Progressive innovation derives from a culture of recognition and direct incentives that align employees with corporate objectives and provide a sense of ownership.

⚠ The use of brainstorming leverages untapped skills, experience, and participation of team members who would otherwise be out of the loop.

CHAPTER 18

Technology

Years ago, when the Internet first hit the scene, there were those in the tech community who were adamant that this technological advancement in global sharing of information and communication was the elixir to everything. Sound familiar? Isn't that what all new technology advocates proclaim about their newest innovation?

The Internet was the technology that was going to give us the tools to leverage the power of the computer to be more efficient, save time, make more money, work smarter. Essentially it was going to radically change our lives for the better. And you could easily argue that this had happened in so many ways that weren't imaginable when it was first introduced.

The Internet unleashed untold possibilities. It freed us up from geography. We can access information and work from anywhere. Theoretically, we don't need to use paper for anything anymore. It's all in the Cloud. Our data is available anytime, anywhere, and accessible from a multitude of electronic devices. Nor do we need the type of phones, pens, watches, clocks, cameras, desks, and a whole host of other physical items that were the mainstay of life and business. All of these to one degree or another have been usurped and replaced through the marvels of modern technology: personal computers, tablets, and mobile devices. The Internet truly is a beast when it comes to HyperLeveraging technology. Stronger than any lever that Aristotle could have imagined.

Take the example of Greneker, a 75-year-old company that specializes in mannequin design and production. Recognizing that the world of retail fashion, especially in the area of sports apparel, was changing dramatically, it sought out technologies that could address the new business landscape it anticipated was developing. Seeing an opportunity to leverage technology to reduce its reliance on the established, labor-intensive methods of clay sculpture to create prototypes, it embraced 3D printing.

As Steve Beckman, President of the company, stated in a recent video, "We positioned ourselves as the experts in this type of mannequin design and transitioned to everything being 3D printed." This dramatically reduced the time to develop a line of mannequins by a factor of 10, from six months to just a couple of weeks. Greneker had reached HyperLeverage by proactively seeking out 3D printing expertise when it first emerged. And it continued to upgrade and refine its 3D equipment and processes even further to reduce time to market dramatically and to be significantly more responsive to market trends. Thanks to technology, Greneker continues to dominate its market niche, working with almost all major sports apparel brands globally.

HyperLeveraging technology requires a significant overlap with other business functions to work. It's not enough to just buy technology off the shelf—like the example of the 3D printer, it means staying abreast of innovation and embracing change.

Before we get to those important topics, let's use our Leverage Prism to deconstruct different components of technology and how they can be used, improved upon, and implemented to create HyperLeverage.

DECONSTRUCTING TECHNOLOGY

TECHNOLOGY

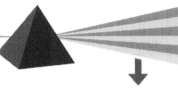

PRODUCT DEVELOPMENT/INNOVATION

DATA COLLECTION & ANALYSIS

COMMUNICATION & FILE SHARING

AUTOMATION & EFFICIENCY

PROTOTYPING & TIME TO MARKET

CONTINUOUS IMPROVEMENT SYSTEMS

PROCESS MONITORING & MODIFICATION

ONLINE COMMERCE & MARKETING

QUALITY & CONSISTENCY

MANAGEMENT & OPERATIONS

FIGURE 24: DECONSTRUCTING TECHNOLOGY

We use the word "technology" to mean quite a few things. In simple terms, it is science or knowledge put into practical use to solve problems or invent useful tools. Without a pragmatic or practical application, there is no way to leverage technology. In any business, there is a multitude of ways that technology makes a difference. It can make processes more efficient and therefore less costly. It can lead to advances in intelligence and data analysis which, in turn, leads to better business decisions.

Technology can also lead to significant disruptions: internally in the displacement of a workforce through automation and robotics, and externally by dramatically changing markets through the introduction of entirely new products or services. Technology is needed for ongoing and real-time improvements to stay current or ahead of the competition. It means recognizing that technology will continuously change and, so, a company must have a systematic mechanism to search out, evaluate, and incorporate these changes into its operations and infrastructure.

Just look at what happened to Internet giant Yahoo. It lost its position as the top echelon of the tech world, its once tight grip on online search, email services, and the web advertising space. Its valuation fell from a high of $125 billion at its pinnacle to only $5 billion when it was sold for literally pennies on the dollar to Verizon in 2016.

Take the fast-growing business areas of Big Data collection, Data Analytics, and Artificial Intelligence. These three areas of technology have significant potential to dramatically change how almost every business does commerce. A company does not have to be directly involved in any of these three to leverage them. Knowing that companies are being formed that can help a company understand its customer interactions and provide the tools to be more responsive to, adaptive, and quicker to market with better solutions will provide a company with a leg up on its competitors. This is the promise that companies like Data.world represent. Unleashing the power of data to inform how companies can and should perform better, in all aspects of business.

The point is that you don't have to understand how the engine in your car works to drive the car. You just must recognize how it makes your car perform better and take advantage of this to drive better and safer. By the same notion, HyperLeveraging most technologies doesn't require a deep understanding of the underlying technology. It's how you use and leverage the technology that matters.

To reach HyperLeverage, one should always be proactively seeking out and learning what new technologies are on the horizon. You don't have to be the first to "cross the chasm" and be the first adopter. Often, it's enough to stay abreast, prepare to adapt to it, and adopt the new technology to your specific problems at the time and situation that fits your specific needs.

HyperLeveraging Your Own Technology

Sometimes the systems you develop for your own internal needs become treasure troves of gold. A gift that keeps on giving. This is what happened at Amazon. Around the year 2000, Amazon was just an e-commerce company struggling to deal with the enormity of scale and hyper-growth that, if not controlled and managed, could have brought the company to its knees. The company was forced to build internal infrastructure and systems like no one had ever created before. The foundation was laid for what became known as AWS (Amazon Web Services). Originally conceived as a solution to issues related to the launch of the e-commerce service Merchant.com, which was designed to help third-party merchants build online shipping sites on top of Amazon's existing e-commerce engine, it became a cash cow for Amazon.

Like the situation with the Denver baggage system, Amazon found that it hadn't planned well for future technological requirements. And instead of the organized development environment it wanted, it had created a big fucking mess. This is how AWS came about as a solution for untangling this mess using well-documented APIs (Application Programming Interfaces). While it drove a smoother development of the Merchant.com program, it also established the discipline for developing tools going forward.

As AWS CEO, Andy Jassy, has said, "We expected all the teams internally from that point on to build in a decoupled, API-access fashion, and then all of the internal teams inside of Amazon expected to be able to consume their peer internal development team services in that way. So very quietly around 2000, we became a services company with really no fanfare."

This is a phenomenal lesson of HyperLeverage. It shows that a lot of the work that goes into building an infrastructure or developing internal technology or management tools can have applications externally as well as become new profit centers.

Wal-Mart may not be at the top of what people consider the most technologically advanced mass market retailer. It was late to react to the threat that Amazon posed and was caught with its pants down as the consumer market rushed to easy to use online retail shopping and the two-day Amazon Prime free shipping policies. It now appears to be applying the tenets of HyperLeverage, by proactively looking for technologies to exploit and being willing to change long-standing business practices.

Consumer technologies are easier to scale when the market is huge. Whether it's advances in video through mobile devices or audio and interactivity through technologies like Alexa, companies can leverage technologies in how they do business. Video cameras, video data collection, and analysis will eventually be the norm as a method to understand buyer behavior. Data Analysis and Artificial Intelligence will eventually be used to make the buying experience much more personalized and adaptive.

HyperLeveraging Business Incubators

The point is that to leverage technology, a company must be cognizant of what's going on and even control it to some degree. It used to be that companies that wanted in on the newest technologies would fund basic research at universities. Now they invest in technology startups or go one major step further and create their own "skunk works"—business incubators and accelerators. In this way, large companies are HyperLeveraging technology in the most proactive and intentional manner.

They are helping to create the technologies of tomorrow by creating an environment in which the innovations can hatch. As early investors in the process, they get to pick and choose who they think can be the winners. They also get the opportunity to corner the market on the technology and lock it up before their competitors might get it. It's the latest iteration of Thomas Edison's modern industrial research and innovation lab.

In 2014, the Disney Company took a big step to leverage its many assets. It created the Disney Accelerator with a vision to help technology startups create an impact on the technologies that will impact the future of media and entertainment. And what a great leverage play this was. Being able to work hand in hand with companies that otherwise pose a direct threat to it down the road, Disney instead HyperLeveraged its infrastructure, its management expertise, and its global brand and distribution to lure and cull out the best of show and bring them under its wings. Over the years, it has invested in companies who have gone through Disney's accelerator with technologies as diverse as robotics, artificial intelligence, wearables, messaging, and augmented reality. All areas that correlate well with the Disney vision and mission. In my view, that's HyperLeverage on so many levels.

Disney is not alone in HyperLeveraging the concept of a business incubator or accelerator. Increasingly, more companies are jumping into the game with their own venture capital arms. Whether Alphabet with its Google Ventures (GV), Microsoft, Oracle, and even companies promoting Fintech technologies, like Deutsche Bank and others, they have leveraged their infrastructure and brand equity to gain early access to the technologies of the future.

HyperLeveraging Automation

We are all aware of the loss of jobs to China, Mexico, and other offshore countries. Job losses have not occurred solely because of cheaper labor and infrastructure costs these countries offer. The real culprit is technology. Yes, the more we innovate and advance our collective knowledge, the more we create situations where the status quo just won't last long.

Automation is one of those areas where technology has forced its hand. The fact is, ever since the start of the industrial revolution in the 1800s, automation and technology have together been leveraged for greater productivity, cost reduction, and higher profits.

How does one go about HyperLeveraging automation, though? Does it mean buying the latest and shiniest new tool off the shelf? Or incorporating the latest software? Perhaps yes to both. Like all other aspects of HyperLeverage, it means deconstructing the problem, looking at the current situation, and seeing what components exist that can be utilized differently or better. I turn to Amazon as an example of a company that has reached HyperLeverage on so many fronts. In the case of automation, it saw its future. It meant a world in which many of the manual human warehouse activities would be replaced with robotics.

Amazon's needs were going to be very specific. They were going to be increasingly large and complex. The company faced a decision point. It could either contract with outside firms to purchase their automation solutions or it could leverage its deep balance sheet and buy the technology outright. Which is exactly what it did. Not being willing to wait for technology to come to it, Amazon had to make it happen by itself.

In 2012, the company bought Kiva Systems—later renamed Amazon Robotics—and started churning out tens of thousands of robots that automate the picking and packing process. The increase in productivity was quick to follow. And even with the continued investment in automation, the company is still growing its warehouse workforce to keep up with the demand. As Martin Ford has written in "Rise of the Robots," a book about automation, "It's certainly true that Amazon would not be able to operate at the costs they have and the costs they provide customers without this automation."

Faced with the challenges of Wal-Mart and Target, who allow customers to order online and pick up at the stores in their vicinity, Amazon continues to invest in technology and infrastructure. The days of free, two-day shipping could soon be replaced with free next-day shipping. Increased and more efficient infrastructure, automation, and location will all be leveraged to make this happen.

Not many companies obviously have the wherewithal to fund, develop, and launch their own proprietary automation solution. Amazon is so dominant in so many areas and certainly stands out in this regard and is the poster child for proactive and intentional exploitation of size, infrastructure, technology, and—you got it—HyperLeverage. But almost every company can find ways to use technology to automate and streamline its processes. Even if it's as simple as a basic CRM system to create better communications with customers. Or accounting or project and time management software that allows coworkers to share and work together.

Takeaways

⚠ HyperLeveraging technology requires a significant overlap with other business functions to work. It means embracing change and preparing your organization accordingly.

⚠ HyperLeveraging most technologies doesn't require a deep understanding of the underlying technology. It's how a company uses the technology that matters.

⚠ A business should always be proactively seeking out and learning what new technologies are on the horizon. HyperLeverage occurs when you can adopt the new technology to your specific problems at the time and conditions that fit your specific needs.

⚠ Automated business processes are a natural extension of how to leverage technology. At some point in a business life cycle, it will be forced upon a company in one form or another to stay viable.

CHAPTER 19

Intellectual Property

When I submitted my first patent application, I felt a real sense of accomplishment. I had performed at the highest level. I had successfully combined all of my training, skills, and experience into an effort that created something new. Truly new—because it wasn't just me that said so, the U.S. Patent Office and its patent lawyer examiners had certified it. It wasn't as if I had invented anything that would change the world, but I knew that I had conceived of something special and was awarded ownership of this intellectual property. It was something that only a very small fraction of people ever accomplishes. Intellectual property is an asset that is often the result of innovation and can be a huge leverageable resource. Let's start with a Leverage Prism view and dissect how this can come about.

We can see from Figure 25 that intellectual property is comprised not just of patents or trademarks, as most people surmise. In fact, in today's online and global economy, these vestiges of recognized and accepted statements of intellectual property ownership just might have less leverage power than ever before. Patent infringement is becoming more common as new products are designed, developed, perfected, assembled, manufactured, distributed, sold, and used in dozens of countries. To leverage patents, therefore, requires

DECONSTRUCTING INTELLECTUAL PROPERTY

INTELLECTUAL PROPERTY

PATENTS

TRADEMARKS

TRADE SECRETS

COPYRIGHTS

SOCIAL MEDIA HANDLES

WEBSITES/DOMAIN NAMES

IMAGES/VIDEOS

BRANDING ELEMENTS/LOGOS/COLORS

SOUNDS/JINGLES

PROCESSES/SYSTEMS/METHODOLOGIES

FIGURE 25: DECONSTRUCTING INTELLECTUAL PROPERTY

a strategic and actual plan for diligent and constant enforcement. A Japanese company can easily develop a new product, manufacture it in the Philippines, and sell it in Europe, only to discover that it infringes a German patent. And we have heard the stories of the herculean efforts, including government intervention, to combat patent infringement by Chinese companies. Technology changes so fast that it's difficult for companies without the resources to dedicate enough time, money, and personnel to develop innovations that lead to groundbreaking patents.

Pharmaceutical companies cite this as a primary reason for expensive drug costs. Unfortunately for the consumer, there is a lot of truth to this. Companies do take significant risk and allocation of non-productive assets to do groundbreaking R&D. And with the limited amount of protection that a patent provides, businesses like Big Pharma must find a way to recoup their investments. Otherwise, no company could afford to leverage this business activity profitably, especially in a business environment that has a shorter time horizon to recoup one's investments. One avenue that has demonstrated success is to limit the scope of the invention and adopt an incremental rather than swing-for-the-fences approach. This is a business move that can leverage existing IP assets and provide for a continuation of protections.

The Internet has become the driver of international commerce, and with it, the concept of intellectual property has expanded to include such items as domain names, Twitter, Instagram handles, social media profiles, and actual websites and mobile apps. Getting a patent approved is one thing, but leveraging it is another. How does one go about taking advantage of the protected rights that a patent represents? The most obvious is to preclude any competitor from copying your product, forcing it to expend resources to develop something new that won't infringe upon your property rights. Patents can be bought and sold as well. They have value like currency. They can be HyperLeveraged defensively to stave off competition as well as sold or licensed for additional revenue streams.

Entire business wars have been fought over these to gain leverage over competitors and corner a market. In the late 2000s and early 2010s, there was a patent war raging on the landscape of American commerce. Companies like Apple, Google, Microsoft, and BlackBerry were trying to box each other out in the growing market for smartphones. They recognized the tremendous upside potential this new technology represented. Furthermore, they knew they didn't have the resources to create this innovation internally. It would cost too much and take too long. But they could leverage their resources differently, by purchasing the patents, unlocking the innovation, and incorporating it into their products and systems, thereby precluding others from using it against them.

The patent battle culminated in 2011 with Google's purchase of Motorola Mobility and its library of over 7500 patents for a tidy sum of $12.5 billion to counteract the previous acquisitions made by Apple and Microsoft to stockpile patents. After selling off the actual Motorola business, Google had spent close to $4 billion just to augment its growing intellectual property library as a defensive move to box out the competition.

As evidenced by Google's purchase of Motorola patents, it is evident that patents are valuable assets. Without patent value or patent assertion, inventors would have no incentive to innovate.

Getting a trademark is a less expensive, time-consuming, and arduous process, yet works similarly to patents. And trademark rights have the added benefit of being renewable, leveraged assets, allowing for extended periods of protection that can be added to a company's balance sheet in the form of an intangible asset.

In many ways, trademarks can be HyperLeveraged more proactively and less expensively than patents because they protect the visual embodiments of a brand. Whether it's a logo, symbol, specific word, or combination of all design elements. You may ask how trademarks can be leveraged. You need to look no further than three of the most known and trusted companies and global brands—Apple, Coca Cola, and Disney. The logo and colors of Coca Cola are recognizable worldwide. Apple's logo is ubiquitous. Disney's distinct font and logo is plastered on toys, videos, clothing, and other children's items. It is obvious when someone is trying to copy them. They leveraged these trademarks in everything they do, thereby reaching HyperLeverage. The Coca Cola and Disney trademarks represent consumer recognition, goodwill, and brand recognition. For example, in 2015, marketing experts, Interbrand, estimated the value of the Apple brand at $170 billion (of a $646 billion market capitalization), Google at $120 billion (of $493 billion), and Coca Cola at $78 billion (of $180 billion).

Copyrights are yet another form of Intellectual Property that can be proactively leveraged both for protection (defensive posturing) and for active marketing. Copyrights cover the intellectual efforts that went into writing books, musical compositions, graphic designs, artwork, and other creative expressions. Like patents and trademarks, they have an intangible value that can be bought and sold. In 1985, Michael Jackson purchased ATV Music for $47.5 million and its 4000-song catalog that included the rights to 250 Lennon-McCartney songs. As the owner of the Beatles song catalog, he now possessed and controlled one of the most sought-after collection of music ever written.

Today, intellectual property takes many different forms: jingles, sounds, visual imagery, video, and even smells. And they can all be leveraged by companies of every size, using the same tools as described previously.

My central point is that Intellectual Property is often viewed as simply a passive and intangible asset when, in fact, the opposite is often true. Intellectual Property has a cost, and therefore it should be treated no differently than any other business asset or resource with an eye to attaining the best return possible. Using the tools of HyperLeverage—actively planning to fully exploit the potential of a company's IP—is not a luxury. It's a business necessity.

Takeaways

⚠ Organizations should consider Intellectual Property, in all its manifestations, as a core business asset and should assign a realistic value to it.

⚠ To find HyperLeverage in intellectual property in a connected business environment means that patents, trademarks, and copyrights may not be the most powerful or cost-effective means to leverage IP.

⚠ The Internet has provided companies of any size the ability to HyperLeverage IP through the intentional acquisition and deployment of websites, social media handles, and apps across multiple communication and branding platforms for business development and market protection from competition.

CHAPTER 20

Change

I n his book, *Crossing the Chasm*, Geoffrey Moore writes about how people adapt or accept new technologies. He defines three categories of individuals: evangelists, early adopters, and late adopters. It is the early adopters that leverage their acceptance of change long before the masses. They recognize that change is inevitable and choose to leverage it intentionally (HyperLeverage) and as soon as possible to minimize the disruption of having it imposed upon them. Now, I'm not advocating for companies to drop everything and make radical changes to how they operate. However, as I've tried to reinforce in this book—and I know it may sound like a broken record—to achieve the highest degree of leverage when making changes, one needs to be proactive, intentional, and strategic. And then you must take action. You can't let change happen to you by surprise. Catch it by the tail, wrangle it to the ground, and put a leash on it.

Embracing Change

It is interesting how few modern companies have truly embraced change as a tool of leverage in their business. Yes, many new companies spring up each year looking to create a disruption in a marketplace that they can leverage for growth. Ten years ago, no one

"Ubered," but today, the taxi business has changed forever because of ride-sharing companies like Uber and Lyft. It will never go back to the situation that existed for decades. Few companies embrace change internally or do so begrudgingly. It's as if only external change to the marketplace is okay, but not "inside the company." Organizations know that change is inevitable and necessary, but so few leverage it. Even fewer ratchet it up a notch to HyperLeverage status by turning change into an intentional business activity.

Achieving HyperLeverage through change requires that someone at the top of your organization take the lead. Business leaders must commit to it and get buy-in at all levels. It can't be a top-down dictate. And most importantly, it requires three key functions: a clear objective for the changes, an easy-to-digest communication message, and honest transparency for the reasons for change.

For example, do you have a Corporate Change Officer in your organization? At a minimum, you should have an individual or, better yet, a team that is tasked with contemplating what changes can or should be incorporated, how it will be communicated and even implemented, and how these changes can be measured and refined.

Change is, after all, a business process no different than others I've written about. It can be planned for, managed, measured, and refined. And how to accept and use it can be taught to employees, both for internal and external business activities. I find it both surprising and somewhat exasperating as a management consultant to find out how few professionals have any formal education in the process of change. Aren't universities chartered to provide the skills and tools for a competitive and modern workplace?

Today, every business needs to be in a constant low boil state of change. Even huge behemoths of industry aren't around forever. They, too, have to embrace a positive approach to change. How quickly competitive companies that fully adopt change can eat away at the underpinnings of their more established competition with a nimbleness that counterbalances all the advantages that these market leaders might have.

Been to any Blockbuster video stores lately? They were as ubiquitous as bluebonnet wildflowers in the Texas springtime. But they were too slow to accept how technology had changed the way that users wanted to get their content. Or what about Polaroid, which got completely wiped out by the changes in digital photography?

The time horizons of the normal business cycles have become compressed, leaving only those companies that can adapt quickly as the winners. Think of the bulky cruise ship that takes a huge wide arc to change course verses the power motorboat that can almost turn on a dime.

I know that change can become a mantra with little substance. Every new manager wants to impose his or her own imprint. Startups or even established, mid-market companies are continuously getting bought or merged. Employees are hesitant and even defensive when it comes to making modifications to how they do their jobs.

How does one HyperLeverage change in a business environment? Especially since so many resources go toward growing a product, a brand, or a company. Besides, you might ask: "Who has got the time or even mindset to live in a state of constant flux?" It goes against the grain of human nature. We strive for the status quo because it's comfortable, predictable, and trustworthy.

Doesn't a company that is always changing risk losing some or all of these characteristics? Of course, it does. I would pose a different question—one that is more apt. Will a company that doesn't embrace and leverage change be around long enough to recover after its competitors and the market have already moved on? Seen anyone use a Blackberry phone lately? It couldn't catch up to the changes in the market that the iPhone and Android smartphones brought on.

Recently, Domino's Pizza grabbed the levers of change. And in a manner that on the surface might seem to be confusing. Then CEO Patrick Doyle had concluded that he didn't want the company to be considered by the investing community as just a pizza company. Rather, he viewed the business as a technology business. How odd. Don't they just sell pizza? A technology business, you say? Really? From the perspective of change and leverage, it makes perfect sense. Domino's product is pizza. But its business model is driven by, and its unique selling proposition is tied directly to, technology. Without it, Domino's would indeed just be a pizza company.

So how is Domino's a technology company? There's a simple logic to it. "We used to be a pizza company that sells online, and we needed to become an e-commerce company that sells pizza," Dennis Maloney, Domino's chief digital officer for the 14,400-store chain based in Ann Arbor, MI is quoted as saying. "That was one of the big ah-ha moments that caused a lot of conversation within the company."

By flipping the switch and stepping outside of its self-imposed box, the company HyperLeveraged change in dramatic fashion. Not only did it redefine itself internally but also externally. Understanding that it was its use of technology that was the real driver of sales, Domino's employed the tenets of HyperLeverage to build on this shift in business model emphasis. It developed apps and other technologies that made it easier for its customers to place an order. It exhibited to its customers that it could embrace the changes that the market demanded before food delivery companies like Grubhub, DoorDash, and UberEats figuratively "ate their lunch."

Changes like the ones at Domino's don't happen out of thin air. They start with a recognition of the necessity to do things differently and instilling the process of change as a pillar of an organization's ethos. Everyone involved with a company, from its employees, new hires, vendors, and even customers, is ready for and even anticipating it. Think back to the section on company culture and community. It must be defined and communicated to everyone at all levels how a company feels about change. Is the company fully embracing the guns blazing, let's blow everything up disruption approach, or is it a conservative slow but steady incrementalistic approach? Borrowing again from the world of sailing, are you talking back and forth into the wind to move forward?

The flip side to not proactively adopting a managed course of change is a surprise—simply an unanticipated change in a short time frame. Even the best surprises leave residues caused by the suddenness. Now, not all change is good or needs to be done in one single act. Recognizing that there is an optimum pace of change reduces the natural disdain for rocking the comfortable boat.

HyperLeveraging the Pace of Change

In the 1987 movie Wall Street, the protagonist Gordon Gecko espouses a business philosophy that *Greed is Good*. What he was referring to was that the profit motive is what drives effective investing and the use of capital. The subtext was more important—that businesses need to change to survive. To borrow and modify the phrase, I state that *Change is Good*.

You may ask, is changing too much or too soon a smart leverage move? Or can it backfire and blow up in one's face? Are companies from startups to huge established market leaders making pivots, changes, and realignment of assets too quickly? Very good questions—and the answers would probably lie in HyperLeveraging the aspects of data and BI from earlier on in this section. There is no pat one size fits all answer.

Here's a story from the period before the age of e-commerce that reinforces the importance of time horizon on reaching HyperLeverage; in this case, not allowing sufficient time for change to happen. It's a lesson that many companies fail to learn as they pivot from one undercooked or misconceived business concept or business model to another before they could possibly realize the potential of the strategic path they had embarked upon. Does that describe any venture you have ever undertaken? Having the rug pulled from under you before you could realize the fruits of your investment?

As much as we want to bend the markets to our schedules, we can't. Every market has certain time cycles that just can't be changed or circumvented at will. A farmer knows this intuitively. It takes time for the seeds to germinate, it takes resources and patience to irrigate and cultivate before a crop can be harvested. Nothing a farmer can do will make the corn grow quicker.

At Colorations®, my first entrepreneurial venture, there were only two ways for teachers and schools to purchase the art materials I produced. They could either find a local parent-teacher supply store or they could order from a mail-order school supply catalog. There were few national companies, as the market was very regional and local in nature. Internet and e-commerce did not exist or was just in its infancy, so as a manufacturer there was absolutely no option of selling directly. I had to learn how to leverage the distribution of the school supply catalogs to sell my products. The problem was, how did one go about getting a new product into these catalogs? After all, they were printed and distributed only once a year. If I missed my opportunity to get "chosen" by the merchandising buyers, I would be waiting another 12 months or more for my opportunity. Nothing I could do would make this cycle shorter.

When I think back on this long cycle and compare it to the instantaneousness of today's online commerce, I'm amazed at the perseverance this took. I could have easily decided to pivot after that first rejection and choose another business model. I believed in my product and, backed up by the hard data and feedback from my existing customers, I decided to stay the course. It was a wise decision to hold off making a change. Over the next 6 years, Colorations® became an award-winning brand of children's art materials that was featured in all major school supply catalogs and used by preschools, elementary grades, and parents throughout the country.

The point is that many sales cycles like this one are years in the making. It's important to plan for an adequate time horizon and understand the sales and market cycles before making changes or pivots. As the story of Colorations® shows, changing too quickly could eliminate any advantage or leverage that might have existed from resisting the pressures to change.

Managing Change Effectively

We assume that everyone accepts change in the same way and knows how to assimilate it into his or her work habits and routines. It's not as if we learned the skills of change. It's almost always assumed that we instinctively know how to do it. We often feel challenged to handle change in the most effective manner in our personal lives. This is often the case from the perspective of business productivity. For a business to HyperLeverage change, it needs to reduce downtime, resistance, and unnecessary costs that are often associated with doing things differently.

The larger the organization, the more resistant it is to change. In my experience, the optimum method to overcome the cemented institutional avoidance to change is to have cross-functional and dedicated teams tasked with implementing how to make changes effective in an organization. Does your organization act that way? Or is it still working on the top-down approach?

Three activities are the core of HyperLeveraging change: Acknowledgement, Communication, and Planning. When there is full management support that dovetails with the strategic goals of the company, the ante is raised into HyperLeverage status.

- Acknowledgment – The cold hard truth is that change is a constant ongoing process, and it is here to stay. We must learn from the past and apply lessons to the future. How did your company successfully deal with change previously? How did it meet the demands of a changing business environment? Can this be duplicated or improved upon?
- Communication – Change can evoke significant emotional responses from employees, vendors, and customers. How a company communicates the reasons for the changes and puts them in a context that relates to the experience of the people who are affected by the change determines the success of HyperLeveraging it for positive gain. Be transparent and honest. Otherwise, people will view the changes with cynicism and reluctance.
- Planning – Managing change successfully starts with establishing new goals with a well-designed plan. We may know best where we are and where we want to be; now we must articulate how we are going to get there. We must clarify goals and expectations. Get feedback from others. Keeping everybody focused on the desired outcome is critical.

What Does the Leverage Prism of Change Reveal?

Change is a business lever that can be controlled by any organization. It can leverage the actual manifestations of change—with its employees, vendors, and even customers. It takes good communication for these groups to both understand and accept the changes an organization might decide to undertake. The more they are aware of, accepting of, and even pushing for some of these changes, the company will realize a powerful gain.

Change in a business context has a multitude of meanings. Which is why I like to take out the Leverage Prism from time to time to deconstruct important concepts. As we can see from the following Leverage Prism diagram, when we deconstruct the concept of change, we find a big pile of change components that may or may not be relevant to every organization.

Figure 26 reveals most of the activities that, taken together, can create a change system approach that works for your specific company. Many organizations like to benchmark or emulate what others have done. There is no point in being a "guinea pig" if you can learn from what others have done beforehand. One way to HyperLeverage that aspect is to query whether anyone else in your organization has ever experienced or gone through that specific change transition and include him or her as part of the change team. This is especially helpful for software integrations.

Being the Driver of Change

A business that controls its own change controls its own destiny. It knows where it's going. It has a leg up on its competitors. And it reduces the chances that it will get caught unprepared. A business

DECONSTRUCTING CHANGE

CHANGE

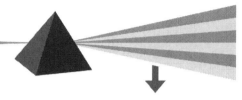

ALLOW FOR SUFFICIENT TIME HORIZON

APPOINT CHANGE TEAMS OR MANAGERS

FREQUENCY, TIMING AND DEGREE OF CHANGE

CHANGE IMPLEMENTATION PLAN

COMMUNICATE REASONS FOR CHANGE

CALCULATED RISK (CHANGE) VS REWARD

BE PROACTIVE AND NOT REACTIVE

EMBRACING CHANGE AT ALL LEVELS

PROVIDE TRAINING & INSTRUCTION

BENCHMARK AND LEARN FROM OTHERS

FIGURE 26: DECONSTRUCTING CHANGE

that plans for and implements change (HyperLeverage change) can bend the market to its advantage rather than have it twisted around its neck.

Steve Jobs understood the concept of change like no other CEO of his day. He made sure that Apple controlled its "ecosystem" and that it could impose its will on the market and bend it to where he wanted it to go. As a market leader, you influence all others to follow suit and fall in line. Few companies will ever come close to reaching these heights.

With the release of the first iPhone back in 2007 and up to the present day, Apple HyperLeverages the changes it makes to its product line like no other technology company, including its major rival in the smartphone marketplace, Samsung. Apple has become the standard-bearer, and the others follow suit, emulate, or copy. Apple is the driver's seat. Android devices make upgrades and changes, but for years these didn't have anywhere near the effect that Apple had on the changing mobile device marketplace. Even when the competitive technology solutions were better and cheaper, they didn't command the same attention or respect from the general population like when Apple introduced a change.

By being the driver of change, your business is less apt to be caught by surprise by your competitors or the changing whims of your customers. When you drive your car, you have your eyes ahead of you, with two hands on the wheel, and are in control of its trajectory and speed. You can turn right or left, accelerate, and brake. Through your rear and side-view mirrors, you have a keen awareness of what's around you. Like Steve Jobs at Apple, you are "bending" the car to arrive at your desired destination. That's what HyperLeverage of change feels like.

Here are three concepts to get your hands firmly on the HyperLeverage change wheel:

- Learn from others. Benchmark, Emulate, and Copy. Don't spend your energy and resources starting from scratch.

- Know your destination and work backwards. I've already written about this in the section on strategic planning. It works the same when it comes to change. Know what you want to change…what change will look like when it's in place and work backwards to put the pieces in place.

- Know when to hit the gas pedal. And when to let up. Driving does not mean going in a forward direction only at maximum speed. Being a good driver of change means also knowing when to ease up or come to a complete halt.

Companies who have reached monopoly status or have patents that provide broad protection from competitors can change markets. Like Apple, they proactively exploit their technology, authority, and demand for their products to affect change in others as well.

Take the example of Luxottica, the $8.5 billion Italian company that designs and retails over 80 percent of the world's eyewear brands, including Ray-Ban, Oakley, and others. With little substantive competition, it is free to hide behind all the brand names and sell its goods at premium markups. The buying public has no idea or even any recourse for purchasing eyeglasses from anyone else.

It doesn't always work out, though, that you can change a market at will even if you are the most dominant brand in the world—Coca Cola. Back in 1985, Coca Cola executives decided to introduce New Coke. They had done all the homework, strategic planning, branding, implementation. The company was indeed HyperLeveraging change, and based on the definitions of this book, it was doing everything right to reach HyperLeverage. The changes to the formula were proactive, intentional, and strategic in that this would be a new formulation for a new generation of Coke drinkers. What could go wrong?

It had it all figured out, or so it thought, only to have it hit it "splat" right in the face in a manner not anticipated. The executives at Coke, from the top management to the marketing teams tasked with the new branding, figured that introducing a new twist on the tried and true taste of Coke—using less expensive high fructose sugar—would be seamless. Their blind taste tests clearly indicated the public was receptive. They had collected and analyzed data to reach well-informed decisions. So why not go for it? Not a small test rollout. No way. This was a time for BIG, BOLD ACTION. After all, Coke figured, the consumer won't notice the difference. It opted to be the driver of change, and New Coke was driven out to the showroom for all to see and taste.

The response was deafening and totally unexpected. Not in the applause but in the uproar. The problem was that no one except the Coca Cola executives wanted a change. Everyone else was okay with the Coke taste that he or she knew and had grown up with for decades. The consumers didn't care about Coke's desire to lower costs by switching to high fructose sugar. That wasn't their problem.

To HyperLeverage change, it must have tangible significance and meaning to all those involved. Being a driver of change requires the skills of conviction, courage, and planning. And, as Coca Cola found out, it's not for the faint of heart. But what successful business is built on being just so-so and mediocre or not embracing change? If you want to be a leader, then you will have to eventually reject the status quo.

Takeaways

⚠ HyperLeveraging change begins by acknowledging and accepting change as a constant component of every business environment and not letting it be imposed upon you without preparation.

⚠ Communicating the reasons for change and putting them into the context of what it means to the people affected by it, reduces the resistance to it and provides a smoother transition to the new paradigm.

⚠ Knowing how to change is not always intuitive. Having specific individuals or teams dedicated to introducing and managing change in an organization brings structure and effectiveness and leads to HyperLeverage.

⚠ The frequency and magnitude of change must be closely monitored to stay within a comfort zone and reduce the risk of backlash from employees, vendors, and customers. Otherwise, a deleveraging effect can occur.

⚠ Being the proactive driver and leader of change in a marketplace can bring great rewards, however, it elevates the risk factor and requires superior coordination across multiple disciplines in a company

The DOIT Leverage Method: Progress
Case Study—Dyson

The application of innovation to solve everyday and even mundane tasks is the most common manifestation of technology. That has been the passion of Sir James Dyson, the creator of the first cyclonic vacuum cleaner that revolutionized and disrupted the relatively stable and low-tech market for vacuums. It wasn't an instant success, nor was it a brainstorm that he whipped up over a weekend in his basement. Dyson leveraged his knowledge of industrial design, coupled with his education as a furniture and interior designer, to apply existing technologies to improve existing household products. This led to his first breakthrough innovation: the Ballbarrow, a modified version of the wheelbarrow that used a ball that could rotate 360 degrees as the fulcrum point instead of the front wheel. While researching different methods to manufacture it, he was introduced to the technology of cyclone centrifuges that were used to collect dirt and dust in industrial settings such as sawmills.

Leveraging his keen eye for practical solutions and underwhelmed by the performance of even the best vacuum cleaners from leading firms such as Hoover and Electrolux, Dyson saw an opportunity to use this technology on a smaller scale to create a different kind of home vacuum. Trying to get his partners in the company he had started to market the Ballbarrow to support this development, he was told to leave the company he had founded. Dyson was undeterred. As he averred, "We get frustrated by-products that don't work properly. As design engineers, we do something about it. We're all about invention and improvement."

This DO-IT analysis is a theoretical look back—with 20/20 vision—at what Dyson faced during that period and how he leveraged progress through Innovation, Technology, and Change—the underpinnings of entrepreneurial progress to a $5.8 billion worldwide consumer product giant with a staff of over 5,800 engineers.

To begin with, Dyson had to deconstruct how to translate the cyclone technology into a practical, smaller scale for use in a home appliance. Armed with the confidence in his own skills at innovation and design, he spent the next five years of his life building over 5,100 prototypes perfecting the cyclone vacuum cleaner. He then had to get it manufactured and distributed, while facing a market too entrenched in existing products to risk taking a chance on this fledgling and unproven entrepreneur and technology. This led him to create his own manufacturing company, Dyson Ltd., and begin marketing the products in the only place that was receptive—Japan. Finally, with the ability to see the long-term horizon and having the necessary perseverance to stick it out, he got his first big breakthrough in the UK market ten years after the initial idea.

Let's bullet item what Dyson may have discovered if he had used a DOIT exercise to understand what he could leverage to secure the future that became a reality. As a reminder, this very general DOIT is based solely on an external examination of the company from available public information.

Deconstruct (A deconstruction of Dyson Ltd.)

- Leverage Design—Applied interior design concepts to create aesthetically attractive and functional modern small appliances.
- Leverage Technology—Utilized existing technologies and re-engineered them for small household appliances.
- Leverage Innovation—Invested in long term R&D by building research center and spending millions yearly on innovation.

- Leverage IP—Utilized the power of patents to protect the company's inventions.
- Leverage Progress & Change—Understood that consumers wanted new products they could trust and were willing to pay a premium for them.
- Leverage a Brand Story—Dyson became the face of the company and distilled his innovations into a relatable and simple story.

Organize (What Dyson organized and reinforced in his company to leverage his resources and market opportunities)

- Continued to innovate and made it a central mission of the company.
- Reinforced the value proposition simple in all products and marketing communication—we combine great design with practical solutions that work.
- Built and increased his own manufacturing and distribution systems.
- Continued to be the main storyteller of the company, making it personal.

Improve (What Dyson improved on to leverage his existing resources)

- Created and invested significant funds into a "brain works" industrial research center, like Thomas Edison's Menlo Park, to create practical innovations.
- Utilized economies of scale to create more "entry" level products.
- Expanded beyond homeowner appliances to commercial markets with the introduction of the AirBlade hand dryer.

- Leveraged research resources to bring innovation to sensing technologies and vision systems.

Take Action (What Dyson acted on to HyperLeverage his resources and opportunities)

- Expanded beyond the vacuum cleaner and the AirBlade.
- Focused on the story rather than the features of the products.
- Kept the company private, thereby shielding it from having to reveal important information to competitors and maintaining control of its operations and future.
- Continued to expand innovation and technology into new areas such as lighting and transportation.

What are the conclusions and results that Dyson realized as a result of this hypothetical DOIT HyperLeverage exercise? First, he recognized that there was a groundswell of demand for well designed, aesthetically pleasing home appliances that utilized more innovative technologies. He proved that the cornerstones of progress—innovation, technology, and change—yield great results if allowed to be developed with enough time horizon. He also learned that the acceptance of new technology takes more time and a different marketing approach to tell a better story.

Dyson was a pioneer in introducing modern industrial design and merging it with existing engineering technologies to produce products whose benefits are easy to see and understand. This allowed him to leverage this difference to establish his brand reputation as a harbinger of technological progress. He was able to command a price premium as a result. Dyson showed that innovation can be leveraged in a scalable fashion, even though it is not sold on price but on performance and aesthetics (same as Apple). And, finally, he demonstrated that HyperLeveraging innovation does not have to be an exercise of self-immolation as most software innovation and technology is through an endless rollout of new software versions. Dyson's products have an extended shelf life, without having to be reinvented continuously, like software.

Finally, Dyson built an innovation machine by opening a research center which has introduced more than 60 consumer products by investing around $10 million per week in product development.

Throughout this book, I have expounded on the difference between leverage and HyperLeverage, and made it clear that developing a HyperLeverage Mindset, and nurturing a corporate culture around that mindset, can be transformative. If you can hardwire this mindset into your company's DNA, you will create a distinct competitive advantage, no matter what your industry. Over time, this shift in thinking will impart a profound impact on all facets of your business.

By definition, a HyperLeverage Mindset requires you to be proactive, not reactive. Instead of waiting for leverage opportunities to come to you, you and your team will consistently discover and exploit leverage opportunities that you would otherwise have missed. If you internalize only one concept from this book, let it be the difference between leverage and HyperLeverage:

Leverage: the ability to influence a business system or environment in a way that multiplies your efforts or magnifies your potential.

HyperLeverage: the proactive, intentional, and systematic search for and acquisition, refinement, and exploitation of leverageable assets and resources.

The HyperLeverage Mindset, Leverage Prism, and DOIT Leverage Method that were presented and explained in Section One are powerful evaluation and analysis tools that can and should be used by anyone who wants to work smarter and multiply their outcomes. There is no question that without active and strategic adoption of a HyperLeverage Mindset, it will always be difficult for a company to achieve HyperLeverage and the many benefits that come with it. Nurturing a business culture that values and strives to develop a HyperLeverage Mindset starts at the top. It's where business leaders can lead by example. The superstars of management past and present—Jack Welch at GE, Jeff Bezos at Amazon, Steve Jobs at Apple, and others—have demonstrated the power of HyperLeverage. They have achieved the exceptional by making more out of what they already have or had at their fingertips. With the tools in this book, you can, too.

As a business leader, you have a charter to strive to achieve exceptional results. Why would you ever consider not getting the most out of what you already have? Leaving "money on the table" may be great for charity, but not when the health, profitability, and longevity of your organization is at stake. It is almost imperative in my mind that HyperLeverage is not something you might get around to. It's something you have to embrace now, not later. It's not complicated or difficult to get started. You can quickly develop the right systems to unlock the underlying leverage in your organization. It's how you take control and bend the levers to your advantage. Don't you want superior results with a minimum expenditure of effort? Go on—take action today.

Most companies don't have a system in place to achieve and experience the benefits of HyperLeverage. They haven't yet assessed their own 4Ps—People, Planning, Performance, and Progress—to see how they can use and enhance what they already have to reap the many benefits of HyperLeverage. It's really not difficult. To begin with, everyone and anyone can avail themselves of the simple Leverage Prism tool to continually uncover the hidden pockets of value. It is often the simple business tools like the Leverage Prism that inform us of far-reaching business potential. The Leverage Prism is truly the first step in HyperLeverage. As an evaluation and analysis tool, it forces us to think critically, examine what we already have, and avoid chasing our tails or wasting time, money, and effort doing things that won't get the desired results.

The most powerful and insightful tool in the new HyperLeverage toolbox is the DOIT Leverage Method. The power of the DOIT Leverage Method lies in its combination of analysis, critical thinking, planning, and action. It's a system that everyone in a company can use. The DOIT Leverage Method is a disciplinary approach to making sure that you understand the core leverage issues and can identify leverage opportunities.

Executive managers tasked with the responsibility for big-picture strategy often de-emphasize the operational and planning components of putting things into action. The "T" (take action) component of the DOIT will be an area they should focus on. The professionals in middle management or with limited areas of responsibility for the development of bigger picture strategies are rarely exercising a wide canvas analysis and end up being tasked with implementation. They should pay special attention to the "O" (organize) and "I" (improve) components of the DOIT Leverage Method. HR managers who shoulder the crucial responsibility of finding, training, and building the workforce of the future will obviously focus on the "D" (deconstruction) component as they take a deep dive into what are the real drivers of employee success.

Like any tool, it's only useful when it's being used correctly. The DOIT Leverage Method is no different. That is why you need to plan for an appropriate and adequate measurement process for any plan of action you take. The DOIT Leverage Method is a closed, continuous loop.

HyperLeverage Really Works

The benefits of HyperLeverage are substantial. I've showcased many wins throughout this book. The phenomenal success of Netflix and TJ Maxx can be attributed to a large degree to their ability to leverage their people through better and different hiring, training, and mentoring. Southwest Airlines refined its planning to shave precious time off its boarding procedures and was able to turn that time into a leverageable asset that yielded more revenue and built a brand reputation for efficiency and value. That's HyperLeverage at work. Amazon has grown into one of America's leading retailers by HyperLeveraging performance. It has taken operational efficiencies and customer service to unprecedented levels of excellence, disrupting a variety of industries along the way. The company's farsighted investment in infrastructure, technology, and automation has created a business engine of unparalleled strength. Amazon has mastered HyperLeverage. And finally, companies like 3M, Google (Google Ventures), and Disney (Disney Accelerator) are prime examples of how HyperLeveraging progress through innovation and intellectual property can pave the road to future growth, profits and business sustainability. It's one more example of how mastering HyperLeverage can lead to accelerated growth and profitability.

Today, HyperLeverage Is the Only Option

Today's business environment is dramatically different from what it was just a decade or two ago. The need to be competitive and at the top of your game is paramount. It's a "survival of the fittest" business marketplace. Technological advances—in data, artificial intelligence, blockchain, and more—guarantee that major changes and disruptions are on the way. It's not just driverless cars or advanced robotics that will paint a different business landscape, it's the sheer speed of innovation in almost every industry. Over time, it's the myriad of smaller changes, layered one on top of the other, that will set a company on a promising trajectory.

Companies that learn how to be proactive, adapt quickly, and make better, more effective decisions will win by turning leverage into a key asset. Teams that adopt a HyperLeverage Mindset will have an important advantage in the marketplace. Already, the carcasses of companies that have squandered their leverage—like Sears, Toys-R-Us, and Kodak—are too numerous to count. In the future, there will be many more, and the death of these companies will be accelerated. Time horizons will be increasingly compressed, making it imperative to squeeze the maximum out of all business assets, resources, and opportunities to achieve the right goals more quickly. This is the reason it is important to grasp the mantle of HyperLeverage. It's not a luxury that can wait anymore. There really is no option but to develop a HyperLeverage Mindset and implement it throughout your organization.

HyperLeverage is present everywhere. Look around and you'll understand that the successful companies are utilizing the tenets of HyperLeverage on a daily basis.

Finding leverage by chance is not a recipe for business success—not today, not ever. Leaving leverage to chance is like letting your business go downriver without a paddle. You're likely to get caught in unseen and dangerous currents that will put you and your company at risk. That is precisely why HyperLeverage is so critical. It allows you to chart an effective course and navigate rough waters with confidence. HyperLeverage helps you to stay agile and achieve exceptional results...repeatedly. Acceptance of the status quo, on the other hand, means your ship is rudderless. You are pushed around and always re-acting to the changing environment. This wastes precious resources, including time and money. Ultimately, a half-baked or myopic plan will inhibit your ability to exploit the leverage that's all around you. You'll never tap into this amazing competitive advantage, and your business will suffer as a result.

Which do you choose for your company's future—HyperLeverage or a status quo that guarantees slow and steady stagnation? As Archimedes might have asked when he discovered the principle of mechanical advantage in the lever, "Are you ready to use your lever-age and move your world?" After reading this book, I hope your answer is "Yes! Bring on the HyperLeverage!"

Joel Goobich is the President of Big Picture Advisors and has founded and led several other ventures. Throughout his career, he has utilized and refined the lessons of HyperLeverage to multiply his efforts and those of his clients.

From successful entrepreneurship, business ownership, business consultancy, and executive management, Joel has worn almost every hat in the businessman's wardrobe. With a multidisciplinary background that covers business development, innovation management, product commercialization, product development, operations, exit planning, quality control, and video marketing, his rock-solid base of experience and seasoned judgment provides him the lens through which to see and understand the big picture canvas. His first company, Colorations®, has become one of the leading children's arts and craft brands in the country.

Additionally, as a recognized problem solver and expert in multiple disciplines, Goobich has received multiple patents, trademarks, copyrights, and trade secrets for his work. As a prolific podcaster, he has launched three successful podcasts on topics ranging from business growth to exit planning and video marketing. He currently resides in Austin, Texas, where he is a sought-after speaker and provides business leverage and growth expertise to established and emerging companies.

Expanding HyperLeverage Beyond the Book

HyperLeverage is the first of a series of resources, such as workbooks and leverage audit guidelines that Joel Goobich will offer through JoelGoobich.com and HyperLeverage.com to further the awareness and use of leverage as a critical tool in business and professional and career development.

You can subscribe and listen to The HyperLeverage Podcast on all major podcast distribution sites or follow the HyperLeverage Blog at HyperLeverage.com for a steady stream of stories about leverage and actionable lessons on how to create HyperLeverage.

As the self-described "Mr. HyperLeverage," Joel Goobich shares his thoughts about the need for a HyperLeverage Mindset and expands on the lessons of HyperLeverage through keynote speeches, talks, workshops, and strategic consulting engagements. To inquire about hiring Joel Goobich for speaking or consulting engagements, please contact Joel Goobich at inquiries@joelgoobich.com

LIST OF FIGURES

ACKNOWLEDGMENTS

This book has been on my drawing board for years, and I had somewhat completed a previous version before I sought the assistance of Kathy Meis, founder and CEO of Bublish. With her professional guidance, astute understanding of the ever-changing world of book publishing, and her patient and insightful coaching, she has been instrumental in getting me to the finish line at last. I am eternally grateful.

A special thanks to Jennifer Ledgerwood for the graphic design of the book figures. She successfully translated my rough ideas into clear and well-presented images.

I would also like to thank my wife Bonnie Goobich, my daughters Sivan Wunder and Dalit Barrett, and my sons-in-law Andy Wunder and Drew Barrett for their invaluable insights, comments, and encouragement during the writing of the book. As the people who know me best and who have partnered with me in some of my business ventures that have shaped my career and business worldview, they have been unflinchingly supportive.

I would like to thank the members of the Austin Toastmasters Club. During the writing of this book, I shared many of the lessons of the book in speech form and received enthusiastic support and positive feedback.

Finally, I'd like to express my appreciation to the many business professionals and colleagues that I interviewed and who provided insight and context to specific chapters in the book.